I0762739

THE PREACHER'S HEBREW / GREEK COMPANION SERIES

General Editor / Old Testament Editor

JONATHAN G. KLINE, PHD
Senior Editor
Hendrickson Publishers

New Testament Editor

SEAN M. MCDONOUGH, PHD
Professor of New Testament
Gordon-Conwell Theological Seminary

The Preacher's Greek Companion Series

Ephesians

THE PREACHER'S GREEK COMPANION TO

Ephesians

A Selective Commentary for
Meditation and Sermon Preparation

Mateus F. de Campos

The Preacher's Greek Companion to Ephesians:
A Selective Commentary for Meditation and Sermon Preparation

Published by Hendrickson Academic
3 Centennial Drive
Peabody, Massachusetts 01960
www.hendricksonpublishers.com

ISBN 979-8-4005-0603-1

Printed in the United States of America

First Printing — April 2025

Library of Congress Control Number: 2024947170

CONTENTS

EPHESIANS 2:11–22

From Alienation to Reconciliation

87

EPHESIANS 3:1–13

The Wisdom of God Revealed Through the Church

115

EPHESIANS 3:14–21

Strengthened by the Spirit, Indwelt by Christ, Filled with the Fullness of God

143

 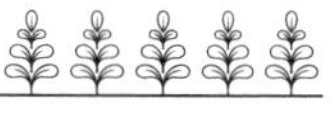

EPHESIANS 4:1–6

Keeping the Unity of the Spirit in the Bond of Peace

159

EPHESIANS 5:21–6:9

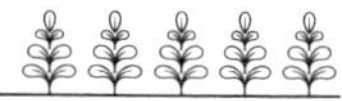

Living in the Household of God

267

EPHESIANS 6:10–24

Standing Strong with the Armor of God

313

SERIES EDITORS' PREFACE

Overview

Like many preachers, you may wish you could use the biblical languages in your sermon preparation, but the task seems daunting. Perhaps you lack confidence in your language skills—especially if it's been a long time since you studied Greek or Hebrew—and when you turn to technical commentaries, you feel overwhelmed. Or perhaps you simply don't have the time to do the laborious work of digging into the original-language texts. To help you overcome these challenges, we designed this series, the Preacher's Greek Companion (as well as its Old Testament counterpart series, the Preacher's Hebrew Companion). In collaboration with the series authors, our goal as series editors is to gently guide you, the busy preacher, through the Greek text of select biblical passages in a way that will empower you to integrate original-language exegesis and homiletics. Our prayer is that you will find this book and the other volumes in this series spiritually and intellectually encouraging as well as pleasant to use. We hope your use of the series will make your sermon preparation a more profound and satisfying process and will invigorate your preaching.

Structure

Each volume in this series includes the following three features for a given biblical book (or portion of a book):

- **a curated selection of passages** we believe many preachers would likely choose to preach on from the biblical book (or portion of the book) in question; **or, for shorter biblical books, the entire book**, broken up into manageable passages
- all the basic **lexical and grammatical tools** you need (whatever your Greek skill level may be) **to work through and meditate on the Greek text** of these passages in a way that strengthens your sermon preparation and empowers you to preach more effectively
- **succinct, select comments** intended to help you responsibly and effectively bridge the gap between reading the Greek text and delivering a sermon on it

The Preacher's Greek Companion is not a traditional commentary series, as is reflected in its title and subtitle: "*Companion*" (not "Commentary") and "*Selected* Passages for *Meditation* and *Sermon Preparation*." That is, we conceived this series as a *supplement* to the wealth of fine commentaries that already exist, not as a replacement for any of them. We recommend using this series alongside traditional commentaries, which by design include helpful information that is not covered in ours.

The Selection of Passages

Each volume in the Preacher's Greek Companion series provides the Greek text of **approximately ten to twelve passages** from a particular biblical book (or portion thereof):

- In addition to having expertise in Greek and exegesis, our series authors typically have extensive preaching experience or are full-time preachers by vocation. Unless the biblical book in question is short enough to be included in full, they chose **passages** they think **preachers would most likely desire to preach**. In order to encourage preaching through the biblical book in an "expository" rather than a thematic manner, these passages are presented in canonical order. That said, for longer books (such as Isaiah or Matthew), we encouraged authors to choose passages that highlight or represent important themes found in the book; for such books, however, the chosen passages are still presented in canonical order. The curated, limited number of passages in each series volume allows you, if you wish, to use the passages as the basis for a "ready-made" sermon series of whatever length suits your schedule (e.g., for a series consisting of, say, four, seven, ten, or twelve sermons). Alternatively, you might choose to preach a series using some of the passages in a volume and then supplement these with passages from the biblical book in question that are not found in the volume.

- The aims of the series guided our decisions about passage length. On the one hand, we encouraged authors to choose **passages that are not too long**, so that the portions of text won't be daunting to you if your Greek skills are rudimentary; nor do we want you to be overwhelmed by wading through dozens of verses in Greek. For this reason, our ideal length for most passages has been approximately ten verses. On the other hand, in order to do justice to the natural boundaries of longer passages, we have taken care not to artificially truncate such texts. Consider, for example, the account of the crossing of the Red Sea (Exod 14–15) or the story of the raising of Lazarus (John 11). Although these texts are far too long to be included in full in a volume in this series, each constituent part of these texts is vital to understanding their narrative development and message. For such passages, we asked authors to focus—as a preacher might typically do when delivering a sermon on a lengthy passage—on what they consider to be the most salient verses from the passage. Accordingly, we have provided the Greek text for only these verses, with the author summarizing the other verses (in English).

- Finally, when authors deemed it helpful (especially for longer biblical books), they have indicated, on the first page devoted to each passage, the **larger literary unit to which the passage belongs**,[1] thus helping you see the passage in question as part of a larger whole rather than as an isolated pericope. In cases where this larger literary context is indicated, we encourage you to pick up a Bible and read and dwell on this context while using this volume to work through the passage.

The Presentation of Each Passage

This volume helps you work through each passage it contains by presenting the Greek text of the passage along with the lexical and grammatical information you need in order to dig into this original-language text. Designed to be highly accessible, this format is intended (1) to enable you to work through the text in manageable chunks and according to your abilities, regardless of your skill level in Greek; (2) to simultaneously facilitate both study and devotion; and (3) in conjunction with the author's commentary, to help you bridge the gap, as easily and seamlessly as possible, between the original-language text and preaching.

More specifically, this volume contains the following five sections for each passage:

- A **brief introduction** to the passage—typically comprising only a few sentences—is included in order to set the stage for the passage and highlight its important themes.

- For ease of reading and to encourage you to slow down and contemplate the text, the passage is typically divided into subunits. For each of these subunits, we provide the **Greek text** of each clause or phrase, along with **transliteration** (as a pronunciation help for those whose Greek is at a rudimentary level) and the author's **translation**.[2]

1. Occasionally, such a literary unit is coterminous with the passage itself.

2. The Greek text used in this series is that of the 1885 Westcott-Hort edition of the New Testament, as printed in B. F. Westcott and F. J. A. Hort, *The Greek New Testament,*

Next, each clause or phrase from the subunit is presented in an interlinear fashion, notably with **a contextual gloss (or multiple contextual glosses) and parsing for each word**.[3] For example:

3a	**Εὐχαριστῶ τῷ θεῷ μου**		
	I give thanks to my God		
Εὐχαριστῶ εὐχαριστέω	I am giving thanks/ give thanks *Eu·cha·ri·**stō***	PRES ACT IND 1ST SG	verb
τῷ ὁ	to the ***tō***	DAT SG MASC	article
θεῷ θεός	(to) God *the·**ō***	DAT SG MASC	noun
μου ἐγώ	of me/my *mou*	1ST GEN SG	personal pron

This formatting allows you to easily analyze each word in the clause or phrase (by helping you on the level of semantics and morphology) and to perceive how the words work together as a whole (by helping you on the level of syntax).

A key feature of each volume in this series is the inclusion of **concise comments** to accompany some clauses and phrases. These have two primary goals: (1) to enable you to understand and exegete the text more deeply than might be possible from reading it in English, and (2) to equip you with insights into the original-language text that will be of direct value for your preaching. To help you focus and not become overwhelmed with too much information, we encouraged our authors to comment only on those clauses and phrases for which they thought doing so would accomplish these two goals. In addition, because the volumes in this series are not only language aids but—ultimately and more importantly—preaching aids, we asked authors to highlight those features in the Greek text that bring out key themes, rhetorical and theological emphasis, narrative de-

with Expanded Dictionary (Peabody, MA: Hendrickson Publishers, 2008). For interested readers, text-critical variants for the passages included in the present volume are presented at the end of the volume.

3. The parsings are derived from an unpublished database created by Mark House and Maurice Robinson for Hendrickson Publishers. The glosses are the author's own, though sometimes they are based on glosses from the aforementioned database. The glosses intentionally err on the "literal" end of the spectrum, in order to help you apprehend the basic meaning(s) of each word in context.

velopment, character development, connections with other biblical texts, and the like. Although noting various other features in the Greek text may have been intrinsically interesting from a grammatical perspective or helpful for strengthening your language skills, authors have generally refrained from commenting on such features when doing so would not be likely to aid you in moving from text to sermon in any substantial way.[4] In short, an author's brief, select comments are intended—in conjunction with the volume's language aids—to provide you both with *focus* and with *space* to slow down, meditate, wonder, and mature in your understanding and experience of the text, as you form your own judgments on it and prepare to proclaim the divine word to your hearers. The author's comments are not intended to circumscribe the possible interpretive options with one single answer (especially for texts whose interpretation is the particular subject of debate among Christian believers). Rather, they are meant to stimulate your thinking, to help you see features of the text (and connections with other texts) that you may not have perceived before, and to prompt you to ask questions that may not have previously occurred to you.

 Each passage ends with a brief section titled **"From Text to Sermon,"** in which our authors, building on their comments, suggest ways you can move from working through the Greek text to the task of homiletics, highlighting potential points of emphasis or particular insights you may wish to share with your audience. In this way, the authors provide you with possible ways to bring the text to life for your audience (e.g., types of illustrations you might use). Because individual preachers (and each of our series authors) bring their own particular skills, perspectives, backgrounds, and oratorial approaches to bear on the homiletical task, and because every biblical text has its own unique features, we encouraged our authors to structure the "From Text to Sermon" section as a free-form series of short paragraphs whose content and emphases are guided by their own personal judgment about what is most helpful for a variety of preachers in different places, cultures, and times. The remarks in this section are always grouped according to rubrics (in the form of inline

4. Another way we have kept the presentation streamlined and uncluttered, so that you can achieve maximum focus, is by intentionally keeping source citations to a minimum. Authors' comments on a given passage are the fruit of their scholarly research on the passage, their personal reflection on it, and their experience preaching and teaching it. They cite secondary sources only when they draw a specific insight from one particular source or wish to point you to a particularly helpful resource for further reading. As stated above, we naturally encourage you to also use traditional commentaries (which typically provide more documentation) in your study and sermon preparation.

headers); but rather than restrict authors with a "one-size-fits-all" set of rubrics, we allowed them to create their own rubrics and even, if helpful, to vary these rubrics across passages within their volume in light of the unique features and emphases of each passage.[5] We view the resulting diversity of approaches and emphases across this series (and even within a given volume) as a strength, and we hope this aspect of the series will encourage you to use your own judgment about how to preach each passage in a way that best suits you and your listeners, being sensitive to the promptings and guidance of the Spirit of God.

Audience and Theological Perspective

Since our hope is that many different kinds of people will find the volumes in this series useful, we have designed the Preacher's Greek Companion to be helpful to a broad spectrum of Christian preachers:

- Our intention is that the series will be **useful and accessible to a large and diverse group of preachers serving a variety of communities throughout the world**. For this reason, we encouraged authors to exercise sensitivity and broad-mindedness in their comments and particularly when writing the "From Text to Sermon" section, in which they could run the risk of being too culturally specific. In particular, we asked authors that any sermon illustrations they included in this section generally be as universal as possible or that, instead of providing specific illustrations, they point to themes from the passage you may wish to illustrate in one way or another. That said, because specificity is essential for good communication, we also allowed authors to suggest—when they deemed it particularly helpful—concrete, culturally specific examples as springboards to help you think about examples that will be relevant for your own context.
- We asked our authors to express any **theological perspectives** in a way that is **consistent with the beliefs stated in the Apostles' Creed**. Because this series aims to meet the needs of Christian preachers of various theological viewpoints, we encouraged a diversity of theological perspectives within these bounds across the volumes in the series. In addition, because the series has a joint focus on exegesis (close attention to what a specific text says) and homiletics (how to preach said text), we advised

5. That said, we suggested the following possible rubrics to authors as starting points to consider: theological themes, themes for application and illustration, integrating the broader historical and literary context, learning from the language, and (as deemed helpful and not reductionistic) "the big idea" of the passage.

authors when making any theological comments to let these flow naturally from the text at hand, rather than using the text as a springboard to discuss issues that would more properly fall under the rubric of systematic theology. Although we asked authors to avoid reading any given passage through the lens of a theological system grounded in other biblical texts, we also strongly encouraged them to discuss allusions to other biblical passages or other innerbiblical literary connections if they felt that doing so would help you understand the message of the text at hand and know how to preach it more effectively.

Acknowledgments

We would like to offer our heartfelt gratitude to the following individuals, who have played a central role in the creation of this series:

- Arley Kangas, Marco Resendes, and Tyler Comer, for their excellent work on various aspects of the making of these volumes, especially transliterating, proofreading, and generating the indexes.
- Phil Frank, for his expert typesetting and for patiently working with us, in our capacity as series editors, to achieve the desired formatting and aesthetic for these volumes.
- The series authors, for joining us in this unique project and for sharing our vision and lending their considerable skills to the task. These volumes are the result of a fruitful collaboration between the Hendrickson team and the series authors (with both parties contributing to the content). We are truly grateful for the opportunity to have worked on this project together.

All of us—the series editors, the series authors, and the team at Hendrickson—pray that the volume you now hold in your hands will empower and encourage you to work through the Greek text of the Bible in order to deepen your sermon preparation and strengthen your proclamation of the word of God. We nurture a deep respect and appreciation for the challenging work that you as a preacher do on the "front lines," and we recognize the many challenges (logistical, mental, emotional, spiritual, and more) that you encounter on a weekly, indeed a daily, basis. We are honored to come alongside you and support you in your important labors, and we pray that your use of this book will bear much fruit for the kingdom of God.

Jonathan G. Kline
Sean M. McDonough

To my father, Waldemar F. de Campos,
and my father-in-law, Cyllas Marins.
May every preacher love the word of God as you do.

AUTHOR'S INTRODUCTION

Among the writings of the New Testament, the letters written by the apostle Paul are some of the most influential for the Christian church in terms of its identity and vocation. A true "pastor-theologian," the apostle articulates the truth of the gospel with remarkable theological depth and pastoral insight. His sophisticated doctrinal teaching is saturated with practical admonitions that have made his writings both the seedbed for Christian doctrine and a foundation for the preaching of the gospel through the centuries.

However, the somewhat complex nature of his writings often makes the task of preaching on them daunting. How can a preacher, as a faithful servant, convey the theological riches of Paul's arguments in a way that both honors the depth of the apostle's thought and remains accessible to a lay Christian audience? How can someone appropriately explore from the pulpit what Paul calls the "mystery of God's will" (Eph 1:9) and bring these lofty truths close to the congregation's hearts without reducing them to manageable practical nuggets?

The letter to the Ephesians—which this commentary assumes was written by the apostle Paul (cf. Hoehner 2002:2–60; Thielman 2010:1–30)—seems particularly challenging in this regard. The letter is packed with long sentences, filled with syntactical and grammatical twists and turns, loaded with complex theological phrases, and saturated with biblical-theological themes. At the same time, however, the mere act of reading the first few chapters of Ephesians out loud can lead the reader to an exhilarating experience of praise and worship.

Ephesians contains some of the most crucial teachings of Paul, and it is understood by many scholars as the crown of Paulinism. In this compact letter, we learn about the election of the saints, salvation by grace through faith, Christ's resurrection and exaltation, union with Christ, the unity of Jews and gentiles, and the work of the Spirit. However, the greatest contribution of the letter lies in its portrayal of the church.

Paul writes his letter to a group of Christians in Ephesus, likely meant to be shared more widely with churches throughout Asia Minor. Paul's history with the Ephesian church is well documented in Acts 18:18–21; 19:1–41; and 20:17–38. His time in Ephesus involves conflicts with Jews in the area, preaching and teaching to gentiles, and a clash with the religious environment of the city—specifically in relation to the pagan cult of the goddess Artemis. On his way back to Jerusalem, Paul summons the Ephesian elders to Miletus and tells them about warnings he has received from the Spirit concerning his future imprisonment.

His predictions are proven accurate as he ends up in prison, first in Caesarea and then in Rome.

Without the direct influence of the apostle, and probably with little news about him, the church in Ephesus begins to experience trials, especially because of the strong pagan context in which they lived. It also begins to grow more and more isolated, avoiding interaction with the Jews, including Jewish Christians.

In light of his absence, Paul writes to the Ephesians from prison to strengthen this predominantly gentile community that is struggling with its identity in relation to both the pagan context in which they live and their understanding of their relationship with the Jews. In doing so, Paul helps this struggling community understand their lives in the context of a cosmic reality. Pulling back the curtain, so to speak, Paul shows his audience how their mundane lives are actually part of an infinitely larger reality where God reigns supreme with the risen Christ at his right hand. Most remarkably, the church, the body of Christ, is portrayed as seated together with Christ in the heavenly places, far above every principality and power. Ordinary Christians, living in the oppressive system of the Roman Empire and surrounded by idolatry, paganism, and corruption on every side, have their eyes opened to a "reality behind the reality"—a realm in which the eternal plan of God is unfolding with absolute precision, to sum up all things in Christ, and to make known the manifold wisdom of God through his church.

This picture is essential for the church in every era. It is by understanding this truth and living into this reality that we are enabled to live a purposeful life, both as individuals and, most importantly, as the body of Christ. This text must be preached repeatedly until our imaginations are transformed and, with them, the way we walk in this world.

Structure of Ephesians

Part 1: The Identity and Vocation of the People of God (1:1–3:21)

Blessed, chosen, and adopted in Christ (1:1–14)
The power of God at work in us (1:15–23)
From death to life (2:1–10)
From alienation to reconciliation (2:11–22)
The wisdom of God revealed through the church (3:1–13)
Strengthened by the Spirit, indwelt by Christ, filled with the fullness of God (3:14–21)

Part 2: The Unity and Conduct of the People of God (4:1–6:24)

Keeping the unity of the Spirit in the bond of peace (4:1–6)
The gift of Christ for the edification of the church (4:7–16)
Living according to the new identity in Christ (4:17–24)
Living as members of one another (4:25–32)
Living as children of light (5:1–20)
Living in the household of God (5:21–6:9)
Standing strong with the armor of God (6:10–24)

I have had the privilege of spending the past twenty-four years preaching, with ten of those years as a pastor in a local church. Nowadays, I have the joy of teaching Scripture and training future pastors and church leaders in a Christian seminary. Although I am thankful for my academic training, it was in the pulpit of a faithful congregation in the countryside of Brazil that my pastoral and theological identity was formed. Therefore, it is my pleasure to contribute a volume on exegesis and preaching for the benefit of preachers. I'm especially thankful for the opportunity to write such a volume on the book of Ephesians. I pray this guide will help inspire sermons by which the beauty of God's plan for his church may be displayed.

There are many people to thank. First and foremost, my wonderful wife, Renata, and my beautiful children, Matt and Zoe, who are a daily source of love and inspiration in my life. The many churches and pastors in Brazil and around the world who have given me the honor of preaching in their pulpits—one of the greatest joys of my life. I also would like to thank Ray Jones Jr. and Alexis Donnelly, my research assistants, who helped revise this volume.

Finally, this book is dedicated to two preachers. My father, Waldemar F. de Campos, who has been a lay preacher most of his life and taught me to love the word of God and the art of preaching from a very young age. I wouldn't be a preacher without his example. Also, my father-in-law, Cyllas Marins, who gave me the opportunity to preach for the first time when I was in my twenties and who remains one of my biggest encouragers.

"To [God] be glory in the church and in Christ Jesus throughout all generations, forever and ever. Amen." (Eph 3:21)

LIST OF ABBREVIATIONS

1ST	first person	INF	infinitive
2ND	second person	interr	interrogative
3RD	third person	MASC	masculine
ACC	accusative	MID	middle
ACT	active	MT	Masoretic Text
adj	adjective	NEUT	neuter
adv	adverb	NOM	nominative
AOR	aorist	num	numerical
comp	comparative	OPT	optative
cond	conditional	PASS	passive
conj	conjunction	PERF	perfect
DAT	dative	PL	plural
demonstr	demonstrative	prep	preposition
FEM	feminine	PRES	present
FUT	future	pron	pronoun
GEN	genitive	PTCP	participle
Heb	Hebrew	SG	singular
IMPF	imperfect	SUBJ	subjunctive
IMPV	imperative	translit	transliteration
IND	indicative	VOC	vocative
indef	indefinite		

NOTE: All Old Testament verse numbers in this volume refer to the Hebrew text. Where the English verse numbering differs, it is listed in brackets following the Hebrew numbering, without any special notation. When the Septuagint (i.e., Greek) version of an Old Testament text is cited and the verse numbering differs from that of the Hebrew text, the Greek reference is listed in brackets following the Hebrew reference, accompanied by the notation "LXX".

EPHESIANS 1:1–14

BLESSED, CHOSEN, AND ADOPTED IN CHRIST

The first part of Ephesians (chs. 1–3) is structured in a liturgical fashion, with two doxologies (1:3–14; 3:20–21) and two prayers (1:15–23; 3:14–19) bookending two discourses (2:1–22; 3:1–13). The section has a christological and ecclesiological orientation. It is about what God has done in Christ for the church and how that shapes their identity. Paul begins his breathtaking theological argument with a doxology, praising God for his blessing of the believers in Christ. At the very outset, Paul situates the election of believers in the eternal good plan of God, who chose them to be his holy daughters and sons through the work of his beloved Son, Jesus Christ, for the praise of his glory.

 1:1–2 

1a Παῦλος ἀπόστολος Χριστοῦ Ἰησοῦ

Paulos apostolos Christou Iēsou

Paul, apostle of Christ Jesus,

1b διὰ θελήματος θεοῦ

dia thelēmatos theou

through the will of God,

1c τοῖς ἁγίοις τοῖς οὖσιν ἐν Ἐφέσῳ

tois hagiois tois ousin en Ephesō

to the holy ones who are in Ephesus

1d καὶ πιστοῖς ἐν Χριστῷ Ἰησοῦ·

kai pistois en Christō Iēsou;

and [the] faithful in Christ Jesus.

2a χάρις ὑμῖν καὶ εἰρήνη

charis hymin kai eirēnē

Grace to you and peace

2b ἀπὸ θεοῦ πατρὸς ἡμῶν

apo theou patros hēmōn

from God our Father

2c καὶ κυρίου Ἰησοῦ Χριστοῦ.

kai kyriou Iēsou Christou.

and the Lord Jesus Christ.

1a	Παῦλος ἀπόστολος Χριστοῦ Ἰησοῦ

Paul, apostle of Christ Jesus,

Παῦλος Παῦλος	Paul ***Pau***·*los*	NOM SG MASC	noun
ἀπόστολος ἀπόστολος	apostle *a*·***po***·*sto*·*los*	NOM SG MASC	noun
Χριστοῦ Χριστός	of Christ *Chri*·***stou***	GEN SG MASC	noun
Ἰησοῦ Ἰησοῦς	(of) Jesus *I*·*ē*·***sou***	GEN SG MASC	noun

Christian audiences are perhaps too familiar with the name Jesus Christ, and some may even think "Christ" is some sort of surname. So it is important to highlight that **Χριστός** corresponds to the title "Messiah," referring to the messianic identity of Jesus, in fulfillment of Old Testament prophecies. This is important in light of Paul's upcoming emphasis on the inclusion of gentiles in the promises made to Israel (2:11–22).

1b	διὰ θελήματος θεοῦ

through the will of God,

διὰ διά	through *di*·***a***	---	prep
θελήματος θέλημα	will *the*·***lē***·*ma*·*tos*	GEN SG NEUT	noun
θεοῦ θεός	of God *the*·***ou***	GEN SG MASC	noun

Θελήματος θεοῦ, the "will of God" (cf. 1:11; 6:6), is part of a prominent cluster of themes in the letter, among which are God's "pleasure" (**εὐδοκία**, 1:9), "predetermination" (**προορίζω**, 1:11), "plan" (**οἰκονομία**), and "purpose" (**πρόθεσις**, 3:11), all referring to the sovereign plan of God. Make sure you track these themes throughout the letter, paying attention to how they influence one another.

1c	τοῖς ἁγίοις τοῖς οὖσιν ἐν Ἐφέσῳ

to the holy ones who are in Ephesus

τοῖς ὁ	to the ***tois***	DAT PL MASC	article

ἁγίοις ἅγιος	(to) holy (ones) *ha·**gi**·ois*	DAT PL MASC	adj
τοῖς ὁ	(to) the (ones) ***tois***	DAT PL MASC	article
οὖσιν εἰμί	(to) those being ***ou**·sin*	PRES ACT PTCP DAT PL MASC	verb
ἐν ἐν	in *en*	---	prep
Ἐφέσῳ Ἔφεσος	Ephesus *E·**phe**·sō*	DAT SG FEM	noun

Rather than a moral designation, **τοῖς ἁγίοις** ("the holy ones") refers to the ecclesiological and covenantal identity of the audience—they are the holy people of God. The term likely draws from the designation of Israel as God's holy people in the Old Testament (cf. Exod 19:3–6; Lev 11:45).

Although the identification of Ephesus is missing from a few important and early manuscripts, it is likely in the original text (Thielman 2010:12–16).

1d **καὶ πιστοῖς ἐν Χριστῷ Ἰησοῦ·**

and [the] faithful in Christ Jesus.

καὶ καί	and ***kai***	---	conj
πιστοῖς πιστός	(to) faithful (ones) *pi·**stois***	DAT PL MASC	adj
ἐν ἐν	in *en*	---	prep
Χριστῷ Χριστός	Christ *Chri·**stō***	DAT SG MASC	noun
Ἰησοῦ Ἰησοῦς	Jesus *I·ē·**sou***	DAT SG MASC	noun

2a **χάρις ὑμῖν καὶ εἰρήνη**

Grace to you and peace

χάρις χάρις	grace ***cha**·ris*	NOM SG FEM	noun
ὑμῖν σύ	to you (all) *hy·**min***	2ND DAT PL	pron

καὶ καί	and ***kai***	---	conj
εἰρήνη εἰρήνη	peace *ei·**rē**·nē*	NOM SG FEM	noun

2b **ἀπὸ θεοῦ πατρὸς ἡμῶν**

from God our Father

ἀπὸ ἀπό	from *a·**po***	---	prep
θεοῦ θεός	God *the·**ou***	GEN SG MASC	noun
πατρὸς πατήρ	father *pa·**tros***	GEN SG MASC	noun
ἡμῶν ἐγώ	of us/our *hē·**mōn***	1ST GEN PL	pron

2c **καὶ κυρίου Ἰησοῦ Χριστοῦ.**

and the Lord Jesus Christ.

καὶ καί	and ***kai***	---	conj
κυρίου κύριος	Lord *ky·**ri**·ou*	GEN SG MASC	noun
Ἰησοῦ Ἰησοῦς	Jesus *I·ē·**sou***	GEN SG MASC	noun
Χριστοῦ Χριστός	Christ *Chri·**stou***	GEN SG MASC	noun

Κύριος ("Lord") is used to translate the name of YHWH in the Septuagint. The parallel coordination (cf. **καὶ**) of **θεοῦ πατρὸς** ("God the Father") and **κυρίου Ἰησοῦ Χριστοῦ** ("Lord Jesus Christ") entails a high christological claim about Jesus that can hardly be overlooked.

 1:3–6 

3a Εὐλογητὸς ὁ θεὸς

*Eulogē**tos** ho the**os***

Blessed is the God

3b καὶ πατὴρ τοῦ κυρίου ἡμῶν Ἰησοῦ Χριστοῦ,

***kai** pa**tēr** **tou** ky**ri**ou hē**mōn** Iē**sou** Chris**tou**,*

and Father of our Lord Jesus Christ,

3c ὁ εὐλογήσας ἡμᾶς

*ho eulo**gē**sas hē**mas***

who blessed us

3d ἐν πάσῃ εὐλογίᾳ πνευματικῇ

*en **pa**sē eulo**gi**a pneumati**kē***

with every spiritual blessing

3e ἐν τοῖς ἐπουρανίοις

*en **tois** epoura**ni**ois*

in the heavenly places

3f ἐν Χριστῷ,

*en Chris**tō**,*

in Christ,

4a καθὼς ἐξελέξατο ἡμᾶς ἐν αὐτῷ

*ka**thōs** exe**le**xato hē**mas** en au**tō***

since he chose us in him

4b πρὸ καταβολῆς κόσμου,

***pro** kata**bo**lēs **kos**mou,*

before the foundation of the world,

4c εἶναι ἡμᾶς ἁγίους καὶ ἀμώμους κατενώπιον αὐτοῦ

einai hēmas hagious kai amōmous katenōpion autou

in order for us to be holy and blameless before him

4d ἐν ἀγάπῃ,

en agapē,

in love

5a προορίσας ἡμᾶς εἰς υἱοθεσίαν

proorisas hēmas eis huiothesian

Having ordained us beforehand for adoption

5b διὰ Ἰησοῦ Χριστοῦ

dia Iēsou Christou

through Jesus Christ

5c εἰς αὐτόν,

eis auton,

in him,

5d κατὰ τὴν εὐδοκίαν τοῦ θελήματος αὐτοῦ,

kata tēn eudokian tou thelēmatos autou,

according to the good pleasure of his will,

6a εἰς ἔπαινον δόξης τῆς χάριτος αὐτοῦ

eis epainon doxēs tēs charitos autou

for the praise of his glorious grace

6b ἧς ἐχαρίτωσεν ἡμᾶς

hēs echaritōsen hēmas

with which he graced us

6c ἐν τῷ ἠγαπημένῳ,

en tō ēgapēmenō,

in the beloved,

3a	**Εὐλογητὸς ὁ θεὸς**		
	Blessed is the God		
Εὐλογητὸς εὐλογητός	blessed *Eu·lo·gē·**tos***	NOM SG MASC	adj
ὁ ὁ	the *ho*	NOM SG MASC	article
θεὸς θεός	God *the**os***	NOM SG MASC	noun

The language **Εὐλογητὸς ὁ θεὸς** ("God is blessed") follows the form of Jewish doxologies (cf. Exod 18:10; 2 Chr 2:11 [12]; Ps 41:3 [2]). The construction is adjectival (the verb "to be" is implied), with **εὐλογητός** ("blessed") denoting a statement of fact rather than an appeal to "bless." It is praise in the form of acknowledgment of God as the blessed one. The statement "God is blessed" is the governing clause upon which the whole argument of 1:3–14 is structured. Everything else is subordinate to this phrase and the next through the relative pronoun that follows in 3c. Therefore, Paul's theology flows from doxology.

3b	**καὶ πατὴρ τοῦ κυρίου ἡμῶν Ἰησοῦ Χριστοῦ,**		
	and Father of our Lord Jesus Christ,		
καὶ καί	and ***kai***	---	conj
πατὴρ πατήρ	father *pa·**tēr***	NOM SG MASC	noun
τοῦ ὁ	of the ***tou***	GEN SG MASC	article
κυρίου κύριος	Lord *ky·**ri**·ou*	GEN SG MASC	noun
ἡμῶν ἐγώ	of us/our *hē·**mōn***	1ST GEN PL	pron
Ἰησοῦ Ἰησοῦς	Jesus *I·ē·**sou***	GEN SG MASC	noun
Χριστοῦ Χριστός	Christ *Chri·**stou***	GEN SG MASC	noun

3c ὁ εὐλογήσας ἡμᾶς

who blessed us

ὁ ὁ	the *ho*	NOM SG MASC	article
εὐλογήσας εὐλογέω	(one) having blessed *eu·lo·**gē**·sas*	AOR ACT PTCP NOM SG MASC	verb
ἡμᾶς ἐγώ	us *hē·**mas***	1ST ACC PL	pron

The relative clause effectively introduces the reason for the doxology: God is blessed because he is **ὁ εὐλογήσας ἡμᾶς**, "the one who blessed us." The verb is an aorist participle, which has a perfective aspect, indicating a completed action at a point in time. The believers have already been blessed in a complete way. God is portrayed here as the ultimate "giver"—an important emphasis in the letter (Eph 1:3, 6–8, 17, 22; 2:4–5, 7–8; 3:2, 7–8, 16; 4:7–8, 11).

3d ἐν πάσῃ εὐλογίᾳ πνευματικῇ

with every spiritual blessing

ἐν ἐν	with *en*	---	prep
πάσῃ πᾶς	all ***pa**·sē*	DAT SG FEM	adj
εὐλογίᾳ εὐλογία	blessing *eu·lo·**gi**·a*	DAT SG FEM	noun
πνευματικῇ πνευματικός	spiritual *pneu·ma·ti·**kē***	DAT SG FEM	adj

In light of the prominence of the Spirit in Ephesians, "spiritual" (**πνευματικῇ**) likely refers to blessings that pertain to and are given by the Holy Spirit.

3e ἐν τοῖς ἐπουρανίοις

in the heavenly places

ἐν ἐν	in *en*	---	prep
τοῖς ὁ	the ***tois***	DAT PL NEUT	article

ἐπουρανίοις ἐπουράνιος	heavenly (places) *e·pou·ra·**ni**·ois*	DAT PL NEUT	adj

Another prominent theme in Ephesians (Eph 1:20; 2:6; 3:10; 6:12), the heavenly places (**ἐν τοῖς ἐπουρανίοις**) are (a) the place of Christ's exaltation (1:20), (b) the place where the church is seated with Christ (2:6), and (c) the realm of principalities and powers (3:10; 6:12). Much of what Paul describes in the letter has the "heavenly places" as a primary perspective. It is as if Paul is looking at reality with his "camera" situated in the heavenly realm.

3f **ἐν Χριστῷ,**

in Christ,

ἐν ἐν	in *en*	---	prep
Χριστῷ Χριστός	Christ *Chri·**stō***	DAT SG MASC	noun

This is Paul's first use of the expression **ἐν Χριστῷ** ("in Christ"), which features nine times in the letter (Eph 1:1, 3; 2:6–7, 10, 13; 3:6, 21; 4:32). The expression occurs another seven times using the pronoun **ἐν αὐτῷ** ("in him"), mostly referring to Christ (Eph 1:4, 9–10; 2:15–16; 4:21; 6:20). The prepositional phrase can have an instrumental sense ("by Christ"), but in several instances, as here, it seems to denote a spatial idea—namely, Christ as the "sphere" of God's blessing of the believers.

4a **καθὼς ἐξελέξατο ἡμᾶς ἐν αὐτῷ**

since he chose us in him

καθὼς καθώς	since *ka·**thōs***	---	adv
ἐξελέξατο ἐκλέγομαι	he chose out *e·xe·**le**·xa·to*	AOR MID IND 3RD SG	verb
ἡμᾶς ἐγώ	us *hē·**mas***	1ST ACC PL	pron
ἐν ἐν	in *en*	---	prep
αὐτῷ αὐτός	him *au·**tō***	3RD DAT SG	personal pron

The adverb **καθὼς** could be read comparatively ("just as") or causally ("since"). If causal, God's blessing is grounded in his election—he blessed because he chose.

The verb **ἐκλέγομαι** ("choose") in the Septuagint commonly describes YHWH's election of Israel (Deut 4:37; 7:7; 10:15; 14:2). In light of other verbal connections the apostle makes with the people of Israel throughout the letter, he likely uses the concept with the narrative of Israel's election in mind.

4b **πρὸ καταβολῆς κόσμου,**

before the foundation of the world,

πρὸ πρό	before ***pro***	---	prep
καταβολῆς καταβολή	foundation *ka·ta·bo·**lēs***	GEN SG FEM	noun
κόσμου κόσμος	(of) (the) world ***kos**·mou*	GEN SG MASC	noun

The two prepositional phrases—**ἐν αὐτῷ** ("in him") from v. 4a and **πρὸ καταβολῆς κόσμου** ("before the foundation of the world") here—indicate the christological sphere and the eternal aspect of election, respectively: believers are elected in Christ, the Elect One, and their election is by an eternal divine determination.

4c **εἶναι ἡμᾶς ἁγίους καὶ ἀμώμους κατενώπιον αὐτοῦ**

in order for us to be holy and blameless before him

εἶναι εἰμί	to be ***ei**·nai*	PRES ACT INF	verb
ἡμᾶς ἐγώ	us *hē·**mas***	1ST ACC PL	pron
ἁγίους ἅγιος	holy *ha·**gi**·ous*	ACC PL MASC	adj
καὶ καί	and ***kai***	---	conj
ἀμώμους ἄμωμος	blameless *a·**mō**·mous*	ACC PL MASC	adj
κατενώπιον κατενώπιον	before *ka·te·**nō**·pi·on*	---	adv.

αὐτοῦ αὐτός	him *au·**tou***	3RD GEN SG	personal pron

The infinitival clause **εἶναι ἡμᾶς ἁγίους** ("in order for us to be holy") completes the thought of the main verb **ἐξελέξατο** ("choose") and identifies its purpose: he chose us in order for us to be holy. Election has a vocational direction.

4d **ἐν ἀγάπῃ,**

in love

ἐν ἐν	in *en*	---	prep
ἀγάπῃ ἀγάπη	love *a·**ga**·pē*	DAT SG FEM	noun

Given its proximity to the infinitive **εἶναι**, **ἐν ἀγάπῃ** ("in love") likely determines the manner in which holiness is expressed. The phrase anticipates the ethical discourse in chs. 4–6. The way holiness is expressed is "in love."

5a **προορίσας ἡμᾶς εἰς υἱοθεσίαν**

Having ordained us beforehand for adoption

προορίσας προορίζω	(he) having determined beforehand *pro·o·**ri**·sas*	AOR ACT PTCP NOM SG MASC	verb
ἡμᾶς ἐγώ	us *hē·**mas***	1ST ACC PL	pron
εἰς εἰς	for *eis*	---	prep
υἱοθεσίαν υἱοθεσία	adoption *hui·o·the·**si**·an*	ACC SG FEM	noun

The participle denotes the manner in which election occurred. The verb **προορίσας** comes from **ὁρίζω**, meaning "to set limits to" or "determine." It is where the English word "horizon" comes from. Here, it carries a sense of determination, expanding on the idea of election. The election of believers entails God's eternal decision to make believers his sons and daughters through Christ. In other words, adoption is the predetermined nature of election—we were chosen as children of God.

5b	**διὰ Ἰησοῦ Χριστοῦ**

through Jesus Christ

διὰ διά	through *di*·***a***	---	prep
Ἰησοῦ Ἰησοῦς	Jesus *I*·*ē*·***sou***	GEN SG MASC	noun
Χριστοῦ Χριστός	Christ *Chri*·***stou***	GEN SG MASC	noun

Whereas elsewhere, Paul uses the term "adoption" (**υἱοθεσία**) to refer to the outcome of the work of Christ and the ministry of the Spirit (Gal 4:4–6; Rom 8:15), here the adoption is **διὰ Ἰησοῦ Χριστοῦ** ("through Jesus Christ"). Christ is the means of adoption. It is through him—with the text likely assuming Christ's redemptive death—that believers have their adoption status granted.

5c	**εἰς αὐτόν,**

in him,

εἰς εἰς	into/in *eis*	---	prep
αὐτόν αὐτός	him *au*·***ton***	3RD ACC SG	personal pron

5d	**κατὰ τὴν εὐδοκίαν τοῦ θελήματος αὐτοῦ,**

according to the good pleasure of his will,

κατὰ κατά	according to *ka*·***ta***	---	prep
τὴν ὁ	the ***tēn***	ACC SG FEM	article
εὐδοκίαν εὐδοκία	good pleasure *eu*·*do*·***ki***·*an*	ACC SG FEM	noun
τοῦ ὁ	of the ***tou***	GEN SG NEUT	article
θελήματος θέλημα	(of) will *the*·***lē***·*ma*·*tos*	GEN SG NEUT	noun
αὐτοῦ αὐτός	of him/his *au*·***tou***	3RD GEN SG	personal pron

This clause refers to God's sovereign and autonomous choice. The prefix **εὐ** ("good") in **εὐδοκίαν** expresses the goodness of God reflected in his plan.

6a	**εἰς ἔπαινον δόξης τῆς χάριτος αὐτοῦ**		
	for the praise of his glorious grace		
εἰς εἰς	for *eis*	---	prep
ἔπαινον ἔπαινος	praise *e·pai·non*	ACC SG MASC	noun
δόξης δόξα	glorious/of glory ***do***·*xēs*	GEN SG FEM	noun
τῆς ὁ	of the ***tēs***	GEN SG FEM	article
χάριτος χάρις	(of) grace ***cha***·*ri·tos*	GEN SG FEM	noun
αὐτοῦ αὐτός	of him/his *au*·***tou***	3RD GEN SG	personal pron

Εἰς ἔπαινον δόξης τῆς χάριτος αὐτοῦ ("for the praise of his glory") is a refrain repeated throughout the blessing (1:6, 12, 14), indicating the ultimate purpose of election: the praise of God's glory. Here God's glory is associated with his grace, another prominent theme in Ephesians.

6b	**ἧς ἐχαρίτωσεν ἡμᾶς**		
	with which he graced us		
ἧς ὅς	which ***hēs***	GEN SG FEM	relative pron
ἐχαρίτωσεν χαριτόω	he gifted *e·cha*·***ri***·*tō·sen*	AOR ACT IND 3RD SG	verb
ἡμᾶς ἐγώ	us *hē*·***mas***	1ST ACC PL	pron

Note the cognate construction—his grace (**τῆς χάριτος αὐτοῦ** [v. 6b]) that he "graced" us (**ἧς ἐχαρίτωσεν ἡμᾶς**)—emphasizing the character of God as the ultimate giver.

6c	**ἐν τῷ ἠγαπημένῳ,**		
	in the beloved,		
ἐν ἐν	in *en*	---	prep
τῷ ὁ	the ***tō***	DAT SG MASC	article
ἠγαπημένῳ ἀγαπάω	beloved/one having been loved *ē·ga·pē·**me**·nō*	PERF PASS PTCP DAT SG MASC	verb

Just as Christ is the "sphere" of the blessing in 1:3, he, as the beloved son, is now the "sphere" (**ἐν τῷ ἠγαπημένῳ**) of that ultimate blessing—the gift of election for adoption.

1:7–10

7a ἐν ᾧ ἔχομεν τὴν ἀπολύτρωσιν

en hō echomen tēn apolytrōsin

In whom we have redemption

7b διὰ τοῦ αἵματος αὐτοῦ,

dia tou haimatos autou,

through his blood,

7c τὴν ἄφεσιν τῶν παραπτωμάτων,

tēn aphesin tōn paraptōmatōn,

the forgiveness of [our] trespasses,

7d κατὰ τὸ πλοῦτος τῆς χάριτος αὐτοῦ

kata to ploutos tēs charitos autou

according to the riches of his grace

8a ἧς ἐπερίσσευσεν εἰς ἡμᾶς

hēs eperisseusen eis hēmas

which he caused to abound in us

8b ἐν πάσῃ σοφίᾳ καὶ φρονήσει,

en pasē sophia kai phronēsei,

in all wisdom and understanding,

9a γνωρίσας ἡμῖν τὸ μυστήριον τοῦ θελήματος αὐτοῦ,

gnōrisas hēmin to mystērion tou thelēmatos autou,

making known to us the mystery of his will,

9b κατὰ τὴν εὐδοκίαν αὐτοῦ

kata tēn eudokian autou

according to his good pleasure

9c ἣν προέθετο ἐν αὐτῷ

hēn proetheto en autō

which he set forth in him

10a εἰς οἰκονομίαν τοῦ πληρώματος τῶν καιρῶν,

eis oikonomian tou plērōmatos tōn kairōn,

as a plan for the fullness of the times,

10b ἀνακεφαλαιώσασθαι τὰ πάντα ἐν τῷ χριστῷ,

anakephalaiōsasthai ta panta en tō christō,

to sum up all things in Christ,

10c τὰ ἐπὶ τοῖς οὐρανοῖς

ta epi tois ouranois

things in heaven

10d καὶ τὰ ἐπὶ τῆς γῆς

kai ta epi tēs gēs

and things on earth.

7a **ἐν ᾧ ἔχομεν τὴν ἀπολύτρωσιν**

In whom we have redemption

ἐν ἐν	in *en*	---	prep
ᾧ ὅς	whom *hō*	DAT SG MASC	relative pron
ἔχομεν ἔχω	we have *e·cho·men*	PRES ACT IND 1ST PL	verb
τὴν ὁ	the *tēn*	ACC SG FEM	article
ἀπολύτρωσιν ἀπολύτρωσις	redemption *a·po·ly·trō·sin*	ACC SG FEM	noun

Verses 7–14 are structured in three blocks marked off by the prepositional phrase **ἐν ᾧ** ("in whom"): "in whom we have redemption" (1:7–10); "in whom we were also chosen" (1:11–12); "in whom you were also sealed (1:13–14)." The relative pronoun refers back to "the beloved" in the previous verse, a reference to Christ. The whole discourse is structured grammatically through the use of relative clauses in a way that conveys the flow from God's agency in blessing us to Christ as the sphere of that blessing. Thus,

Blessed is *God*

who blessed us . . . just as he (God) chose us . . . having determined us beforehand for adoption . . . for the praise of the glory of his *grace*

which he graced us in the *beloved* (i.e., Christ)

in *whom* we have redemption

in *whom* we were also chosen

in *whom* you were also sealed

Besides functioning as rhetorical emphases, providing a sense of rhythm to the discourse, the phrase "in whom" establishes the christological tenor of God's act of blessing. Everything God does for the believers, he does "in Christ." God is the ultimate agent; Christ the ultimate means of this blessing.

7b **διὰ τοῦ αἵματος αὐτοῦ,**

through his blood,

διὰ διά	through *di·**a***	---	prep
τοῦ ὁ	the ***tou***	GEN SG NEUT	article
αἵματος αἷμα	blood ***hai**·ma·tos*	GEN SG NEUT	noun
αὐτοῦ αὐτός	of him/his *au·**tou***	3RD GEN SG	personal pron

The noun **ἀπολύτρωσις** ("redemption" [v. 7a]) is somewhat rare in the Septuagint, but its verbal root, **λυτρόω**, appears more prominently. An important occurrence is in Exod 13:13–16, which describes the redemption of the firstborn, recalling the killing of the firstborn in Egypt. Although the text does not specify the exact means of redemption of the human firstborn, it is likely that the command to redeem them envisions a substitutional sacrifice (Davies 2020:181), perhaps following the same rationale of Exod 12:1–13, where the blood of lambs were put on the doorposts of the houses of the Israelites at the occasion of the killing of the firstborn in Egypt. In Exodus, the sense of deliverance from Egypt and, very likely, of a substitutional sacrifice are part of the meaning of redemption. Paul's use of the word "redemption," particularly with the reference to blood, likely interprets Christ's sacrifice against this backdrop of substitution and deliverance (cf. Rom 3:21–25).

7c	**τὴν ἄφεσιν τῶν παραπτωμάτων,**		
	the forgiveness of [our] trespasses,		
τὴν ὁ	the *tēn*	ACC SG FEM	article
ἄφεσιν ἄφεσις	forgiveness *a·phe·sin*	ACC SG FEM	noun
τῶν ὁ	of the *tōn*	GEN PL NEUT	article
παραπτωμάτων παράπτωμα	(of) trespasses *pa·rap·tō·ma·tōn*	GEN PL NEUT	noun

7d	**κατὰ τὸ πλοῦτος τῆς χάριτος αὐτοῦ**		
	according to the riches of his grace		
κατὰ κατά	according to *ka·ta*	---	prep
τὸ ὁ	the *to*	ACC SG NEUT	article
πλοῦτος πλοῦτος	riches *plou·tos*	ACC SG NEUT	noun
τῆς ὁ	of the *tēs*	GEN SG FEM	article
χάριτος χάρις	(of) grace *cha·ri·tos*	GEN SG FEM	noun
αὐτοῦ αὐτός	of him/his *au·tou*	3RD GEN SG	personal pron

The redemption by blood follows the pattern (**κατά**) of the abundant grace of God. Rather than an act of violence, as it is sometimes wrongly perceived, Christ's sacrifice is the gracious provision of a loving God.

8a	ἧς ἐπερίσσευσεν εἰς ἡμᾶς

which he caused to abound in us

ἧς ὅς	(of) which ***hēs***	GEN SG FEM	relative pron
ἐπερίσσευσεν περισσεύω	he caused to abound *e·pe·**ris**·seu·sen*	AOR ACT IND 3RD SG	verb
εἰς εἰς	in *eis*	---	prep
ἡμᾶς ἐγώ	us ***hē**·mas*	1ST ACC PL	pron

8b	ἐν πάσῃ σοφίᾳ καὶ φρονήσει,

in all wisdom and understanding,

ἐν ἐν	in *en*	---	prep
πάσῃ πᾶς	all ***pa**·sē*	DAT SG FEM	adj
σοφίᾳ σοφία	wisdom *so·**phi**·a*	DAT SG FEM	noun
καὶ καί	and ***kai***	---	conj
φρονήσει φρόνησις	understanding *phro·**nē**·sei*	DAT SG FEM	noun

If on the one hand grace is the cause of redemption, then on the other hand it results in wisdom and insight into the mystery of God's will. Note that the verb **ἐπερίσσευσεν** ("abound" [v. 8a]) is in the aorist tense, which in conjunction with the adjective **πᾶς** ("all" [v. 8b]), denotes a completed and all-encompassing action. The knowledge and understanding of God's mysterious actions on behalf of the believer is a primary emphasis in Ephesians. The phrase here anticipates Paul's prayer for the believers to receive the spirit of wisdom and revelation in the knowledge of God (1:16–21).

9a	γνωρίσας ἡμῖν τὸ μυστήριον τοῦ θελήματος αὐτοῦ,

making known to us the mystery of his will,

γνωρίσας γνωρίζω	(he) making known *gnō·**ri**·sas*	AOR ACT PTCP NOM SG MASC	verb

ἡμῖν ἐγώ	to us *hē·**min***	1ST DAT PL	pron
τὸ ὁ	the ***to***	ACC SG NEUT	article
μυστήριον μυστήριον	mystery *my·**stē**·ri·on*	ACC SG NEUT	noun
τοῦ ὁ	of the ***tou***	GEN SG NEUT	article
θελήματος θέλημα	will *the·**lē**·ma·tos*	GEN SG NEUT	noun
αὐτοῦ αὐτός	of him/his *au·**tou***	3RD GEN SG	personal pron

The word **μυστήριον** ("mystery") has an esoteric sense both in Greco-Roman and Jewish literature, referring to a special knowledge given to some but not to others (cf. Mark 4:11). It has multiple referents in Paul's writings in general (Rom 11:25; 16:25–26; 1 Cor 2:7; 4:1; 14:2; 15:51; Col 1:27; 2:2; 2 Thess 2:7; 1 Tim 3:16) as well as in Ephesians (Eph 1:9; 3:3–4, 9; 5:32; 6:19). Here, it refers to the summing up of all things in Christ. The expression **τὸ μυστήριον τοῦ θελήματος αὐτοῦ** ("the mystery of his will") refers not only to the inability of humans to grasp cognitively and on their own effort the significance of God's work (it is a mystery!) but also to the fact that the knowledge of such work is obtained by God's intentional revelation.

9b **κατὰ τὴν εὐδοκίαν αὐτοῦ**

according to his good pleasure

κατὰ κατά	according to *ka·**ta***	---	prep
τὴν ὁ	the ***tēn***	ACC SG FEM	article
εὐδοκίαν εὐδοκία	good pleasure *eu·do·**ki**·an*	ACC SG FEM	noun
αὐτοῦ αὐτός	of him/his *au·**tou***	3RD GEN SG	personal pron

9c ἣν προέθετο ἐν αὐτῷ

which he set forth in him

ἣν ὅς	which ***hēn***	ACC SG FEM	relative pron
προέθετο προτίθημι	he set forth *pro·**e**·the·to*	AOR MID IND 3RD SG	verb
ἐν ἐν	in *en*	---	prep
αὐτῷ αὐτός	him *au·**tō***	3RD DAT SG	personal pron

Revealing his mystery in Christ (**ἐν αὐτῷ**) is according to God's good pleasure and, like the election of his children (1:5–6), an aspect of his gracious blessing.

10a εἰς οἰκονομίαν τοῦ πληρώματος τῶν καιρῶν,

as a plan for the fullness of the times,

εἰς εἰς	toward *eis*	---	prep
οἰκονομίαν οἰκονομία	plan *oi·ko·no·**mi**·an*	ACC SG FEM	noun
τοῦ ὁ	for the ***tou***	GEN SG NEUT	article
πληρώματος πλήρωμα	(for) fullness *plē·**rō**·ma·tos*	GEN SG NEUT	noun
τῶν ὁ	of the ***tōn***	GEN PL MASC	article
καιρῶν καιρός	(of) times *kai·**rōn***	GEN PL MASC	noun

The term **οἰκονομία** ("plan") denotes careful administration, management, economy, or planning. It has its origins in the idea of the management of the household (**οἰκος**). The fullness of time (**τοῦ πληρώματος τῶν καιρῶν**) is eschatological terminology reflecting the unfolding and ultimate completion of God's plan in history. Along with the reference to God's will and his administration, the phrase underscores God's absolute control in bringing all things to their appointed goal in his appointed time.

10b ἀνακεφαλαιώσασθαι τὰ πάντα ἐν τῷ χριστῷ,

to sum up all things in Christ,

ἀνακεφαλαιώσασθαι ἀνακεφαλαιόω	to sum up *a·na·ke·pha·lai·**ō**·sas·thai*	AOR MID INF	verb
τὰ ὁ	the ***ta***	ACC PL NEUT	article
πάντα πᾶς	all (things) ***pan**·ta*	ACC PL NEUT	adj
ἐν ἐν	in *en*	---	prep
τῷ ὁ	the ***tō***	DAT SG MASC	article
χριστῷ Χριστός	Christ *chri·**stō***	DAT SG MASC	noun

The infinitive **ἀνακεφαλαιώσασθαι** ("to sum up") likely has an appositional sense, revealing the content of the mystery. In other words, the mystery *is* the "summing up of all things in Christ." The verb stems from the noun **κεφαλή**, meaning "head," which is a prominent metaphor to denote Christ's headship over all things and the church (1:22; 4:15; 5:23). More directly, the word **ἀνακεφαλαιόω** is commonly used to identify the summary of an argument. In this metaphorical sense, Christ is understood as the point of convergence of all things, the point at which all things find their ultimate sense and purpose.

10c τὰ ἐπὶ τοῖς οὐρανοῖς

things in heaven

τὰ ὁ	the (things) ***ta***	ACC PL NEUT	article
ἐπὶ ἐπί	in *e·**pi***	---	prep
τοῖς ὁ	the ***tois***	DAT PL MASC	article
οὐρανοῖς οὐρανός	heaven *ou·ra·**nois***	DAT PL MASC	noun

10d **καὶ τὰ ἐπὶ τῆς γῆς**

and things on earth.

καὶ καί	and ***kai***	---	conj
τὰ ὁ	the (things) ***ta***	ACC PL NEUT	article
ἐπὶ ἐπί	on *e*·***pi***	---	prep
τῆς ὁ	the ***tēs***	GEN SG FEM	article
γῆς γῆ	earth ***gēs***	GEN SG FEM	noun

1:11–12

11a ἐν αὐτῷ,

*en au**tō**,*

In him,

11b ἐν ᾧ καὶ ἐκληρώθημεν

*en **hō kai** eklē**rō**thēmen*

in whom we were also chosen [as God's possession],

11c προορισθέντες κατὰ πρόθεσιν

*proori**sthen**tes ka**ta** **pro**thesin*

having been determined beforehand according to the purpose

11d τοῦ τὰ πάντα ἐνεργοῦντος

***tou ta pan**ta ener**goun**tos*

κατὰ τὴν βουλὴν τοῦ θελήματος αὐτοῦ,

*ka**ta tēn** bou**lēn tou** the**lē**matos au**tou**,*

of the one working all things according to the counsel of his will

12a εἰς τὸ εἶναι ἡμᾶς εἰς ἔπαινον δόξης αὐτοῦ

*eis **to ei**nai hē**mas** eis **e**painon **do**xēs au**tou***

in order for us to be for the praise of his glory,

12b τοὺς προηλπικότας ἐν τῷ χριστῷ·

***tous** proēlpi**ko**tas en **tō** chri**stō**;*

the ones who first hoped in Christ.

11a	**ἐν αὐτῷ,**
	In him,

ἐν ἐν	in *en*	---	prep
αὐτῷ αὐτός	him *au·**tō***	3RD DAT SG	personal pron

Ἐν αὐτῷ adds emphasis to **ἐν τῷ χριστῷ**, and ends the first block (1:7–11a, see comment on v. 7a above). The next clause begins with the second relative clause marker **ἐν ᾧ** in 11b.

11b	**ἐν ᾧ καὶ ἐκληρώθημεν**
	in whom we were also chosen [as God's possession],

ἐν ἐν	in *en*	---	prep
ᾧ ὅς	whom ***hō***	DAT SG MASC	relative pron
καὶ καί	also ***kai***	---	conj
ἐκληρώθημεν κληρόω	we were chosen *e·klē·**rō**·thē·men*	AOR PASS IND 1ST PL	verb

The verb **κληρόω**, which has the sense of "appointing by lot," appears only here in the New Testament and is rare in the Septuagint. A related word **ἔγκληρον** ("one who has an inheritance") is used in the Septuagint in Deut 4:20 to refer to Israel as God's chosen inheritance. The verb continues Paul's emphasis initiated in the previous verses on God's election of believers, but now with the added nuance of inheritance.

11c	**προορισθέντες κατὰ πρόθεσιν**
	having been determined beforehand according to the purpose

προορισθέντες προορίζω	(we) having been determined beforehand *pro·o·ris·**then**·tes*	AOR PASS PTCP NOM PL MASC	verb
κατὰ κατά	according to *ka·**ta***	---	prep
πρόθεσιν πρόθεσις	purpose ***pro**·the·sin*	ACC SG FEM	noun

11d **τοῦ τὰ πάντα ἐνεργοῦντος κατὰ τὴν βουλὴν τοῦ θελήματος αὐτοῦ,**

of the one working all things according to the counsel of his will

τοῦ ὁ	of the ***tou***	GEN SG MASC	article
τὰ ὁ	the ***ta***	ACC PL NEUT	article
πάντα πᾶς	all (things) ***pan***·*ta*	ACC PL NEUT	adj
ἐνεργοῦντος ἐνεργέω	(of) (one) working *en*·*er*·***goun***·*tos*	PRES ACT PTCP GEN SG MASC	verb
κατὰ κατά	according to *ka*·***ta***	---	prep
τὴν ὁ	the ***tēn***	ACC SG FEM	article
βουλὴν βουλή	counsel *bou*·***lēn***	ACC SG FEM	noun
τοῦ ὁ	of the ***tou***	GEN SG NEUT	article
θελήματος θέλημα	(of) will *the*·***lē***·*ma*·*tos*	GEN SG NEUT	noun
αὐτοῦ αὐτός	of him/his *au*·***tou***	3RD GEN SG	personal pron

Several terms here—**πρόθεσιν** (“purpose”), **ἐνεργοῦντος** (“the one who works”), **βουλὴν** (“counsel”), **θελήματος** (“will”)—continue the emphasis on God’s absolute sovereignty and autonomy in carrying out his purposes.

12a **εἰς τὸ εἶναι ἡμᾶς εἰς ἔπαινον δόξης αὐτοῦ**

in order for us to be for the praise of his glory,

εἰς εἰς	in order for *eis*	---	prep
τὸ ὁ	*(sign of articular infinitive)* ***to***	ACC SG NEUT	article
εἶναι εἰμί	to be ***ei***·*nai*	PRES ACT INF	verb
ἡμᾶς ἐγώ	us *hē*·***mas***	1ST ACC PL	pron
εἰς εἰς	for *eis*	---	prep
ἔπαινον ἔπαινος	praise ***e***·*pai*·*non*	ACC SG MASC	noun

δόξης δόξα	of glory/glorious ***do**·xēs*	GEN SG FEM	noun
αὐτοῦ αὐτός	of him/his *au·**tou***	3RD GEN SG	personal pron

The phrase **εἰς ἔπαινον δόξης τῆς χάριτος αὐτοῦ** ("for the praise of his glorious grace") from 1:6 is repeated here (minus the adjective "glorious") in the context of God's predetermined election. The ultimate purpose of the believer's election is the glory of God.

Notice the very similar construction to 1:4–6 but with a different order: 1:4–6: Election (**ἐκλέγομαι**)—vocation (**εἶναι ἡμᾶς ἁγίους**)—predetermination (**προορίζω**); 1:11–12: Election (**κληρόω**)—predetermination (**προορίζω**)—vocation (**εἰς τὸ εἶναι ἡμᾶς εἰς ἔπαινον δόξης αὐτοῦ**). Thus, two aspects of election are highlighted: (a) the origin of election in God's sovereign will (having been predetermined according to the plan of God); (b) the vocational purpose of election (in order for us to be holy and for the praise of his glory).

12b **τοὺς προηλπικότας ἐν τῷ χριστῷ·**

the ones who first hoped in Christ.

τοὺς ὁ	the (ones) ***tous***	ACC PL MASC	article
προηλπικότας προελπίζω	who first hoped *pro·ēl·pi·**ko**·tas*	PERF ACT PTCP ACC PL MASC	verb
ἐν ἐν	in *en*	---	prep
τῷ ὁ	the ***tō***	DAT SG MASC	article
χριστῷ Χριστός	Christ *chri·**stō***	DAT SG MASC	noun

1:13–14

13a ἐν ᾧ καὶ ὑμεῖς ἀκούσαντες τὸν λόγον τῆς ἀληθείας,

en hō kai hymeis akousantes ton logon tēs alētheias,

In whom you also—having heard the word of truth,

13b τὸ εὐαγγέλιον τῆς σωτηρίας ὑμῶν,

to euangelion tēs sōtērias hymōn,

the gospel of your salvation—

13c ἐν ᾧ καὶ πιστεύσαντες

en hō kai pisteusantes

in whom you also, having believed,

13d ἐσφραγίσθητε τῷ πνεύματι τῆς ἐπαγγελίας τῷ ἁγίῳ,

esphragisthēte tō pneumati tēs epangelias tō hagiō,

were sealed with the promised Holy Spirit,

14a ὅ ἐστιν ἀρραβὼν τῆς κληρονομίας ἡμῶν,

ho estin arrhabōn tēs klēronomias hēmōn,

who is the down payment of our inheritance,

14b εἰς ἀπολύτρωσιν τῆς περιποιήσεως,

eis apolytrōsin tēs peripoiēseōs,

until the redemption of [God's] possession,

14c εἰς ἔπαινον τῆς δόξης αὐτοῦ.

eis epainon tēs doxēs autou.

for the praise of his glory.

13a	**ἐν ᾧ καὶ ὑμεῖς ἀκούσαντες τὸν λόγον τῆς ἀληθείας,**

In whom you also—having heard the word of truth,

ἐν ἐν	in *en*	---	prep
ᾧ ὅς	whom ***hō***	DAT SG MASC	relative pron
καὶ καί	also ***kai***	---	conj
ὑμεῖς σύ	you (all) *hy*·***meis***	2ND NOM PL	pron
ἀκούσαντες ἀκούω	(you all) having heard *a*·***kou***·*san*·*tes*	AOR ACT PTCP NOM PL MASC	verb
τὸν ὁ	the ***ton***	ACC SG MASC	article
λόγον λόγος	word ***lo***·*gon*	ACC SG MASC	noun
τῆς ὁ	of the ***tēs***	GEN SG FEM	article
ἀληθείας ἀλήθεια	(of) truth *a*·*lē*·***thei***·*as*	GEN SG FEM	noun

Note the emphatic pronoun in the second-person plural **ὑμεῖς** (a change from the first-person plural pronouns in the previous blocks). While the first two blocks (1:7–10, 11–12) describe a broader reality pertaining to believers in general, the third (1:13–14) focuses on the experience of the audience, tying their "being sealed" with their experience of hearing the gospel and believing in Jesus. Paul wants the audience to think about the specific events involved in their conversion.

13b	**τὸ εὐαγγέλιον τῆς σωτηρίας ὑμῶν,**

the gospel of your salvation—

τὸ ὁ	the ***to***	ACC SG NEUT	article
εὐαγγέλιον εὐαγγέλιον	gospel *eu*·*an*·***ge***·*li*·*on*	ACC SG NEUT	noun
τῆς ὁ	of the ***tēs***	GEN SG FEM	article
σωτηρίας σωτηρία	(of) salvation *sō*·*tē*·***ri***·*as*	GEN SG FEM	noun
ὑμῶν σύ	of you (all)/your *hy*·***mōn***	2ND GEN PL	pron

13c	**ἐν ᾧ καὶ πιστεύσαντες**		
	in whom you also, having believed,		
ἐν ἐν	in *en*	---	prep
ᾧ ὅς	whom ***hō***	DAT SG MASC	relative pron
καὶ καί	also ***kai***	---	conj
πιστεύσαντες πιστεύω	(you all) having believed *pi·**steu**·san·tes*	AOR ACT PTCP NOM PL MASC	verb

13d	**ἐσφραγίσθητε τῷ πνεύματι τῆς ἐπαγγελίας τῷ ἁγίῳ,**		
	were sealed with the promised Holy Spirit,		
ἐσφραγίσθητε σφραγίζω	you (all) were sealed *es·phra·**gis**·thē·te*	AOR PASS IND 2ND PL	verb
τῷ ὁ	with the ***tō***	DAT SG NEUT	article
πνεύματι πνεῦμα	(with) Spirit ***pneu**·ma·ti*	DAT SG NEUT	noun
τῆς ὁ	of the ***tēs***	GEN SG FEM	article
ἐπαγγελίας ἐπαγγελία	(of) promise/promised *e·pan·ge·**li**·as*	GEN SG FEM	noun
τῷ ὁ	(of) the ***tō***	DAT SG NEUT	article
ἁγίῳ ἅγιος	(of) holy *ha·**gi**·ō*	DAT SG NEUT	adj

The two aorist participles, **ἀκούσαντες** ("hearing") in v. 13a and **πιστεύσαντες** ("believing") in v. 13c, modify the main aorist passive verb **ἐσφραγίσθητε** ("being sealed") in v. 13d temporally, with a causal nuance. Having heard the gospel and believed in Christ (and because they heard and believed), the believers have been already sealed in Christ. "Hearing" and "believing" put an emphasis on the human response to the gospel. Even though, from start to finish, salvation is a sovereign act of God's grace, there is also emphasis on the human response to this grace. The two aspects are not in tension in Paul's theology.

Ἐν ᾧ ("in whom" [v. 13c]) refers to Christ, following the constructions in vv. 7 and 11. Christ is now portrayed as the "sphere" of the sealing, with the Holy Spirit being the instrument. There is, therefore, Trinitarian activity: the believers were sealed by God, in Christ, with the Spirit.

14a	**ὅ ἐστιν ἀρραβὼν τῆς κληρονομίας ἡμῶν,**		
	who is the down payment of our inheritance,		
ὅ ὅς	who ***ho***	NOM SG NEUT	relative pron
ἐστιν εἰμί	is *e·stin*	PRES ACT IND 3RD SG	verb
ἀρραβὼν ἀρραβών	down payment *ar·rha·**bōn***	NOM SG MASC	noun
τῆς ὁ	of the ***tēs***	GEN SG FEM	article
κληρονομίας κληρονομία	(of) inheritance *klē·ro·no·**mi**·as*	GEN SG FEM	noun
ἡμῶν ἐγώ	of us (all)/our *hē·**mōn***	1ST GEN PL	pron

The noun **ἀρραβών** means "down payment" or "pledge." It was used in commercial contexts denoting an initial payment that stands as a pledge of a payment in full in the future. Theologically, it is a sign that a future reality is already guaranteed. This brings forward the inaugurated eschatology of Paul's theology. The Spirit is the guarantee that the eschatological reality is already the inheritance of the people of God.

14b	**εἰς ἀπολύτρωσιν τῆς περιποιήσεως,**		
	until the redemption of [God's] possession,		
εἰς εἰς	until *eis*	---	prep
ἀπολύτρωσιν ἀπολύτρωσις	redemption *a·po·**ly**·trō·sin*	ACC SG FEM	noun
τῆς ὁ	of the ***tēs***	GEN SG FEM	article
περιποιήσεως περιποίησις	(of) possession *pe·ri·poi·**ē**·se·ōs*	GEN SG FEM	noun

This prepositional phrase concludes the thought of **ἐκληρώθημεν** ("we were chosen") in 1:11. God has chosen the believers as his own inheritance and sealed them with his Holy Spirit, which guarantees that they will be his possession in the end.

14c	**εἰς ἔπαινον τῆς δόξης αὐτοῦ.**

for the praise of his glory.

εἰς εἰς	for *eis*	---	prep
ἔπαινον ἔπαινος	praise ***e**·pai·non*	ACC SG MASC	noun
τῆς ὁ	of the ***tēs***	GEN SG FEM	article
δόξης δόξα	(of) glory ***do**·xēs*	GEN SG FEM	noun
αὐτοῦ αὐτός	of him/his *au·**tou***	3RD GEN SG	personal pron

From Text to Sermon

Main Exegetical Idea. God has blessed us in Christ, by choosing us as his children to be holy before him, for the praise of his glory.

Bridge to Theology. The central theological idea of the passage is election, yet there are several other theological ideas that give shape to it. First, election is a blessing by a benevolent God. Paul describes God as the ultimate giver who lavishes his abundant grace upon his people. Second, election is an act of God's sovereign predetermination. Paul emphasizes the initiative of God's will and his eternal determination. Third, election is vocational. We are chosen for a purpose, to be holy and blameless before God. Fourth, election is an act of adoption. We are chosen to be children of a loving Father. Fifth, election is christological. It is only "in Christ"—namely, by participating in Christ—that we gain our status as the elect people of God. Finally, election is doxological. It is ultimately for the praise of God's glory, which is why the whole passage is structured as a doxology ("God is blessed . . .").

Preaching on this passage can be an excellent opportunity to explore what it means to be chosen as God's children. Perhaps you can spend two weeks on this passage with the congregation, considering these different aspects. The christological facet, elaborated in the three "in whom" phrases (as discussed in the comments above), likely warrants a sermon of its own.

Possible Sermon Structure. There are different ways to structure a sermon in this passage. Since it is a long passage, it might be wise to approach it as a two-part miniseries within a series, or even as its own series on election. You could structure it using the six theological aspects of election outlined above. Alternatively, a verse-by-verse exposition of the text will lead you to all six theological aspects. However, due to the somewhat circular rhetoric, you will find yourself revisiting the same themes throughout the passage. This demands some creativity to avoid being repetitive. Another option is to structure your sermons following Paul's rhetoric. Thus:

Sermon 1—1:3–6: God blessed us with all spiritual blessing (1:3). What is that spiritual blessing?

1 He chose us (1:4)

    1.1 before the foundation of the world

    1.2 so that we may be holy

2 He adopted us (1:5–6)

  2.1 according to the purpose of his will
  2.2 to the praise of his glorious grace

Sermon 2 — 1:7–14: We are blessed *in Christ*

1 We have been redeemed by his blood (1:7–10).

  1.1 we have been forgiven (1:7a)
  1.2 we have been given wisdom and insight into the mystery of God's will (1:7b–10)

2 We have been chosen as God's possession (1:11–12)

3 We have been sealed with the Holy Spirit (1:13–14)

For the sake of effective communication, dividing the passage into two sermons will provide you with a better opportunity to do justice to its rich theology. However, since this entire passage revolves around the theme of election, it is beneficial to maintain both sections in the congregation's mind so that they appreciate the overall theme. One way of doing this is to read the full passage in both sermons.

Points of Application. There are several points of application in this passage, and you might want to focus on one or two. An important observation is that the entire passage is framed as a doxology. Our election is ultimately for God's glory. Furthermore, the explanation for God blessing us with every spiritual blessing in the heavenly realm is rooted in our election and adoption. Reflecting on what it means to be blessed can be very meaningful, especially in a time when being blessed is often understood in material terms. Lastly, one cannot overlook the vocational orientation of the passage. We are not chosen just to blissfully enjoy our status but to live holy lives before God.

Illustration Opportunities. The concept of election is not easily illustrated, and political elections are not appropriate as an illustration except as a point of contrast. For example, election for office relies on a majority vote, while God's election is God's alone; he acts in accordance with the counsel of his will. Another point of contrast is that political elections are normally based on merit, or people's perception thereof. We, however, are elected in Christ, and on the basis of his merits alone—in him we have redemption through his blood. There are probably other points of contrast that you can use along these lines.

Adoption is perhaps better illustrated through familiar stories about the adoption of children. While these stories vary and might require sensitivity in some congregations, they often show how adoptive parents intentionally pour their love onto a child they choose to embrace as their own. That would be a good entry point to explore the immeasurably greater benevolence of God the Father, who chose us to be his children before the foundation of the world. Here, God's choice of Israel as his people (see comments above) also makes for a great biblical illustration, although it is not a mere illustration but a biblical-theological concept.

Finally, the concept of believers being God's own possession and the Spirit serving as the guarantee can be likened to the commercial idea of a down payment (see comments above). When someone offers a down payment on a house, they signal their possession of it, even if it has not been fully "redeemed" yet. The Spirit is the down payment on our inheritance as God's children, the sign that we already belong to him, even as we wait for our full redemption.

EPHESIANS 1:15–23

KNOWING THE POWER OF GOD AT WORK IN US

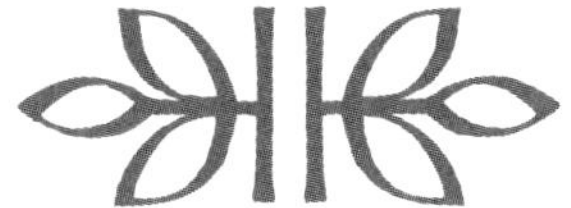

After the blessing, Paul offers a prayer for the believers, continuing the liturgical tone of the first part of the letter. The apostle will repeat several theological elements of the blessing in the prayer. In effect, Paul prays for the audience to appropriate the reality already made available by God's grace. More specifically, he prays that the mystery that has already been made known in all wisdom and insight (1:8–10) will now be fully grasped by an enlightened church. In both the blessing and the prayer, the object of revelation is Christ's supremacy, but in the prayer, Paul emphasizes the outcome of God's power at work in the believers. The prayer can be divided into two blocks: 1:15–18a—prayer for revelation; 1:18b–23—the explanation of what is revealed.

1:15–19

15a Διὰ τοῦτο κἀγώ,

Dia touto kagō,

For this reason, I also,

15b ἀκούσας τὴν καθ᾽ ὑμᾶς πίστιν ἐν τῷ κυρίῳ Ἰησοῦ

akousas tēn kath' hymas pistin en tō kyriō Iēsou

having heard of your own faith in the Lord Jesus,

15c καὶ τὴν ἀγάπην τὴν εἰς πάντας τοὺς ἁγίους,

kai tēn agapēn tēn eis pantas tous hagious,

and the love which you have for all the saints,

16a οὐ παύομαι εὐχαριστῶν ὑπὲρ ὑμῶν

ou pauomai eucharistōn hyper hymōn

do not cease giving thanks on your behalf,

16b μνείαν ποιούμενος ἐπὶ τῶν προσευχῶν μου,

mneian poioumenos epi tōn proseuchōn mou,

mentioning [you] in my prayers,

17a ἵνα ὁ θεὸς τοῦ κυρίου ἡμῶν Ἰησοῦ Χριστοῦ,

hina ho theos tou kyriou hēmōn Iēsou Christou,

so that the God of our Lord Jesus Christ,

17b ὁ πατὴρ τῆς δόξης,

ho patēr tēs doxēs,

the Father of glory,

17c δώῃ ὑμῖν πνεῦμα σοφίας καὶ ἀποκαλύψεως

dōē hymin pneuma sophias kai apokalypseōs

might give you [the] Spirit of wisdom and revelation

17d ἐν ἐπιγνώσει αὐτοῦ,

en epignōsei autou,

in the knowledge of him,

18a πεφωτισμένους τοὺς ὀφθαλμοὺς τῆς καρδίας ὑμῶν

pephōtismenous tous ophthalmous tēs kardias hymōn

having had the eyes of your hearts enlightened,

18b εἰς τὸ εἰδέναι ὑμᾶς τίς ἐστιν ἡ ἐλπὶς τῆς κλήσεως αὐτοῦ,

eis to eidenai hymas tis estin hē elpis tēs klēseōs autou,

that you may know what is the hope of his calling,

18c τίς ὁ πλοῦτος τῆς δόξης τῆς κληρονομίας αὐτοῦ

tis ho ploutos tēs doxēs tēs klēronomias autou

ἐν τοῖς ἁγίοις,

en tois hagiois,

what are the riches of his glorious inheritance in the saints,

19a καὶ τί τὸ ὑπερβάλλον μέγεθος τῆς δυνάμεως αὐτοῦ

kai ti to hyperballon megethos tēs dynameōs autou

and what is the surpassing greatness of his power

19b εἰς ἡμᾶς τοὺς πιστεύοντας

eis hēmas tous pisteuontas

for us who believe

19c κατὰ τὴν ἐνέργειαν τοῦ κράτους τῆς ἰσχύος αὐτοῦ

kata tēn energeian tou kratous tēs ischyos autou

according to the working of the might of his strength

15a	**Διὰ τοῦτο κἀγώ,**
	For this reason, I also,

Διὰ διά	for *Di·**a***	---	prep
τοῦτο οὗτος	this (reason) ***tou**·to*	ACC SG NEUT	demonstr pron
κἀγώ κἀγώ	I also *ka·**gō***	1ST NOM SG	pron

The prepositional phrase **διὰ τοῦτο** ("for this reason") looks back at 1:3–14 as the basis of the prayer. Paul has just praised God for what he has done in Christ for the believers. Now, grounded on that reality he goes on to express his wish that the believers will be able to appropriate it. The prayer has several thematic links with the blessing: Spirit of wisdom and revelation, wisdom and insight, believing/hoping in Christ, calling and inheritance, the supremacy of Christ over all things. This is an excellent model for prayer. Prayer should always be grounded in praise, because praise sets our hearts in the right perspective to ask. So we begin with praise for what God has done and pray for God to help us appropriate and live into the reality he has already made possible.

15b	**ἀκούσας τὴν καθ' ὑμᾶς πίστιν ἐν τῷ κυρίῳ Ἰησοῦ**
	having heard of your own faith in the Lord Jesus,

ἀκούσας ἀκούω	(I) having heard *a·**kou**·sas*	AOR ACT PTCP NOM SG MASC	verb
τὴν ὁ	of the ***tēn***	ACC SG FEM	article
καθ' κατά	according to *kath'*	---	prep
ὑμᾶς σύ	you (all) *hy·**mas***	2ND ACC PL	pron
πίστιν πίστις	faith ***pi**·stin*	ACC SG FEM	noun
ἐν ἐν	in *en*	---	prep
τῷ ὁ	the ***tō***	DAT SG MASC	article
κυρίῳ κύριος	Lord *ky·**ri**·ō*	DAT SG MASC	noun
Ἰησοῦ Ἰησοῦς	Jesus *I·ē·**sou***	DAT SG MASC	noun

15c καὶ τὴν ἀγάπην τὴν εἰς πάντας τοὺς ἁγίους,

and the love which you have for all the saints,

καὶ καί	and ***kai***	---	conj
τὴν ὁ	the ***tēn***	ACC SG FEM	article
ἀγάπην ἀγάπη	love *a·**ga**·pēn*	ACC SG FEM	noun
τὴν ὁ	the ***tēn***	ACC SG FEM	article
εἰς εἰς	for *eis*	---	prep
πάντας πᾶς	all ***pan**·tas*	ACC PL MASC	adj
τοὺς ὁ	of the ***tous***	ACC PL MASC	article
ἁγίους ἅγιος	(of) saints *ha·**gi**·ous*	ACC PL MASC	adj

The noun **τὴν ἀγάπην** ("love") is not present in the earliest manuscripts. However, it is likely that the repetition of the accusative article **τὴν . . . τὴν** might have confused an early scribe, who accidentally omitted the noun present in the original text. Faith (**πίστιν** [v. 15b]) and love (**ἀγάπην** [v. 15c]) are associated elsewhere in Ephesians (cf. 3:17; 6:23. Cf. also 1 Cor 13:2, 13; Gal 5:6), highlighting the vertical and horizontal directions of the Christian life (cf. Mark 12:29).

16a οὐ παύομαι εὐχαριστῶν ὑπὲρ ὑμῶν

do not cease giving thanks on your behalf,

οὐ οὐ	not *ou*	---	particle
παύομαι παύω	I cease ***pau**·o·mai*	PRES MID IND 1ST SG	verb
εὐχαριστῶν εὐχαριστέω	(I) giving thanks *eu·cha·ri·**stōn***	PRES ACT PTCP NOM SG MASC	verb
ὑπὲρ ὑπέρ	on behalf of *hy·**per***	---	prep
ὑμῶν σύ	you (all) *hy·**mōn***	2ND GEN PL	pron

16b	**μνείαν ποιούμενος ἐπὶ τῶν προσευχῶν μου,**

mentioning [you] in my prayers,

μνείαν μνεία	mention/remembrance *mnei·an*	ACC SG FEM	noun
ποιούμενος ποιέω	(I) making *poi·ou·me·nos*	PRES MID PTCP NOM SG MASC	verb
ἐπὶ ἐπί	in *e·pi*	---	prep
τῶν ὁ	the *tōn*	GEN PL FEM	article
προσευχῶν προσευχή	prayers *pros·eu·chōn*	GEN PL FEM	noun
μου ἐγώ	of me/my *mou*	1ST GEN SG	pron

Although Paul follows the ancient epistolary convention of beginning the letter with prayer (here) and thanksgiving ("**εὐχαριστῶν**" [v. 16a]), he expands on the prayer significantly, adding key theological concepts that are developed throughout the letter.

17a	**ἵνα ὁ θεὸς τοῦ κυρίου ἡμῶν Ἰησοῦ Χριστοῦ,**

so that the God of our Lord Jesus Christ,

ἵνα ἵνα	so that *hi·na*	---	conj
ὁ ὁ	the *ho*	NOM SG MASC	article
θεὸς θεός	God *the·os*	NOM SG MASC	noun
τοῦ ὁ	of the *tou*	GEN SG MASC	article
κυρίου κύριος	Lord *ky·ri·ou*	GEN SG MASC	noun
ἡμῶν ἐγώ	of us/our *hē·mōn*	1ST GEN PL	pron
Ἰησοῦ Ἰησοῦς	Jesus *I·ē·sou*	GEN SG MASC	noun
Χριστοῦ Χριστός	Christ *Chri·stou*	GEN SG MASC	noun

Here Paul begins to turn to the purpose (**ἵνα**) of the prayer and its theological core. It is a direct request to God. What Paul wants the Ephesians to know can only come by direct revelation from God through the Spirit. Paul can say what it is, but only God can reveal what it means.

17b	**ὁ πατὴρ τῆς δόξης,**		
	the Father of glory,		
ὁ ὁ	the *ho*	NOM SG MASC	article
πατὴρ πατήρ	father *pa·**tēr***	NOM SG MASC	noun
τῆς ὁ	of the ***tēs***	GEN SG FEM	article
δόξης δόξα	(of) glory ***do**·xēs*	GEN SG FEM	noun

The association of the concepts of the fatherhood of God (**ὁ πατὴρ**) and his glory (**τῆς δόξης**) is not common in the Old Testament, but they were often employed by Jesus (Matt 16:27; Mark 8:38; John 8:54; 17:5, 24). The genitive construction makes God's glory an attribute of his fatherhood.

17c	**δώῃ ὑμῖν πνεῦμα σοφίας καὶ ἀποκαλύψεως**		
	might give you [the] Spirit of wisdom and revelation		
δώῃ δίδωμι	(he) might give ***dō**·ē*	AOR ACT OPT 3RD SG	verb
ὑμῖν σύ	to you (all) *hy·**min***	2ND DAT PL	pron
πνεῦμα πνεῦμα	spirit ***pneu**·ma*	ACC SG NEUT	noun
σοφίας σοφία	of wisdom *so·**phi**·as*	GEN SG FEM	noun
καὶ καί	and ***kai***	---	conj
ἀποκαλύψεως ἀποκάλυψις	(of) revelation *a·po·ka·**ly**·pse·ōs*	GEN SG FEM	noun

17d	**ἐν ἐπιγνώσει αὐτοῦ,**		
	in the knowledge of him,		
ἐν ἐν	in *en*	---	prep
ἐπιγνώσει ἐπίγνωσις	knowledge *e·pi·**gnō**·sei*	DAT SG FEM	noun
αὐτοῦ αὐτός	of him *au·**tou***	3RD GEN SG	personal pron

"Giving" (**δώῃ**) is a prominent theme in Ephesians (1:3, 6–8, 17, 22; 2:4–5, 7–8; 3:2, 7–8, 16; 4:7–8, 11). God is the gracious giver.

The noun **πνεῦμα** ("spirit") is likely a reference to the Holy Spirit rather than a general reference to an internal disposition. Wisdom and revelation (**σοφίας καὶ ἀποκαλύψεως**) are coordinated. Therefore wisdom is more specifically understood as greater insight into the knowledge (**ἐπιγνώσις**) of God rather than a reference to wisdom as a virtue in general.

18a	**πεφωτισμένους τοὺς ὀφθαλμοὺς τῆς καρδίας ὑμῶν**		
	having had the eyes of your hearts enlightened,		
πεφωτισμένους φωτίζω	(them) having been enlightened *pe·phō·tis·**me**·nous*	PERF PASS PTCP ACC PL MASC	verb
τοὺς ὁ	the ***tous***	ACC PL MASC	article
ὀφθαλμοὺς ὀφθαλμός	eyes *oph·thal·**mous***	ACC PL MASC	noun
τῆς ὁ	of the ***tēs***	GEN SG FEM	article
καρδίας καρδία	(of) hearts *kar·**di**·as*	GEN SG FEM	noun
ὑμῶν σύ	of you (all)/your *hy·**mōn***	2ND GEN PL	pron

The syntax of the clause is difficult because of the participle **πεφωτισμένους** ("having been enlightened"), whose function is ambiguous, but since it is in the accusative, it likely looks forward to the accusative **ὑμᾶς** (you) in the following sentence. The perfect participle, which refers to an accomplished event with ongoing results, likely points to the experience of conversion. Later Paul will refer to the Ephesians as those who once "lived in darkness" (5:8). In the Greco-Roman understanding, the "inner eye" was a metaphor for mystical insight. In Jewish thought, the heart is the seat of reason. Blindness and hardened hearts are often combined to denote obduracy and rebellion (cf. Eph 4:17–18), which are sometimes associated with idolatry (cf. Isa 6:9–10; Rom 1:18–32). Many in the Ephesian church had come from the pagan practice of idolatry of Artemis, but when the eyes of their hearts had been enlightened by the gospel, they turned from the idolatrous practices of the gentiles to allegiance to Jesus. Paul, therefore, prays they will be able to know (**εἰδέναι** [18b]), among other things, the supremacy of Christ over the powers (cf. 1:20–23).

18b **εἰς τὸ εἰδέναι ὑμᾶς τίς ἐστιν ἡ ἐλπὶς τῆς κλήσεως αὐτοῦ,**

that you may know what is the hope of his calling,

εἰς εἰς	to *eis*	---	prep
τὸ ὁ	*(sign of articular infinitive)* ***to***	ACC SG NEUT	article
εἰδέναι εἰδῶ	know *ei·**de**·nai*	PERF ACT INF	verb
ὑμᾶς σύ	you (all) *hy·**mas***	2ND ACC PL	pron
τίς τίς~2	what ***tis***	NOM SG FEM	interr pron
ἐστιν εἰμί	is *e·stin*	PRES ACT IND 3RD SG	verb
ἡ ὁ	the ***hē***	NOM SG FEM	article
ἐλπὶς ἐλπίς	hope *el·**pis***	NOM SG FEM	noun
τῆς ὁ	of the ***tēs***	GEN SG FEM	article
κλήσεως κλῆσις	(of) calling ***klē**·se·ōs*	GEN SG FEM	noun
αὐτοῦ αὐτός	of him/his *au·**tou***	3RD GEN SG	personal pron

18c **τίς ὁ πλοῦτος τῆς δόξης τῆς κληρονομίας αὐτοῦ ἐν τοῖς ἁγίοις,**

what are the riches of his glorious inheritance in the saints,

τίς τίς~2	what ***tis***	NOM SG MASC	interr pron
ὁ ὁ	the *ho*	NOM SG MASC	article
πλοῦτος πλοῦτος	riches ***plou*** · *tos*	NOM SG MASC	noun
τῆς ὁ	of the ***tēs***	GEN SG FEM	article
δόξης δόξα	(of) glory/glorious ***do*** · *xēs*	GEN SG FEM	noun
τῆς ὁ	(of) the ***tēs***	GEN SG FEM	article
κληρονομίας κληρονομία	inheritance *klē* · *ro* · *no* · ***mi*** · *as*	GEN SG FEM	noun
αὐτοῦ αὐτός	of him/his *au* · ***tou***	3RD GEN SG	personal pron
ἐν ἐν	in *en*	---	prep
τοῖς ὁ	the ***tois***	DAT PL MASC	article
ἁγίοις ἅγιος	saints *ha* · ***gi*** · *ois*	DAT PL MASC	adj

19a **καὶ τί τὸ ὑπερβάλλον μέγεθος τῆς δυνάμεως αὐτοῦ**

and what is the surpassing greatness of his power

καὶ καί	and ***kai***	---	conj
τί τίς~2	what ***ti***	NOM SG NEUT	interr pron
τὸ ὁ	the ***to***	NOM SG NEUT	article
ὑπερβάλλον ὑπερβάλλω	surpassing *hy* · *per* · ***bal*** · *lon*	PRES ACT PTCP NOM SG NEUT	verb
μέγεθος μέγεθος	greatness ***me*** · *ge* · *thos*	NOM SG NEUT	noun
τῆς ὁ	of the ***tēs***	GEN SG FEM	article

δυνάμεως δύναμις	(of) power *dy·**na**·me·ōs*	GEN SG FEM	noun
αὐτοῦ αὐτός	of him/his *au·**tou***	3RD GEN SG	personal pron

Election (**κλήσεως** [v. 18b]) and inheritance (**κληρονομίας** [v. 18c]) pick up on the concepts previously developed in the blessing. Paul now adds "power" (**δύναμις**), which he emphasizes with hyperbolic rhetoric, piling up nouns and adjectives in genitive constructions: **τὸ ὑπερβάλλον μέγεθος τῆς δυνάμεως αὐτοῦ** ("the surpassing greatness of his power"). Paul will unpack the meaning of this power in vv. 20–23.

19b **εἰς ἡμᾶς τοὺς πιστεύοντας**

for us who believe

εἰς εἰς	for *eis*	---	prep
ἡμᾶς ἐγώ	us *hē·**mas***	1ST ACC PL	pron
τοὺς ὁ	the ***tous***	ACC PL MASC	article
πιστεύοντας πιστεύω	ones believing *pi·**steu**·on·tas*	PRES ACT PTCP ACC PL MASC	verb

This prepositional phrase likely indicates advantage: the power is for the benefit of the ones who believe. This frames Paul's discourse on God's power. In vv. 20–21, he will unpack the significance of God's power at work in Christ's resurrection and exaltation, after which he will land on the significance of this power in the life of the church (vv. 22–23), moving from Christology to ecclesiology.

19c **κατὰ τὴν ἐνέργειαν τοῦ κράτους τῆς ἰσχύος αὐτοῦ**

according to the working of the might of his strength

κατὰ κατά	according to *ka·**ta***	---	prep
τὴν ὁ	the ***tēn***	ACC SG FEM	article
ἐνέργειαν ἐνέργεια	working *en·**er**·gei·an*	ACC SG FEM	noun

τοῦ ὁ	of the ***tou***	GEN SG NEUT	article
κράτους κράτος	(of) might ***kra***·*tous*	GEN SG NEUT	noun
τῆς ὁ	of the ***tēs***	GEN SG FEM	article
ἰσχύος ἰσχύς	(of) strength *is*·***chy***·*os*	GEN SG FEM	noun
αὐτοῦ αὐτός	of him/his *au*·***tou***	3RD GEN SG	personal pron

20a ἣν ἐνήργησεν ἐν τῷ χριστῷ

hēn enērgēsen en tō christō

which he worked in Christ,

20b ἐγείρας αὐτὸν ἐκ νεκρῶν,

egeiras auton ek nekrōn,

when he raised him from the dead,

20c καὶ καθίσας ἐν δεξιᾷ αὐτοῦ ἐν τοῖς ἐπουρανίοις

kai kathisas en dexia autou en tois epouraniois

and seated [him] at his right hand in the heavenly places

21a ὑπεράνω πάσης ἀρχῆς καὶ ἐξουσίας

hyperanō pasēs archēs kai exousias

καὶ δυνάμεως καὶ κυριότητος

kai dynameōs kai kyriotētos

far above every ruler and authority and power and dominion

21b καὶ παντὸς ὀνόματος ὀνομαζομένου

kai pantos onomatos onomazomenou

and every name being named

21c οὐ μόνον ἐν τῷ αἰῶνι τούτῳ

ou monon en tō aiōni toutō

not only in this age

21d ἀλλὰ καὶ ἐν τῷ μέλλοντι·

alla kai en tō mellonti;

but also in the one to come

22a καὶ πάντα ὑπέταξεν ὑπὸ τοὺς πόδας αὐτοῦ,

kai panta hypetaxen hypo tous podas autou,

and he subjected all things under his feet,

22b καὶ αὐτὸν ἔδωκεν κεφαλὴν

kai auton edōken kephalēn

and gave him to be head

22c ὑπὲρ πάντα

hyper panta

over all things

22d τῇ ἐκκλησίᾳ,

tē ekklēsia,

to the church,

23a ἥτις ἐστὶν τὸ σῶμα αὐτοῦ,

hētis estin to sōma autou,

which is his body,

23b τὸ πλήρωμα τοῦ τὰ πάντα ἐν πᾶσιν πληρουμένου.

to plērōma tou ta panta en pasin plēroumenou.

the fullness of the one filling all things in every way.

20a **ἣν ἐνήργησεν ἐν τῷ χριστῷ**

which he worked in Christ,

ἣν ὅς	which *hēn*	ACC SG FEM	relative pron
ἐνήργησεν ἐνεργέω	he worked *en·ēr·gē·sen*	AOR ACT IND 3RD SG	verb
ἐν ἐν	in *en*	---	prep
τῷ ὁ	the *tō*	DAT SG MASC	article
χριστῷ Χριστός	Christ *chri·stō*	DAT SG MASC	noun

More than a theological digression, vv. 20–23 explain the affirmation made in 1:15–19. It is an expansion on the third element the Ephesians are to grasp by revelation; namely, the "surpassing power" for the benefit of the believers. This power is expressed in three elements: (1) God's resurrection and exaltation of the Messiah; (2) God's subjection of all things under the Messiah's feet; and (3) God's giving of the Messiah as head over all things to the church.

20b **ἐγείρας αὐτὸν ἐκ νεκρῶν,**

when he raised him from the dead,

ἐγείρας ἐγείρω	(he) having raised *e·**gei**·ras*	AOR ACT PTCP NOM SG MASC	verb
αὐτὸν αὐτός	him *au·**ton***	3RD ACC SG	personal pron
ἐκ ἐκ	from *ek*	---	prep
νεκρῶν νεκρός	dead *ne·**krōn***	GEN PL MASC	adj

20c **καὶ καθίσας ἐν δεξιᾷ αὐτοῦ ἐν τοῖς ἐπουρανίοις**

and seated [him] at his right hand in the heavenly places

καὶ καί	and ***kai***	---	conj
καθίσας καθίζω	(he) having seated *ka·**thi**·sas*	AOR ACT PTCP NOM SG MASC	verb
ἐν ἐν	in *en*	---	prep
δεξιᾷ δεξιός	right hand *de·xi·**a***	DAT SG FEM	adj
αὐτοῦ αὐτός	of him/his *au·**tou***	3RD GEN SG	personal pron
ἐν ἐν	in *en*	---	prep
τοῖς ὁ	the ***tois***	DAT PL NEUT	article
ἐπουρανίοις ἐπουράνιος	heavenly (places) *e·pou·ra·**ni**·ois*	DAT PL NEUT	adj

Resurrection (**ἐγείρας** [20b]) and exaltation (**καὶ καθίσας ἐν δεξιᾷ αὐτοῦ**) are often associated in Paul's Christology (cf. 1 Cor 15:20, 25–28; Rom 1:3–4; 8:34; Phil 2:8–11). Together they constitute God's vindication of Jesus. The reference to God's right hand (**δεξιᾷ**) recalls Ps 110:1, a messianic psalm with divine warfare imagery (cf. Mark 12:35–37), where God is portrayed as shattering the kings and chiefs of the earth. The psalm fits well with the portrayal of Jesus as exalted far above rulers and authorities.

21a **ὑπεράνω πάσης ἀρχῆς καὶ ἐξουσίας καὶ δυνάμεως καὶ κυριότητος**

far above every ruler and authority and power and dominion

ὑπεράνω ὑπεράνω	far above *hy·pe·**ra**·nō*	---	adv
πάσης πᾶς	every ***pa**·sēs*	GEN SG FEM	adj
ἀρχῆς ἀρχή	ruler *ar·**chēs***	GEN SG FEM	noun
καὶ καί	and ***kai***	---	conj
ἐξουσίας ἐξουσία	authority *e·xou·**si**·as*	GEN SG FEM	noun
καὶ καί	and ***kai***	---	conj
δυνάμεως δύναμις	power *dy·**na**·me·ōs*	GEN SG FEM	noun
καὶ καί	and ***kai***	---	conj
κυριότητος κυριότης	dominion *ky·ri·**o**·tē·tos*	GEN SG FEM	noun

21b **καὶ παντὸς ὀνόματος ὀνομαζομένου**

and every name being named

καὶ καί	and ***kai***	---	conj
παντὸς πᾶς	every *pan·**tos***	GEN SG NEUT	adj
ὀνόματος ὄνομα	name *o·**no**·ma·tos*	GEN SG NEUT	noun

ὀνομαζομένου ὀνομάζω	(it) being named *o·no·ma·zo·**me**·nou*	PRES PASS PTCP GEN SG NEUT	verb

Even though there are slightly different nuances in the terms used above—**ἀρχῆς** ("ruler"), **ἐξουσίας** ("authority"), **δυνάμεως** ("power"), **κυριότητος** ("dominion"), and **ὀνόματος** ("name")—together they indicate a comprehensive reality (note the repetition of **πᾶς** here and in the following verse). In other words, these are not necessarily distinct entities with distinct characteristics but part of a rhetorical redundancy meant to create a sense of completeness. The terms encompass both spiritual and human powers. It would have been perceived in both senses in Ephesus, where both Artemis and emperor cults coexisted.

21c **οὐ μόνον ἐν τῷ αἰῶνι τούτῳ**

not only in this age

οὐ οὐ	not *ou*	---	particle
μόνον μόνον	only ***mo**·non*	---	adv
ἐν ἐν	in *en*	---	prep
τῷ ὁ	the ***tō***	DAT SG MASC	article
αἰῶνι αἰών	age *ai·**ō**·ni*	DAT SG MASC	noun
τούτῳ οὗτος	this ***tou**·tō*	DAT SG MASC	demonstr pron

21d **ἀλλὰ καὶ ἐν τῷ μέλλοντι·**

but also in the one to come

ἀλλὰ ἀλλά	but *al·**la***	---	conj
καὶ καί	also ***kai***	---	conj
ἐν ἐν	in *en*	---	prep
τῷ ὁ	the ***tō***	DAT SG MASC	article

μέλλοντι μέλλω	one to come *__mel__·lon·ti*	PRES ACT PTCP DAT SG MASC	verb

22a	**καὶ πάντα ὑπέταξεν ὑπὸ τοὺς πόδας αὐτοῦ,**
	and he subjected all things under his feet,

καὶ καί	and ***kai***	---	conj
πάντα πᾶς	all (things) *__pan__·ta*	ACC PL NEUT	adj
ὑπέταξεν ὑποτάσσω	he subjected *hy·__pe__·ta·xen*	AOR ACT IND 3RD SG	verb
ὑπὸ ὑπό	under *hy·__po__*	---	prep
τοὺς ὁ	the ***tous***	ACC PL MASC	article
πόδας πούς	feet *__po__·das*	ACC PL MASC	noun
αὐτοῦ αὐτός	of him/his *au·__tou__*	3RD GEN SG	personal pron

This is a reference to Ps 8:6, which reflects on God granting mankind dominion over creation (cf. 1 Cor 15:27). Paul uses a "new Adam" Christology, in which Christ recovers the dominion mankind had lost. However, while the psalm goes on to identify **πάντα ὑπέταξεν** ("all things") with created beings (sheep, oxen, birds, fish), Paul heightens the image of Christ's exaltation, emphasizing his dominion over principalities and powers.

22b	**καὶ αὐτὸν ἔδωκεν κεφαλὴν**
	and gave him to be head

καὶ καί	and ***kai***	---	conj
αὐτὸν αὐτός	him *au·__ton__*	3RD ACC SG	personal pron
ἔδωκεν δίδωμι	he gave *__e__·dō·ken*	AOR ACT IND 3RD SG	verb
κεφαλὴν κεφαλή	(as) head *ke·pha·__lēn__*	ACC SG FEM	noun

22c	**ὑπὲρ πάντα**		
	over all things		
ὑπὲρ ὑπέρ	over *hy*·***per***	---	prep
πάντα πᾶς	all (things) ***pan***·*ta*	ACC PL NEUT	adj

22d	**τῇ ἐκκλησίᾳ,**		
	to the church,		
τῇ ὁ	to the *tē*	DAT SG FEM	article
ἐκκλησίᾳ ἐκκλησία	(to) church *ek*·*klē*·***si***·*a*	DAT SG FEM	noun

The word **ἐκκλησία** ("church") is used nine times in Ephesians, proportionally more than in any other Pauline epistle. In all instances, Paul refers to the church as the corporate body of Christ rather than a specific local congregation. The word literally means "assembly" and was used to identify the gathering of people in public spaces for a specific purpose. In the Septuagint it is used to identify the congregation of Israel as the people of God.

The grammar here is important: **αὐτόν** ("him") is in the accusative, making Jesus the direct object of God's action, while **τῇ ἐκκλησίᾳ** ("the church") is in the dative and thus the indirect object. The noun **κεφαλή** ("head"), denoting authority, is a predicate accusative followed by the prepositional phrase **ὑπὲρ πάντα** ("over all"). Thus, God gave Christ *as* head *over* all things *to* the church. Even though Paul will later mention Christ's headship over the church (5:23), and the body metaphor (1:23) implies already that Christ is the head of the church, here the emphasis is on Christ's supremacy *over all things*, which is accomplished by Jesus being given *to the church*. Christ's exaltation is therefore described as both a christological and an ecclesiological event, whereby Christ's supremacy is expressed through the church (cf. 3:10).

23a	ἥτις ἐστὶν τὸ σῶμα αὐτοῦ,

which is his body,

ἥτις ὅστις	which *hē·tis*	NOM SG FEM	relative pron
ἐστὶν εἰμί	is *e·stin*	PRES ACT IND 3RD SG	verb
τὸ ὁ	the *to*	NOM SG NEUT	article
σῶμα σῶμα	body *sō·ma*	NOM SG NEUT	noun
αὐτοῦ αὐτός	of him/his *au·tou*	3RD GEN SG	personal pron

The body (**τὸ σῶμα**) is one of Paul's favorite metaphors for the relationship between Christ and his church (Rom 12:4–5; 1 Cor 10:16–17; 12:12–13; Eph 2:16; 4:4, 12, 16; 5:23, 28, 30; Col 1:18, 24; 2:19; 3:15). The metaphor is used to convey several ideas, including unity, diversity, participation, and extension. Here, the church is the corporate extension and expression of Christ.

23b	τὸ πλήρωμα τοῦ τὰ πάντα ἐν πᾶσιν πληρουμένου.

the fullness of the one filling all things in every way.

τὸ ὁ	the *to*	NOM SG NEUT	article
πλήρωμα πλήρωμα	fullness *plē·rō·ma*	NOM SG NEUT	noun
τοῦ ὁ	of the *tou*	GEN SG MASC	article
τὰ ὁ	the *ta*	ACC PL NEUT	article
πάντα πᾶς	all (things) *pan·ta*	ACC PL NEUT	adj
ἐν ἐν	in *en*	---	prep
πᾶσιν πᾶς	every (way) *pa·sin*	DAT PL NEUT	adj
πληρουμένου πληρόω	(of) (one) filling *plē·rou·me·nou*	PRES MID PTCP GEN SG MASC	verb

The meaning of the cognate phrase "the fullness of the one filling all in all" is difficult. The verbal noun **πλήρωμα** ("fullness") is followed by a subjective genitive—Christ fills the church. The phrase **τὰ πάντα ἐν πᾶσιν** likely entails an object (**τὰ πάντα** ["all things"]) and a dative of manner (**ἐν πᾶσιν** ["in every way"]). Since Christ fills the church, the church is the full expression of Christ, who himself fills all things in every way. The phrase conveys Christ's absolute supremacy and also the church's incredibly elevated status as the full expression of Christ, something Paul will unpack in the next segment.

 From Text to Sermon 

 ***Main Exegetical Idea.*** Believers should realize that God's power at work in them—the same power at work in Christ—enables them, as the body of Christ, to express his supremacy over all things.

Bridge to Theology. Once again, Paul packs many rich theological themes in a well-crafted argument. The first theme is *revelation*. As a result of their conversion, believers should have insight given by God's revelation through the Spirit into the realities that are now true of their existence. The content of that revelation prompts the other theological themes: the *hope of election*, the glorious *inheritance* they now have, and the *power* of God at work in them.

Election and inheritance were developed in 1:1–14, so Paul now focuses on the power of God. This is the most important theological theme of the passage. Paul points to Christ's resurrection from the dead and his exaltation over all principalities and powers as the points of reference for the power that is now at work in the church. The apostle uses Ps 110:1 and Ps 8:6 to make significant theological assertions about Christ's supremacy, but those are not simply theological digressions. Rather, they serve to explain that the same divine power that accomplished these events is now at work in the church. So, he moves from Christology—depicting what God's power has done for Christ—to ecclesiology—illustrating what God's power has done for the church. Even more astounding is the affirmation that Christ's supremacy over all things is expressed through his body, the church.

Possible Sermon Structure. A good way to structure the sermon is to follow Paul's rhetoric.

1 We need revelation (1:15–17)

2 What we need to know (1:18–23)

- 2.1 The hope of our calling
- 2.2 Our inheritance in the saints
- 2.3 The power of God at work in us (main theological emphasis)
  - 2.3.1 The same power that raised Christ from the dead and exalted him above the authorities

2.3.2 The same power that subjected all things under Christ's feet

2.3.3 The same power that gave Christ as head over all things to the church

 ***Points of Application.*** Although there are several possible points of application in the passage, two are probably central. First, conversion must result in the transformation of our understanding. Since we have been adopted by God in Christ, we now have to understand what that means—namely, the reality in which we now participate. Even though the knowledge of these things—the hope, the inheritance, and the power of God at work in us—is the result of God's revelation by the Spirit, the fact that Paul prays for the Ephesians to acquire such knowledge means that we can and should also pray that God will reveal this powerful reality to us. Our effective witness of Christ's supremacy over all things depends on our understanding of this reality.

The second main point of application is the understanding of God's power. In a post-Christian world, it doesn't look like the church has a lot of power. In fact, it may seem like the church is losing her voice in the proclamation of the gospel. However, Paul reminds the Ephesians, who were struggling with the paganism and idolatry of their day, that the same power that raised Christ from the dead and placed him above every principality and power is "for us who believe." And most importantly, Christ's supremacy over all things is expressed through the church. The impact of this truth is transformative and should be boldly preached. It is also worth noting that it is through the corporate body of Christ that this power is expressed. It is only as a body that we become an effective demonstration of Christ's supremacy.

 ***Illustration Opportunities.*** Paul uses the language of the "enlightenment of the eyes of the heart." The metaphor is full of possibilities for illustrations. For example, people who were once blind and went through corrective surgery often relate that even though their eyesight is restored, they need time to adjust to processing cognitively what they see. In other words, their brain has to assimilate the new reality they perceive. This could be an illustration of the need for an assimilation of the realities made available to us in Christ after conversion. God has already blessed us with every spiritual blessing in Christ, but we need his revelation to appropriate and live into that reality. Inspirational stories about people

who change their posture in life once they realize their potential can also serve as illustrations. Just make sure to emphasize that this realization is the result of God's revelation through the Spirit and not of a mere act of self-suggestion.

EPHESIANS 2:1–10

FROM DEATH TO LIFE

Paul now moves more intently from Christology to ecclesiology, which is the main emphasis in the letter. In his prayer, Paul describes a reality in which Christ is exalted above all rulers and authorities. Moreover, the church is presented as the body of Christ and his full expression. The picture is a lofty one and raises the question: how can the church be the full expression of Christ? Paul goes on to explain two ways in which this becomes a reality, both moving from plight to solution. First (2:1–10), Paul expounds on salvation by grace, describing how those who were dead in their sins have been raised and exalted with Christ. Second (2:11–22), he explains reconciliation by the cross, describing how gentiles, once alienated from the covenant, have been reconciled with God and his people.

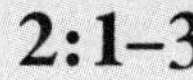

2:1–3

1 καὶ ὑμᾶς ὄντας νεκροὺς

kai hymas ontas nekrous

τοῖς παραπτώμασιν καὶ ταῖς ἁμαρτίαις ὑμῶν,

tois paraptōmasin kai tais hamartiais hymōn,

And you were dead in your trespasses and sins,

2a ἐν αἷς ποτὲ περιεπατήσατε

en hais pote periepatēsate

in which you once walked

2b κατὰ τὸν αἰῶνα τοῦ κόσμου τούτου,

kata ton aiōna tou kosmou toutou,

according to the age of this world,

2c κατὰ τὸν ἄρχοντα τῆς ἐξουσίας τοῦ ἀέρος,

kata ton archonta tēs exousias tou aeros,

according to the ruler of the authority of the air,

2d τοῦ πνεύματος τοῦ νῦν ἐνεργοῦντος

tou pneumatos tou nyn energountos

ἐν τοῖς υἱοῖς τῆς ἀπειθίας·

en tois huiois tēs apeithias;

the spirit which is now working in the sons of disobedience,

3a ἐν οἷς καὶ ἡμεῖς πάντες ἀνεστράφημέν ποτε

en hois kai hēmeis pantes anestraphēmen pote

among whom we all once lived

3b ἐν ταῖς ἐπιθυμίαις τῆς σαρκὸς ἡμῶν,

en tais epithymiais tēs sarkos hēmōn,

in the desires of our flesh,

3c ποιοῦντες τὰ θελήματα τῆς σαρκὸς καὶ τῶν διανοιῶν,

*poiountes **ta** thelēmata **tēs** sarkos **kai tōn** dianoiōn,*

doing the will of the flesh and of the thoughts,

3d καὶ ἤμεθα τέκνα φύσει ὀργῆς ὡς καὶ οἱ λοιποί·—

***kai** ēmetha **tekna physei** orgēs **hōs kai** hoi loipoi;—*

**and we were by nature children of wrath,
as also the rest [of mankind].**

1 **καὶ ὑμᾶς ὄντας νεκροὺς τοῖς παραπτώμασιν καὶ ταῖς ἁμαρτίαις ὑμῶν,**

And you were dead in your trespasses and sins,

καὶ καί	and ***kai***	---	conj
ὑμᾶς σύ	you (all) *hy·**mas***	2ND ACC PL	pron
ὄντας εἰμί	(you all) being/were *__on__·tas*	PRES ACT PTCP ACC PL MASC	verb
νεκροὺς νεκρός	dead *ne·**krous***	ACC PL MASC	adj
τοῖς ὁ	in the ***tois***	DAT PL NEUT	article
παραπτώμασιν παράπτωμα	(in) trespasses *pa·rap·**tō**·ma·sin*	DAT PL NEUT	noun
καὶ καί	and ***kai***	---	conj
ταῖς ὁ	in the ***tais***	DAT PL FEM	article
ἁμαρτίαις ἁμαρτία	(in) sins *ha·mar·**ti**·ais*	DAT PL FEM	noun
ὑμῶν σύ	of you (all)/your *hy·**mōn***	2ND GEN PL	pron

Paul begins with the plight of humanity. However, he uses the second plural **ὑμᾶς** ("you") to personalize this plight specifically to his audience. The participle **ὄντας** ("were") is a rare instance of the accusative absolute, indicating time or cause. Syntactically, the construction leaves the sentence unresolved, creating the expectation for the resolution in v. 4.

Νεκροὺς ("dead") is used here in an existential sense. Paul modifies the adjective with the dative of sphere, **τοῖς παραπτώμασιν καὶ ταῖς ἁμαρτίαις ὑμῶν** ("in your trespasses and sins"), indicating sin as the realm in which his audience experienced this existential death.

2a	**ἐν αἷς ποτὲ περιεπατήσατε**		
	in which you once walked		
ἐν ἐν	in *en*	---	prep
αἷς ὅς	which ***hais***	DAT PL FEM	relative pron
ποτὲ ποτέ	once *po·**te***	---	particle
περιεπατήσατε περιπατέω	you (all) walked about *pe·ri·e·pa·**tē**·sa·te*	AOR ACT IND 2ND PL	verb

"Walked" (**περιεπατήσατε**) is a verb with an ethical connotation, relating to a person's conduct and manner of living. For Paul this existential death is expressed in concrete terms as an ethical failure.

2b	**κατὰ τὸν αἰῶνα τοῦ κόσμου τούτου,**		
	according to the age of this world,		
κατὰ κατά	according to *ka·**ta***	---	prep
τὸν ὁ	the ***ton***	ACC SG MASC	article
αἰῶνα αἰών	age *ai·**ō**·na*	ACC SG MASC	noun
τοῦ ὁ	of the ***tou***	GEN SG MASC	article
κόσμου κόσμος	(of) world ***kos**·mou*	GEN SG MASC	noun
τούτου οὗτος	(of) this ***tou**·tou*	GEN SG MASC	demonstr pron

Paul identifies two patterns or norms according to which sinners live using two phrases that begin with **κατά** ("according to"). The first is **τὸν**

αἰῶνα τοῦ κόσμου τούτου ("the age of this world"). The noun **αἰών** normally carries a sense of time, referring to the "age" characterized by this "world," but here, it probably has a more personalized meaning—a force of agency in the world. The noun **κόσμος** refers to a worldly system.

2c **κατὰ τὸν ἄρχοντα τῆς ἐξουσίας τοῦ ἀέρος,**

according to the ruler of the authority of the air,

κατὰ κατά	according to *ka·**ta***	---	prep
τὸν ὁ	the ***ton***	ACC SG MASC	article
ἄρχοντα ἄρχων	ruler ***ar**·chon·ta*	ACC SG MASC	noun
τῆς ὁ	of the ***tēs***	GEN SG FEM	article
ἐξουσίας ἐξουσία	(of) authority *e·xou·**si**·as*	GEN SG FEM	noun
τοῦ ὁ	of the ***tou***	GEN SG MASC	article
ἀέρος ἀήρ	(of) air *a·**e**·ros*	GEN SG MASC	noun

2d **τοῦ πνεύματος τοῦ νῦν ἐνεργοῦντος ἐν τοῖς υἱοῖς τῆς ἀπειθίας·**

the spirit which is now working in the sons of disobedience,

τοῦ ὁ	of the ***tou***	GEN SG NEUT	article
πνεύματος πνεῦμα	(of) spirit ***pneu**·ma·tos*	GEN SG NEUT	noun
τοῦ ὁ	which ***tou***	GEN SG NEUT	article
νῦν νῦν	now ***nyn***	---	adv
ἐνεργοῦντος ἐνεργέω	(it) (is) working *en·er·**goun**·tos*	PRES ACT PTCP GEN SG NEUT	verb
ἐν ἐν	in *en*	---	prep
τοῖς ὁ	the ***tois***	DAT PL MASC	article

υἱοῖς υἱός	sons *hui·**ois***	DAT PL MASC	noun
τῆς ὁ	of the ***tēs***	GEN SG FEM	article
ἀπειθίας ἀπείθεια	(of) disobedience *a·pei·**thi**·as*	GEN SG FEM	noun

The second pattern at work is even more personalized—**κατὰ τὸν ἄρχοντα τῆς ἐξουσίας τοῦ ἀέρος** ("according to the ruler of the authority of the air" [2c]). The "air" (**ἀήρ**) for the Greeks was the dwelling place of spirits. The chief ruler of this realm, then, is understood to be the devil (cf. John 12:31; 14:30; 16:11). In 2d, Paul further qualifies this ruler of the air as the "spirit at work in the sons of disobedience." Disobedience (**ἀπειθίας**) entails a rebellious, willful act. Therefore, the spirit is at work in those who choose to rebel against God.

3a **ἐν οἷς καὶ ἡμεῖς πάντες ἀνεστράφημέν ποτε**

among whom we all once lived

ἐν ἐν	among *en*	---	prep
οἷς ὅς	whom ***hois***	DAT PL MASC	relative pron
καὶ καί	also ***kai***	---	conj
ἡμεῖς ἐγώ	we *hē·**meis***	1ST NOM PL	pron
πάντες πᾶς	all ***pan**·tes*	NOM PL MASC	adj
ἀνεστράφημέν ἀναστρέφω	we lived *a·ne·**stra**·phē·**men***	AOR PASS IND 1ST PL	verb
ποτε ποτέ	once *po·te*	---	particle

3b **ἐν ταῖς ἐπιθυμίαις τῆς σαρκὸς ἡμῶν,**

in the desires of our flesh,

ἐν ἐν	in *en*	---	prep
ταῖς ὁ	the ***tais***	DAT PL FEM	article

ἐπιθυμίαις ἐπιθυμία	desires *e·pi·thy·**mi**·ais*	DAT PL FEM	noun
τῆς ὁ	of the ***tēs***	GEN SG FEM	article
σαρκὸς σάρξ	(of) flesh *sar·**kos***	GEN SG FEM	noun
ἡμῶν ἐγώ	of us/our *hē·**mōn***	1ST GEN PL	pron

3c **ποιοῦντες τὰ θελήματα τῆς σαρκὸς καὶ τῶν διανοιῶν,**

doing the will of the flesh and of the thoughts,

ποιοῦντες ποιέω	(we) doing *poi·**oun**·tes*	PRES ACT PTCP NOM PL MASC	verb
τὰ ὁ	the ***ta***	ACC PL NEUT	article
θελήματα θέλημα	will *the·**lē**·ma·ta*	ACC PL NEUT	noun
τῆς ὁ	of the ***tēs***	GEN SG FEM	article
σαρκὸς σάρξ	(of) flesh *sar·**kos***	GEN SG FEM	noun
καὶ καί	and ***kai***	---	conj
τῶν ὁ	of the ***tōn***	GEN PL FEM	article
διανοιῶν διάνοια	(of) thoughts *di·a·noi·**ōn***	GEN PL FEM	noun

Having highlighted external influences in v. 2 (the age of this world and the ruler of the authority of the air), Paul now turns to the inward realities of the individual. Verse 3b, **ταῖς ἐπιθυμίαις τῆς σαρκὸς ἡμῶν** ("the desires of *our* flesh"), makes human culpability clear. Even if sponsored by the world and the devil, sin originates within the human will. The "will of the flesh and of the thoughts" (**τὰ θελήματα τῆς σαρκὸς καὶ τῶν διανοιῶν**) in this context stands in contrast to the will of God (1:1, 5, 9, 11). "Flesh" and "thoughts" encompass both sensual sins and those produced in the mind or imagination.

3d	**καὶ ἤμεθα τέκνα φύσει ὀργῆς ὡς καὶ οἱ λοιποί·—**

and we were by nature children of wrath,
as also the rest [of mankind].

καὶ καί	and ***kai***	---	conj
ἤμεθα εἰμί	we were *ē·me·tha*	IMPF MID IND 1ST PL	verb
τέκνα τέκνον	children ***tek***·*na*	NOM PL NEUT	noun
φύσει φύσις	by nature ***phy***·*sei*	DAT SG FEM	noun
ὀργῆς ὀργή	of wrath *or*·***gēs***	GEN SG FEM	noun
ὡς ὡς	as ***hōs***	---	adv
καὶ καί	also ***kai***	---	conj
οἱ ὁ	the *hoi*	NOM PL MASC	article
λοιποί λοιπός	rest *loi*·***poi***	NOM PL MASC	adj

Paul shifts to the first-person plural in 3a and here includes **οἱ λοιποί** ("the rest" of mankind) to emphasize the universality of the problem. All are destined to wrath (cf. Rom 1:18; 3:23).

2:4–7

4a ὁ δὲ θεὸς πλούσιος ὢν ἐν ἐλέει,

ho de theos plousios ōn en eleei,

But God, being rich in mercy,

4b διὰ τὴν πολλὴν ἀγάπην αὐτοῦ ἣν ἠγάπησεν ἡμᾶς,

dia tēn pollēn agapēn autou hēn ēgapēsen hēmas,

because of his great love [with] which he loved us,

5a καὶ ὄντας ἡμᾶς νεκροὺς τοῖς παραπτώμασιν

kai ontas hēmas nekrous tois paraptōmasin

and when we were dead in [our] trespasses,

5b συνεζωοποίησεν τῷ χριστῷ,—

synezōopoiēsen tō christō,—

he made us alive together with Christ—

5c χάριτί ἐστε σεσωσμένοι,—

chariti este sesōsmenoi,—

by grace you have been saved.

6a καὶ συνήγειρεν καὶ συνεκάθισεν

kai synēgeiren kai synekathisen

And he raised [us] together and seated [us] together

6b ἐν τοῖς ἐπουρανίοις

en tois epouraniois

in the heavenly places

6c ἐν Χριστῷ Ἰησοῦ,

en Christō Iēsou,

with Christ Jesus,

7a ἵνα ἐνδείξηται

hina endeixētai

so that he might show

7b ἐν τοῖς αἰῶσιν τοῖς ἐπερχομένοις

*en **tois** aiōsin **tois** eperchomenois*

in the coming ages

7c τὸ ὑπερβάλλον πλοῦτος τῆς χάριτος αὐτοῦ

to** hyper**ball**on **plou**tos **tēs charitos** au**tou

the exceeding riches of his grace

7d ἐν χρηστότητι ἐφ᾽ ἡμᾶς

*en chrēs**to**tēti eph' hē**mas***

in kindness toward us

7e ἐν Χριστῷ Ἰησοῦ.

*en Chris**tō** Iē**sou**.*

in Christ Jesus.

4a	**ὁ δὲ θεὸς πλούσιος ὢν ἐν ἐλέει,**		
	But God, being rich in mercy,		
ὁ ὁ	the *ho*	NOM SG MASC	article
δὲ δέ	but ***de***	---	conj
θεὸς θεός	God *the·**os***	NOM SG MASC	noun
πλούσιος πλούσιος	rich ***plou**·si·os*	NOM SG MASC	adj
ὢν εἰμί	being ***ōn***	PRES ACT PTCP NOM SG MASC	verb
ἐν ἐν	in *en*	---	prep
ἐλέει ἔλεος	mercy *e·**le**·ei*	DAT SG NEUT	noun

Because of the suspended sentence that began with the accusative absolute in v. 1 and continued through v. 3, this sentence comes with added rhetorical force. The colorful description of the human tragedy begs for the adversative conjunction "but" (**δέ**).

4b	**διὰ τὴν πολλὴν ἀγάπην αὐτοῦ ἣν ἠγάπησεν ἡμᾶς,**
	because of his great love [with] which he loved us,

διὰ διά	because of *di·**a***	---	prep
τὴν ὁ	the ***tēn***	ACC SG FEM	article
πολλὴν πολύς	great *pol·**lēn***	ACC SG FEM	adj
ἀγάπην ἀγάπη	love *a·**ga**·pēn*	ACC SG FEM	noun
αὐτοῦ αὐτός	of him/his *au·**tou***	3RD GEN SG	personal pron
ἣν ὅς	which ***hēn***	ACC SG FEM	relative pron
ἠγάπησεν ἀγαπάω	he loved *ē·**ga**·pē·sen*	AOR ACT IND 3RD SG	verb
ἡμᾶς ἐγώ	us *hē·**mas***	1ST ACC PL	pron

Mercy (**ἐλέει** [v. 4a]), great love (**πολλὴν ἀγάπην** [v. 4b]), and grace (**χάριτί** [v. 5c]), along with the "exceeding riches of his grace in kindness" in v. 7, show Paul's overwhelming emphasis on God's love and generosity, a theme established from the very beginning of the letter (cf. 1:3–6).

5a	**καὶ ὄντας ἡμᾶς νεκροὺς τοῖς παραπτώμασιν**
	and when we were dead in [our] trespasses,

καὶ καί	and ***kai***	---	conj
ὄντας εἰμί	(we) being/when (we) were ***on**·tas*	PRES ACT PTCP ACC PL MASC	verb
ἡμᾶς ἐγώ	we *hē·**mas***	1ST ACC PL	pron
νεκροὺς νεκρός	dead *ne·**krous***	ACC PL MASC	adj

τοῖς ὁ	in the ***tois***	DAT PL NEUT	article
παραπτώμασιν παράπτωμα	(in) trespasses *pa·rap·**tō**·ma·sin*	DAT PL NEUT	noun

This repetition of the participial phrase from v. 1 emphasizes the absolutely unmerited and unconditional aspect of God's gracious salvation. It can also be read with a concessive meaning: "although we were dead . . ."

5b **συνεζωοποίησεν τῷ χριστῷ,—**

he made us alive together with Christ—

συνεζωοποίησεν συζωοποιέω	he made alive together *syn·e·zō·o·**poi**·ē·sen*	AOR ACT IND 3RD SG	verb
τῷ ὁ	with the ***tō***	DAT SG MASC	article
χριστῷ Χριστός	(with) Christ *chri·**stō***	DAT SG MASC	noun

This is the first of three **συν-** ("with") verbs. Paul describes what God has done for believers in intrinsic association with Christ. "Making alive" (**συνεζωοποίησεν**) implies union with Christ in his resurrection, which reverses the reality of death he just described. In Col 2:11–15, a parallel passage, Paul expands this idea, explaining it in terms of association with Christ through baptism.

5c **χάριτί ἐστε σεσωσμένοι,—**

by grace you have been saved.

χάριτί χάρις	by grace ***cha**·ri·**ti***	DAT SG FEM	noun
ἐστε εἰμί	you (all) have been *e·ste*	PRES ACT IND 2ND PL	verb
σεσωσμένοι σῴζω	(you all) (having been) saved *se·sōs·**me**·noi*	PERF PASS PTCP NOM PL MASC	verb

Paul signals here the grounds of salvation: God's grace (**χάρις**). He will unpack this phrase in 2:8–10 (see below).

6a	**καὶ συνήγειρεν καὶ συνεκάθισεν**		
	And he raised [us] together and seated [us] together		
καὶ καί	and ***kai***	---	conj
συνήγειρεν συνεγείρω	he raised together *syn·**ē**·gei·ren*	AOR ACT IND 3RD SG	verb
καὶ καί	and ***kai***	---	conj
συνεκάθισεν συγκαθίζω	(he) seated together *syn·e·**ka**·thi·sen*	AOR ACT IND 3RD SG	verb

Here, we find the second and third **συν-** verbs. Although "making alive" (**συνεζωοποίησεν** [5b]) already signals Christ's resurrection as a point of reference, "raising" (**συνήγειρεν**) denotes the vindication aspect of resurrection, which is completed in the exaltation language of "sitting" (**συνεκάθισεν**). These two verbs are used in reference to Christ (cf. 1:20 above). The image is astonishing. What happened to Christ is now extended to believers, who are placed with Christ in the heavenly realms, above the rulers and authorities. Note the aorist tense of the verbs, denoting a completed action. Paul is providing a "snapshot" of a spiritual reality. Obviously, Paul is aware that the church in Ephesus still deals with very earthly challenges, but in a spiritual sense, they also participate in this triumphant reality with Christ. The reference to the "coming ages" in the next verse indicates that Paul sees this as an unfolding reality in an eschatological "already/not yet" framework.

6b	**ἐν τοῖς ἐπουρανίοις**		
	in the heavenly places		
ἐν ἐν	in *en*	---	prep
τοῖς ὁ	the ***tois***	DAT PL NEUT	article
ἐπουρανίοις ἐπουράνιος	heavenly (places) *e·pou·ra·**ni**·ois*	DAT PL NEUT	adj

6c	**ἐν Χριστῷ Ἰησοῦ,**		
	with Christ Jesus,		

ἐν ἐν	in *en*	---	prep
Χριστῷ Χριστός	Christ *Chri·**stō***	DAT SG MASC	noun
Ἰησοῦ Ἰησοῦς	Jesus *I·ē·**sou***	DAT SG MASC	noun

7a	**ἵνα ἐνδείξηται**		
	so that he might show		

ἵνα ἵνα	so that ***hi**·na*	---	conj
ἐνδείξηται ἐνδείκνυμι	he might show *en·**dei**·xē·tai*	AOR MID SUBJ 3RD SG	verb

Showing (**ἐνδείξηται**) grace in kindness is God's ultimate purpose (**ἵνα**) of salvation. Salvation is a self-disclosing act of God, making his character known.

7b	**ἐν τοῖς αἰῶσιν τοῖς ἐπερχομένοις**		
	in the coming ages		

ἐν ἐν	in *en*	---	prep
τοῖς ὁ	the ***tois***	DAT PL MASC	article
αἰῶσιν αἰών	ages *ai·**ō**·sin*	DAT PL MASC	noun
τοῖς ὁ	the ***tois***	DAT PL MASC	article
ἐπερχομένοις ἐπέρχομαι	coming *ep·er·cho·**me**·nois*	PRES MID/PASS PTCP DAT PL MASC	verb

7c	**τὸ ὑπερβάλλον πλοῦτος τῆς χάριτος αὐτοῦ**

the exceeding riches of his grace

τὸ ὁ	the ***to***	ACC SG NEUT	article
ὑπερβάλλον ὑπερβάλλω	exceeding *hy·per·**bal**·lon*	PRES ACT PTCP ACC SG NEUT	verb
πλοῦτος πλοῦτος	riches ***plou**·tos*	ACC SG NEUT	noun
τῆς ὁ	of (the) ***tēs***	GEN SG FEM	article
χάριτος χάρις	(of) grace ***cha**·ri·tos*	GEN SG FEM	noun
αὐτοῦ αὐτός	of him/his *au·**tou***	3RD GEN SG	personal pron

7d	**ἐν χρηστότητι ἐφ᾽ ἡμᾶς**

in kindness toward us

ἐν ἐν	in *en*	---	prep
χρηστότητι χρηστότης	kindness *chrēs·**to**·tē·ti*	DAT SG FEM	noun
ἐφ᾽ ἐπί	toward *eph᾽*	---	prep
ἡμᾶς ἐγώ	us *hē·**mas***	1ST ACC PL	pron

7e	**ἐν Χριστῷ Ἰησοῦ.**

in Christ Jesus.

ἐν ἐν	in *en*	---	prep
Χριστῷ Χριστός	Christ *Chri·**stō***	DAT SG MASC	noun
Ἰησοῦ Ἰησοῦς	Jesus *I·ē·**sou***	DAT SG MASC	noun

2:8–10

8a τῇ γὰρ χάριτί ἐστε σεσωσμένοι διὰ πίστεως·

tē gar chariti este sesōsmenoi dia pisteōs;

For by grace you have been saved through faith.

8b καὶ τοῦτο οὐκ ἐξ ὑμῶν,

kai touto ouk ex hymōn,

And this is not from you,

8c θεοῦ τὸ δῶρον·

theou to dōron;

[it is] a gift from God,

9a οὐκ ἐξ ἔργων,

ouk ex ergōn,

not from works,

9b ἵνα μή τις καυχήσηται.

hina mē tis kauchēsētai.

so that no one may boast.

10a αὐτοῦ γάρ ἐσμεν ποίημα,

autou gar esmen poiēma,

For we are his workmanship,

10b κτισθέντες ἐν Χριστῷ Ἰησοῦ ἐπὶ ἔργοις ἀγαθοῖς

ktisthentes en Christō Iēsou epi ergois agathois

created in Christ Jesus for good works,

10c οἷς προητοίμασεν ὁ θεὸς

hois proētoimasen ho theos

which God prepared beforehand

10d ἵνα ἐν αὐτοῖς περιπατήσωμεν.

hina en autois peripatēsōmen.

in order that we should walk in them.

8a **τῇ γὰρ χάριτί ἐστε σεσωσμένοι διὰ πίστεως·**

For by grace you have been saved through faith.

τῇ ὁ	by (the) *tē*	DAT SG FEM	article
γὰρ γάρ	for *gar*	---	conj
χάριτί χάρις	(by) grace *cha·ri·ti*	DAT SG FEM	noun
ἐστε εἰμί	you (all) have been *e·ste*	PRES ACT IND 2ND PL	verb
σεσωσμένοι σῴζω	saved *se·sōs·me·noi*	PERF PASS PTCP NOM PL MASC	verb
διὰ διά	through *di·a*	---	prep
πίστεως πίστις	faith *pi·ste·ōs*	GEN SG FEM	noun

Both the dative **τῇ χάριτί** ("by grace") and the prepositional phrase **διὰ πίστεως** ("through faith") indicate means. Salvation is both by means of grace and by means of faith, and it comes solely from God. Grace (or gift) is a multivalent concept in both the ancient Greco-Roman context and Pauline theology (Barclay 2015). In the present context, Paul emphasizes the incongruity of grace: it is an undeserved (**οὐκ ἐξ ὑμῶν**, "not from you" [8b]) gift from God (**θεοῦ τὸ δῶρον** [8c]). The participle **σεσωσμένοι** ("have been saved") is in the perfect tense, indicating a past action with ongoing results, but the periphrastic construction (with the verb "to be," **ἐστε**) puts the emphasis on the continuous effects of salvation.

8b	**καὶ τοῦτο οὐκ ἐξ ὑμῶν,**		
	And this is not from you,		
καὶ καί	and ***kai***	---	conj
τοῦτο οὗτος	this ***tou***·*to*	NOM SG NEUT	demonstr pron
οὐκ οὐ	not *ouk*	---	particle
ἐξ ἐκ	from *ex*	---	prep
ὑμῶν σύ	you (all) *hy*·***mōn***	2ND GEN PL	pron

8c	**θεοῦ τὸ δῶρον·**		
	[it is] a gift from God,		
θεοῦ θεός	from God *the*·***ou***	GEN SG MASC	noun
τὸ ὁ	the ***to***	NOM SG NEUT	article
δῶρον δῶρον	gift ***dō***·*ron*	NOM SG NEUT	noun

9a	**οὐκ ἐξ ἔργων,**		
	not from works,		
οὐκ οὐ	not *ouk*	---	particle
ἐξ ἐκ	from *ex*	---	prep
ἔργων ἔργον	works ***er***·*gōn*	GEN PL NEUT	noun

9b	**ἵνα μή τις καυχήσηται.**		
	so that no one may boast.		
ἵνα ἵνα	so that ***hi***·*na*	---	conj

μή μή	no *mē*	---	particle
τις τίς~1	one *tis*	NOM SG MASC	indef pron
καυχήσηται καυχάομαι	(he/she) may boast *kau·**chē**·sē·tai*	AOR MID SUBJ 3RD SG	verb

Pauline interpreters have discussed the issue of works at length (although few include Ephesians in the discussion). Some scholars from the interpretive position known as the New Perspective on Paul argue that references to works in Paul, especially works of the law, refer to ethnic badges such as circumcision, adherence to food laws, and Sabbath keeping, but they do not generally relate to actual deeds of obedience that one would rely on for justification. While it is true that in the next section Paul discusses circumcision, the reference to "boasting" (**καυχήσηται**) and the parallel constructions in 8b and 9a, "not from you" (**οὐκ ἐξ ὑμῶν**) // "not from works" (**οὐκ ἐξ ἔργων**), imply human effort. Paul is emphasizing that salvation is solely from God and not accomplished by human works.

10a **αὐτοῦ γάρ ἐσμεν ποίημα,**

For we are his workmanship,

αὐτοῦ αὐτός	of him *au·**tou***	3RD GEN SG	personal pron
γάρ γάρ	for ***gar***	---	conj
ἐσμεν εἰμί	we are *es·men*	PRES ACT IND 1ST PL	verb
ποίημα ποίημα	workmanship ***poi**·ē·ma*	NOM SG NEUT	noun

10b **κτισθέντες ἐν Χριστῷ Ἰησοῦ ἐπὶ ἔργοις ἀγαθοῖς**

created in Christ Jesus for good works,

κτισθέντες κτίζω	created *ktis·**then**·tes*	AOR PASS PTCP NOM PL MASC	verb
ἐν ἐν	in *en*	---	prep
Χριστῷ Χριστός	Christ *Chri·**stō***	DAT SG MASC	noun

Ἰησοῦ Ἰησοῦς	Jesus *I·ē·**sou***	DAT SG MASC	noun
ἐπὶ ἐπί	for *e·**pi***	---	prep
ἔργοις ἔργον	works ***er**·gois*	DAT PL NEUT	noun
ἀγαθοῖς ἀγαθός	good *a·ga·**thois***	DAT PL NEUT	adj

The word **ποίημα** ("workmanship" [10a]) is used in the Septuagint often to refer to the work of God (Pss 91:5 [MT 92:5, Eng. 92:4]; 142:5 [MT/Eng. 143:5]; Eccl 3:11; 7:13; Isa 29:16). It is also sometimes used in classical literature with an artistic sense, denoting the work of a craftsman. The association with the participle **κτισθέντες** ("created") evokes creation, more specifically, new creation, which establishes an important contrast with v. 3, where sinners were "by nature children of wrath." God's work of recreation reverses the "natural" fallenness of humanity. God's standard for the believer is not "nature" but "new creation."

10c **οἷς προητοίμασεν ὁ θεὸς**

which God prepared beforehand

οἷς ὅς	which ***hois***	DAT PL NEUT	relative pron
προητοίμασεν προετοιμάζω	(he) prepared beforehand *pro·ē·**toi**·ma·sen*	AOR ACT IND 3RD SG	verb
ὁ ὁ	the *ho*	NOM SG MASC	article
θεὸς θεός	God *the·**os***	NOM SG MASC	noun

10d **ἵνα ἐν αὐτοῖς περιπατήσωμεν.**

in order that we should walk in them.

ἵνα ἵνα	in order that ***hi**·na*	---	conj
ἐν ἐν	in *en*	---	prep
αὐτοῖς αὐτός	them *au·**tois***	3RD DAT PL	personal pron

περιπατήσωμεν περιπατέω	we should walk *pe·ri·pa·**tē**·sō·men*	AOR ACT SUBJ 1ST PL	verb

Several statements here are in contrast with previous statements. Sinners, who "walked" (**περιεπατήσατε**) in trespasses and sins (2:1) are recreated to "walk" (**περιπατήσωμεν**) in good works. Salvation is not "from works" (**ἐξ ἔργων** [2:9]), but in the new creation "good works" (**ἔργοις ἀγαθοῖς**) are the very purpose of the believers' new lives in Christ. Additionally, notice the verb **προετοιμάζω** ("to prepare beforehand" [10a]), which belongs with the thematic thread of election (1:4–5, 11). That believers should walk in good works is part of God's eternal purpose.

 From Text to Sermon 

 ***Main Exegetical Idea.*** Although we were dead in our sins, God, by his great love and grace, made us alive in Christ, so that we should walk in the good works that he has prepared beforehand for us.

Bridge to Theology. As can be seen in the main exegetical idea, this passage is a summary of the gospel. It affirms two core theological doctrines. First, it expounds the doctrine of original sin, describing the devastating reality sin brought about for humanity. Second, it describes the doctrine of salvation by grace through faith, an unmerited demonstration of God's love for the sinner.

The way Paul expounds these two doctrines is very profound. In vv. 1–3, describing the plight of humanity, Paul alludes to the world, the flesh, and the devil (i.e., the ruler of the power of the air)—the three enemies of the believer according to Christian tradition. In doing so, Paul highlights both external temptations and internal willful dispositions as sinful influences. In vv. 4–10, describing God's salvation, the apostle not only describes the reversal of the existential death through the believers' being made alive with Christ, but also, astoundingly, he describes the believers as seated with Christ in the heavenly places. Thus, the two events Paul highlighted in 1:20 about Christ—his resurrection and exaltation—he now applies to the church through the concept of participation. This might be a difficult concept to explain, but it is a mysterious truth about the church that needs to be emphasized. In a mysterious but real way, those saved by God's grace already enjoy participation with the risen and exalted Christ.

Finally, one should not overlook the theology of new creation for good works, which Paul is keen to emphasize. The move from walking in sin (2:1–2) to walking in good works (2:10) completes the narrative of salvation. Just as those who are dead in their sins cannot help but walk in disobedience, those who are made alive in Christ are recreated to walk in good works. Furthermore, the contrast between "not being saved by works" and "being created for good works" sets the role of ethical living in the right theological perspective.

 ***Possible Sermon Structure.*** The passage moves very clearly from plight to solution. Thus,

1 The plight of humanity: dead in sin (2:1–3)

2 God's solution: salvation by grace through faith (2:4–10)

One can also make use of the elements Paul highlights as subsections:

1 The plight of humanity: three enemies (2:1–3)
   1.1 The world (2:1–2a)
   1.2 The devil (2:2b)
   1.3 The flesh (2:3)
2 God's solution: salvation by grace through faith (2:4–10)
   2.1 God's love (2:4)
   2.2 God's salvation (2:5–9)
   2.3 God's design (2:10)

Finally, the structure of Paul's rhetoric—"You once were . . . but God"—makes for a great way to develop the passage.

 ***Points of Application.*** This passage creates a great opportunity to go deep into core theological truths to strengthen old-time Christians who may have grown accustomed to hearing and singing them over and over throughout their long journeys with Christ. The preacher will do well in spending good time painting the picture of absolute death that Paul emphasizes in the beginning, reminding the audience that this is the reality of every human being before being saved. In fact, the brightness of God's salvation cannot be understood apart from the bleak reality of sin.

But bear in mind that this passage also provides a wonderful opportunity to preach God's love and grace to those who might not have heard the gospel and may never have thought of their lives in these negative terms. Highlighting that the original audience may not have perceived the seriousness of their situation prior to their conversion might help to put the listener in a position to reflect on their own situation. In a way, it's only after one sees the light that they are able to realize the darkness in which they find themselves. Many might mentally object that they are not that bad—a natural human response—and you might even want to anticipate that in your sermon. The emphasis should be on sin as an inevitable existential reality of all humankind. The bleak picture will make God's gracious salvation shine brighter. It goes without saying that convincing the sinner is the supernatural work of the Holy Spirit, so pray for his work to be done as you preach these powerful truths.

The preacher should also make sure to emphasize God's design for those who are saved to walk in good works. Sometimes the hesitation about works' righteousness causes us not to dwell too much on this. But the way Paul describes it creates the perfect balance between God's gracious salvation of undeserving sinners and his expectation that those who are saved will live in the way he has designed for them from before the foundation of the world.

Illustration Opportunities. The image of people dead in their sins is already vivid on its own. Speaking of the reality of death may be heavy, but it is not a coincidence that Paul uses the image of a corpse to illustrate humanity's condition. A corpse is subject to decay, and regardless of the degree to which decay is evidenced in the corpse, the reality of death is the same. Similarly, some who are dead may have more evidence of death than others, but all who are without Christ are equally dead. For a younger audience, referring to the pop-culture image of zombies might be humorous and effective since Paul speaks of a "dead corpse" who is "walking."

Also readily available is the image of the gift. Reflecting on the dynamics of gift giving and reciprocity might render good applications. What do you do when you receive a completely undeserving gift? Some refuse to accept it because they feel they do not deserve it. Others accept and try to convince themselves they do deserve it. These are two ways of rejecting the gift as a gift. The only proper posture is one of humble acceptance of the gift as an unmerited and outrageously gracious gift.

Finally, the artistic connotations of the word ποίημα ("workmanship") may also fund good illustrations. A work of art often reflects the heart of the artist. You may want to show a painting that reflects that. A few years ago, I had the opportunity of visiting the Louvre in Paris. We had little time, so I made my way intently to the exhibition where the *Mona Lisa* by Leonardo da Vinci was displayed. The room was packed with people surrounding this small painting. The reason for the fame of this painting obviously is not the subject, whose identity remains a mystery. Rather, it is a display of the genius of da Vinci as an artist. In the same way, we are created to be God's workmanship, a display of the genius of the Great Artist to the world.

EPHESIANS 2:11–22

FROM ALIENATION TO RECONCILIATION

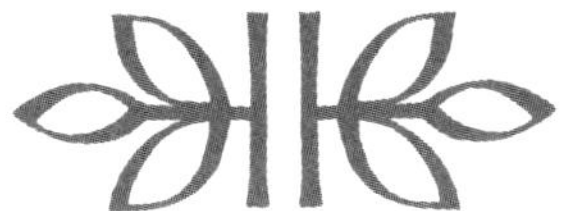

Having addressed the reality of death in sin and God's response of salvation, Paul describes another aspect of God's work in Christ. Using another plight-to-solution structure, the apostle now focuses on both the reality of the gentiles' alienation from the covenant and God's work of reconciliation in Christ Jesus, which would produce out of Jews and gentiles a new corporate "person" and a holy temple for God's dwelling. The ecclesiological overtones of Paul's theology come even more to the surface.

2:11–13

11a Διὸ μνημονεύετε ὅτι ποτὲ ὑμεῖς τὰ ἔθνη ἐν σαρκί,

Dio mnēmoneuete hoti pote hymeis ta ethnē en sarki,

Therefore remember that formerly you gentiles in the flesh—

11b οἱ λεγόμενοι ἀκροβυστία

hoi legomenoi akrobystia

the ones called uncircumcision

11c ὑπὸ τῆς λεγομένης περιτομῆς ἐν σαρκὶ χειροποιήτου,—

hypo tēs legomenēs peritomēs en sarki cheiropoiētou,

by the so-called circumcision made by hands in the flesh—

12a ὅτι ἦτε τῷ καιρῷ ἐκείνῳ χωρὶς Χριστοῦ,

hoti ēte tō kairō ekeinō chōris Christou,

you were at that time without Christ,

12b ἀπηλλοτριωμένοι τῆς πολιτείας τοῦ Ἰσραὴλ

apēllotriōmenoi tēs politeias tou Israēl

alienated from the citizenship of Israel

12c καὶ ξένοι τῶν διαθηκῶν τῆς ἐπαγγελίας,

kai xenoi tōn diathēkōn tēs epangelias,

and strangers to the covenants of the promise,

12d ἐλπίδα μὴ ἔχοντες

elpida mē echontes

having no hope

12e καὶ ἄθεοι ἐν τῷ κόσμῳ.

kai atheoi en tō kosmō.

and without God in the world.

13a νυνὶ δὲ ἐν Χριστῷ Ἰησοῦ ὑμεῖς

nyni de en Christō Iēsou hymeis

But now, in Christ, you,

13b οἵ ποτε ὄντες μακρὰν

hoi pote ontes makran

who were once far away,

13c ἐγενήθητε ἐγγὺς

egenēthēte engys

have come near

13d ἐν τῷ αἵματι τοῦ χριστοῦ.

en tō haimati tou christou,

by the blood of Christ.

11a **Διὸ μνημονεύετε ὅτι ποτὲ ὑμεῖς τὰ ἔθνη ἐν σαρκί,**

Therefore remember that formerly you gentiles in the flesh—

Διὸ διό	therefore *Di·o*	---	conj
μνημονεύετε μνημονεύω	(you all) remember *mnē·mo·neu·e·te*	PRES ACT IMPV 2ND PL	verb
ὅτι ὅτι	that *ho·ti*	---	conj
ποτὲ ποτέ	formerly *po·te*	---	particle
ὑμεῖς σύ	you (all) *hy·meis*	2ND NOM PL	pron
τὰ ὁ	the *ta*	NOM PL NEUT	article
ἔθνη ἔθνος	gentiles *eth·nē*	NOM PL NEUT	noun
ἐν ἐν	in *en*	---	prep

σαρκί σάρξ	flesh *sar·**ki***	DAT SG FEM	noun

11b **οἱ λεγόμενοι ἀκροβυστία**

the ones called uncircumcision

οἱ ὁ	the ones *hoi*	NOM PL MASC	article
λεγόμενοι λέγω	called *le·**go**·me·noi*	PRES PASS PTCP NOM PL MASC	verb
ἀκροβυστία ἀκροβυστία	uncircumcision *a·kro·by·**sti**·a*	NOM SG FEM	noun

11c **ὑπὸ τῆς λεγομένης περιτομῆς ἐν σαρκὶ χειροποιήτου,—**

by the so-called circumcision made by hands in the flesh—

ὑπὸ ὑπό	by *hy·**po***	---	prep
τῆς ὁ	the ***tēs***	GEN SG FEM	article
λεγομένης λέγω	ones called *le·go·**me**·nēs*	PRES PASS PTCP GEN SG FEM	verb
περιτομῆς περιτομή	circumcision *pe·ri·to·**mēs***	GEN SG FEM	noun
ἐν ἐν	in *en*	---	prep
σαρκὶ σάρξ	flesh *sar·**ki***	DAT SG FEM	noun
χειροποιήτου χειροποίητος	made by hands *chei·ro·poi·**ē**·tou*	GEN SG FEM	adj

Note the ironic wordplay in Paul's use of **λεγόμενοι/λεγομένης** ("called"/"so called") in 11b and 11c, respectively. Paul reproaches the Jews' rejection of the gentiles on the basis of circumcision, indicating that their perception of circumcision is faulty (cf. Rom 2:25–29; Gal 5:6). Thus, Paul first highlights the *perceived* alienation the gentiles experience, which is established on a faulty perception of covenant identity by the Jews.

12a	ὅτι ἦτε τῷ καιρῷ ἐκείνῳ χωρὶς Χριστοῦ,

you were at that time without Christ,

ὅτι ὅτι	that *ho·ti*	---	conj
ἦτε εἰμί	you (all) were *ē·te*	IMPF ACT IND 2ND PL	verb
τῷ ὁ	at (the) *tō*	DAT SG MASC	article
καιρῷ καιρός	(at) time *kai·rō*	DAT SG MASC	noun
ἐκείνῳ ἐκεῖνος	(at) that *e·kei·nō*	DAT SG MASC	demonstr pron
χωρὶς χωρίς	without *chō·ris*	---	adv
Χριστοῦ Χριστός	Christ *Chri·stou*	GEN SG MASC	noun

The phrase **χωρὶς Χριστοῦ** ("without Christ") contrasts with the prominent phrase **ἐν Χριστῷ** ("in Christ") repeated throughout the letter. Paul now describes the *real* alienation of gentiles with five statements, bookended by the phrases "without Christ" (here) and "without God in the world" (**ἄθεοι ἐν τῷ κόσμῳ**) in 12e. In between, there are descriptions of the alienation of gentiles in relation to Israel. Their estrangement from the people of Israel and the covenant is fundamentally connected to their alienation from God and Christ.

12b	ἀπηλλοτριωμένοι τῆς πολιτείας τοῦ Ἰσραὴλ

alienated from the citizenship of Israel

ἀπηλλοτριωμένοι ἀπαλλοτριόω	(you all) alienated *ap·ēl·lo·tri·ō·me·noi*	PERF PASS PTCP NOM PL MASC	verb
τῆς ὁ	from the *tēs*	GEN SG FEM	article
πολιτείας πολιτεία	(from) citzenship *po·li·tei·as*	GEN SG FEM	noun
τοῦ ὁ	of (the) *tou*	GEN SG MASC	article
Ἰσραὴλ Ἰσραήλ	(of) Israel *Is·ra·ēl*	INDECLINABLE	noun

Given Paul's later use of this language (cf. **συμπολῖται**, 2:19), **πολιτείας** ("citizenship") carries a political connotation. This term would have captured the attention of the Ephesian audience, given the importance of Roman citizenship in their context. Furthermore, the irony of Paul's use of the term in reference to Israel would not have been lost on the audience since Roman citizenship would have been considered far superior to Israelite citizenship in their context. Roman citizens took pride in their status, and suggesting that their core issue was not being citizens of Israel would have challenged their sense of privilege.

12c	**καὶ ξένοι τῶν διαθηκῶν τῆς ἐπαγγελίας,**		
	and strangers to the covenants of the promise,		
καὶ καί	and *kai*	---	conj
ξένοι ξένος	strangers *xe·noi*	NOM PL MASC	adj
τῶν ὁ	to the *tōn*	GEN PL FEM	article
διαθηκῶν διαθήκη	(to) covenants *di·a·thē·kōn*	GEN PL FEM	noun
τῆς ὁ	of the *tēs*	GEN SG FEM	article
ἐπαγγελίας ἐπαγγελία	(of) promise *e·pan·ge·li·as*	GEN SG FEM	noun

Again, given the political overtones, **ξένοι** ("strangers") would evoke the image of someone from another country. However, with the reference to the covenants of the promise, Paul frames the issue of alienation as a covenantal estrangement rather than simply a political one. Paul does not specify which covenants he has in mind with the use of the plural, but it likely refers to the Abrahamic (Gen 15:18) and new covenants (Jer 31:31–33; cf. 2 Cor 3:6).

12d	**ἐλπίδα μὴ ἔχοντες**		
	having no hope		
ἐλπίδα ἐλπίς	hope *el·pi·da*	ACC SG FEM	noun
μὴ μή	no *mē*	---	particle
ἔχοντες ἔχω	having *e·chon·tes*	PRES ACT PTCP NOM PL MASC	verb

12e	**καὶ ἄθεοι ἐν τῷ κόσμῳ.**

and without God in the world.

καὶ καί	and ***kai***	---	conj
ἄθεοι ἄθεος	without God ***a***·*the*·*oi*	NOM PL MASC	adj
ἐν ἐν	in *en*	---	prep
τῷ ὁ	the ***tō***	DAT SG MASC	article
κόσμῳ κόσμος	world ***kos***·*mō*	DAT SG MASC	noun

The term **ἄθεοι** ("without gods") was one commonly used by pagans to slander Jews for not acknowledging their gods, yet here Paul turns the tables and says it is the Ephesians who are **ἄθεοι** ("without God"). Given the profoundly pagan and polytheistic culture in Asia Minor, the term would also be perceived as ironic. Despite all their gods, they are without God in the world.

13a	**νυνὶ δὲ ἐν Χριστῷ Ἰησοῦ ὑμεῖς**

But now, in Christ, you,

νυνὶ νυνί	now *ny*·***ni***	---	adv
δὲ δέ	but ***de***	---	conj
ἐν ἐν	in *en*	---	prep
Χριστῷ Χριστός	Christ *Chri*·***stō***	DAT SG MASC	noun
Ἰησοῦ Ἰησοῦς	Jesus *I*·*ē*·***sou***	DAT SG MASC	noun
ὑμεῖς σύ	you (all) *hy*·***meis***	2ND NOM PL	pron

13b	**οἵ ποτε ὄντες μακρὰν**

who were once far away,

οἵ ὁ	the (ones) ***hoi***	NOM PL MASC	article
ποτε ποτέ	once *po·te*	---	particle
ὄντες εἰμί	being ***on***·*tes*	PRES ACT PTCP NOM PL MASC	verb
μακρὰν μακράν	far away *ma*·***kran***	---	adv

13c	**ἐγενήθητε ἐγγὺς**

have come near

ἐγενήθητε γίνομαι	(you all) have come *e·ge·nē·thē·te*	AOR PASS IND 2ND PL	verb
ἐγγὺς ἐγγύς	near *en*·***gys***	---	adv

Along with the reference to peace in the next verse, the language of **μακρὰν** ("far") and **ἐγγὺς** ("near") echoes Isa 57:19—a promise of the regathering of the exiled people of Israel. Paul applies this promise to the gentiles, which makes sense since the Isaianic oracles also envision the inclusion of gentiles (cf. Isa 56:6–8).

13d	**ἐν τῷ αἵματι τοῦ χριστοῦ.**

by the blood of Christ.

ἐν ἐν	by *en*	---	prep
τῷ ὁ	the ***tō***	DAT SG NEUT	article
αἵματι αἷμα	blood ***hai***·*ma·ti*	DAT SG NEUT	noun
τοῦ ὁ	of (the) ***tou***	GEN SG MASC	article
χριστοῦ Χριστός	(of) Christ *chri*·***stou***	GEN SG MASC	noun

The blood of Christ (**αἷμα τοῦ χριστοῦ**), identified with redemption in 1:7, is now considered for its effects in the reconciliation between Jews and gentiles.

 2:14–18 

14a Αὐτὸς γάρ ἐστιν ἡ εἰρήνη ἡμῶν,

Autos gar estin hē eirēnē hēmōn,

For he is our peace,

14b ὁ ποιήσας τὰ ἀμφότερα ἓν

ho poiēsas ta amphotera hen

the one who made both [into] one

14c καὶ τὸ μεσότοιχον τοῦ φραγμοῦ λύσας,

kai to mesotoichon tou phragmou lysas,

τὴν ἔχθραν ἐν τῇ σαρκὶ αὐτοῦ,

tēn echthran en tē sarki autou,

and destroyed the dividing wall,
[namely] the enmity, in his flesh

15a τὸν νόμον τῶν ἐντολῶν ἐν δόγμασιν καταργήσας,

ton nomon tōn entolōn en dogmasin katargēsas,

by causing to pass away the law of commandments
[expressed] in regulations,

15b ἵνα τοὺς δύο κτίσῃ ἐν αὐτῷ εἰς ἕνα καινὸν ἄνθρωπον

hina tous dyo ktisē en hautō eis hena kainon anthrōpon

that he might create the two into one new person in him,

15d ποιῶν εἰρήνην,

poiōn eirēnēn,

[thus] making peace,

16a καὶ ἀποκαταλλάξῃ τοὺς ἀμφοτέρους ἐν ἑνὶ σώματι τῷ θεῷ

kai apokatallaxē tous amphoterous en heni sōmati tō theō

and that he might reconcile both into one body to God

16b διὰ τοῦ σταυροῦ

dia tou staurou

through the cross,

16c ἀποκτείνας τὴν ἔχθραν

apokteinas tēn echthran

thus killing the hostility

16d ἐν αὐτῷ·

en autō;

in him.

17a καὶ ἐλθὼν εὐηγγελίσατο εἰρήνην ὑμῖν

kai elthōn euēngelisato eirēnēn hymin

And he came and proclaimed peace to you,

17b τοῖς μακρὰν καὶ εἰρήνην τοῖς ἐγγύς·

tois makran kai eirēnēn tois engys;

those far away, and peace to those [who were] near,

18a ὅτι δι᾽ αὐτοῦ ἔχομεν τὴν προσαγωγὴν οἱ ἀμφότεροι

hoti di' autou echomen tēn prosagōgēn hoi amphoteroi

ἐν ἑνὶ πνεύματι πρὸς τὸν πατέρα.

en heni pneumati pros ton patēra.

for through him we both have access in one spirit to the Father.

14a **Αὐτὸς γάρ ἐστιν ἡ εἰρήνη ἡμῶν,**

For he is our peace,

Αὐτὸς αὐτός	he *Au·tos*	3RD NOM SG	personal pron
γάρ γάρ	for *gar*	---	conj

ἐστιν εἰμί	(he) is *e·stin*	PRES ACT IND 3RD SG	verb
ἡ ὁ	the *hē*	NOM SG FEM	article
εἰρήνη εἰρήνη	peace *ei·**rē**·nē*	NOM SG FEM	noun
ἡμῶν ἐγώ	of us/our *hē·**mōn***	1ST GEN PL	pron

14b **ὁ ποιήσας τὰ ἀμφότερα ἓν**

the one who made both [into] one

ὁ ὁ	the *ho*	NOM SG MASC	article
ποιήσας ποιέω	one who made *poi·**ē**·sas*	AOR ACT PTCP NOM SG MASC	verb
τὰ ὁ	the ***ta***	ACC PL NEUT	article
ἀμφότερα ἀμφότεροι	both *am·**pho**·te·ra*	ACC PL NEUT	adj
ἓν εἷς	one ***hen***	ACC SG NEUT	adj

14c **καὶ τὸ μεσότοιχον τοῦ φραγμοῦ λύσας,**
τὴν ἔχθραν ἐν τῇ σαρκὶ αὐτοῦ,

and destroyed the dividing wall,
[namely] the enmity, in his flesh

καὶ καί	and ***kai***	---	conj
τὸ ὁ	the ***to***	ACC SG NEUT	article
μεσότοιχον μεσότοιχον	dividing wall *me·**so**·toi·chon*	ACC SG NEUT	noun
τοῦ ὁ	of the ***tou***	GEN SG MASC	article
φραγμοῦ φραγμός	of a wall *phrag·**mou***	GEN SG MASC	noun
λύσας λύω	having destroyed ***ly**·sas*	AOR ACT PTCP NOM SG MASC	verb

τὴν ὁ	the *tēn*	ACC SG FEM	article
ἔχθραν ἔχθρα	enmity ***ech*** · *thran*	ACC SG FEM	noun
ἐν ἐν	in *en*	---	prep
τῇ ὁ	the *tē*	DAT SG FEM	article
σαρκὶ σάρξ	flesh *sar* · ***ki***	DAT SG FEM	noun
αὐτοῦ αὐτός	of him *au* · ***tou***	3RD GEN SG	personal pron

The "dividing wall" (**τὸ μεσότοιχον**) may be drawing from the image of the Jerusalem temple, where a wall separated the courtyard of the gentiles from the part of the temple reserved for Jews only. Notice that Paul will end this section with the image of a holy temple made of Jews and gentiles. In context, the wall is more directly a metaphor for the enmity (**ἔχθραν**) between the two groups.

15a **τὸν νόμον τῶν ἐντολῶν ἐν δόγμασιν καταργήσας,**

by causing to pass away the law of commandments [expressed] in regulations,

τὸν ὁ	the *ton*	ACC SG MASC	article
νόμον νόμος	law ***no*** · *mon*	ACC SG MASC	noun
τῶν ὁ	of the *tōn*	GEN PL FEM	article
ἐντολῶν ἐντολή	(of) commandments *en* · *to* · ***lōn***	GEN PL FEM	noun
ἐν ἐν	in *en*	---	prep
δόγμασιν δόγμα	regulations ***dog*** · *ma* · *sin*	DAT PL NEUT	noun
καταργήσας καταργέω	causing to pass away *ka* · *tar* · ***gē*** · *sas*	AOR ACT PTCP NOM SG MASC	verb

A good Pauline commentary on the meaning of the word **καταργήσας** ("causing to pass away") is 2 Cor 3:7–11, where Paul talks about the fading away of the Mosaic law using the same word. One should refrain from reading in this statement a complete rejection of the law (cf. Rom 7:12), but rather as a statement that it has been superseded by the new covenant in Christ (cf. Gal 3:25). The law should still be considered for its moral values (cf. Eph 6:1–3), but it is not the basis of the covenantal relationship between God and those who are in Christ.

15b	**ἵνα τοὺς δύο κτίσῃ ἐν αὐτῷ εἰς ἕνα καινὸν ἄνθρωπον**
	that he might create the two into one new person in him,

Greek	English	Parsing	Part of speech
ἵνα ἵνα	that ***hi***·*na*	---	conj
τοὺς ὁ	the ***tous***	ACC PL MASC	article
δύο δύο	two ***dy***·*o*	---	number
κτίσῃ κτίζω	he might create ***kti***·*sē*	AOR ACT SUBJ 3RD SG	verb
ἐν ἐν	in ***en***	---	prep
αὐτῷ αὐτοῦ	him *hau*·***tō***	3RD DAT SG	personal pron
εἰς εἰς	into *eis*	---	prep
ἕνα εἷς	one ***he***·*na*	ACC SG MASC	adj
καινὸν καινός	new *kai*·***non***	ACC SG MASC	adj
ἄνθρωπον ἄνθρωπος	man ***an***·*thrō*·*pon*	ACC SG MASC	noun

The word "two" (**δύο**) is the object of the verb "to create" (**κτίσῃ**), and "one new person" (**ἕνα καινὸν ἄνθρωπον**) is the object of the preposition "into" (**εἰς**). God, in this new creation (**κτίσῃ**, cf. 2:10), makes one new "person" *out of the two groups*.

15d	**ποιῶν εἰρήνην,**
	[thus] making peace,

Greek	English	Parsing	Part of speech
ποιῶν ποιέω	making *poi*·***ōn***	PRES ACT PTCP NOM SG MASC	verb
εἰρήνην εἰρήνη	peace *ei*·***rē***·*nēn*	ACC SG FEM	noun

16a	**καὶ ἀποκαταλλάξῃ τοὺς ἀμφοτέρους ἐν ἑνὶ σώματι τῷ θεῷ**

and that he might reconcile both into one body to God

καὶ καί	and ***kai***	---	conj
ἀποκαταλλάξῃ ἀποκαταλλάσσω	he might reconcile *a·po·ka·tal·**la**·xē*	AOR ACT SUBJ 3RD SG	verb
τοὺς ὁ	the ***tous***	ACC PL MASC	article
ἀμφοτέρους ἀμφότεροι	both *am·pho·**te**·rous*	ACC PL MASC	adj
ἐν ἐν	into *en*	---	prep
ἑνὶ εἷς	one ***he**·ni*	DAT SG NEUT	adj
σώματι σῶμα	body *sō·ma·ti*	DAT SG NEUT	noun
τῷ ὁ	to the ***tō***	DAT SG MASC	article
θεῷ θεός	(to) God *the·**ō***	DAT SG MASC	noun

This "new person" of 15c is a corporate entity with a unified identity, a metaphor that goes alongside the idea of the "body" (**σώματι**). The unity, emphasized by the repetition of the word "one," is key. These two groups are unified by the reconciling work of Christ to the point of being recognized collectively as a single individual.

Even though the main focus of the passage is reconciliation to one another, both groups are ultimately presented as reconciled **τῷ θεῷ** ("to God"). This echoes vv. 11–12, where being alienated from Israel is framed in terms of being "without God." This is a complete reconciliation. Both levels of alienation are now resolved in Christ.

16b	**διὰ τοῦ σταυροῦ**

through the cross,

διὰ διά	through *di·**a***	---	prep
τοῦ ὁ	the ***tou***	GEN SG MASC	article
σταυροῦ σταυρός	cross *stau·**rou***	GEN SG MASC	noun

16c	**ἀποκτείνας τὴν ἔχθραν**		
	thus killing the hostility		
ἀποκτείνας ἀποκτείνω	killing *a·po·**ktei**·nas*	AOR ACT PTCP NOM SG MASC	verb
τὴν ὁ	the ***tēn***	ACC SG FEM	article
ἔχθραν ἔχθρα	hostility ***ech**·thran*	ACC SG FEM	noun

16d	**ἐν αὐτῷ·**		
	in him.		
ἐν ἐν	in/by *en*	---	prep
αὐτῷ αὐτός	it/him *au·**tō***	3RD DAT SG	personal pron

17a	**καὶ ἐλθὼν εὐηγγελίσατο εἰρήνην ὑμῖν**		
	And he came and proclaimed peace to you,		
καὶ καί	and ***kai***	---	conj
ἐλθὼν ἔρχομαι	having come *el·**thōn***	AOR ACT PTCP NOM SG MASC	verb
εὐηγγελίσατο εὐαγγελίζω	he proclaimed *eu·ēn·ge·**li**·sa·to*	AOR MID IND 3RD SG	verb
εἰρήνην εἰρήνη	peace *ei·**rē**·nēn*	ACC SG FEM	noun
ὑμῖν σύ	to you (all) *hy·**min***	2ND DAT PL	pron

Εὐηγγελίσατο is from the root **εὐαγγελίζω**, "to proclaim good news." Note the echoes of Isa 52:7 and 57:18–19.

17b	**τοῖς μακρὰν καὶ εἰρήνην τοῖς ἐγγύς·**

those far away, and peace to those [who were] near,

τοῖς ὁ	(to) the (ones)/those ***tois***	DAT PL MASC	article
μακρὰν μακράν	far away *ma*·***kran***	---	adv
καὶ καί	and ***kai***	---	conj
εἰρήνην εἰρήνη	peace *ei*·***rē***·*nēn*	ACC SG FEM	noun
τοῖς ὁ	to those ***tois***	DAT PL MASC	article
ἐγγύς ἐγγύς	near *en*·***gys***	---	adv

18a	**ὅτι δι᾽ αὐτοῦ ἔχομεν τὴν προσαγωγὴν οἱ ἀμφότεροι ἐν ἑνὶ πνεύματι πρὸς τὸν πατέρα.**

for through him we both have access in one spirit to the Father.

ὅτι ὅτι	for ***ho***·*ti*	---	conj
δι᾽ διά	through *di᾽*	---	prep
αὐτοῦ αὐτός	him *au*·***tou***	3RD GEN SG	personal pron
ἔχομεν ἔχω	we have ***e***·*cho*·*men*	PRES ACT IND 1ST PL	verb
τὴν ὁ	the ***tēn***	ACC SG FEM	article
προσαγωγὴν προσαγωγή	access *pros*·*a*·*gō*·***gēn***	ACC SG FEM	noun
οἱ ὁ	the *hoi*	NOM PL MASC	article
ἀμφότεροι ἀμφότεροι	both *am*·***pho***·*te*·*roi*	NOM PL MASC	adj
ἐν ἐν	in *en*	---	prep
ἑνὶ εἷς	one *he*·***ni***	DAT SG NEUT	adj
πνεύματι πνεῦμα	spirit ***pneu***·*ma*·*ti*	DAT SG NEUT	noun

πρὸς πρός	to ***pros***	---	prep
τὸν ὁ	the ***ton***	ACC SG MASC	article
πατέρα πατήρ	father *pa·**tē**·ra*	ACC SG MASC	noun

2:19–22

19a Ἄρα οὖν οὐκέτι ἐστὲ ξένοι καὶ πάροικοι,

Ara oun ouketi este xenoi kai paroikoi,

So then you are no longer strangers and aliens,

19b ἀλλὰ ἐστὲ συνπολῖται τῶν ἁγίων καὶ οἰκεῖοι τοῦ θεοῦ,

alla este synpolitai tōn hagiōn kai oikeioi tou theou,

but you are co-citizens with the saints
and members of the household of God,

20a ἐποικοδομηθέντες ἐπὶ τῷ θεμελίῳ

epoikodomēthentes epi tō themeliō

τῶν ἀποστόλων καὶ προφητῶν,

tōn apostolōn kai prophētōn,

built upon the foundation of the apostles and prophets,

20b ὄντος ἀκρογωνιαίου αὐτοῦ Χριστοῦ Ἰησοῦ,

ontos akrogōniaiou autou Christou Iēsou,

Christ Jesus himself being the cornerstone,

21a ἐν ᾧ πᾶσα οἰκοδομὴ συναρμολογουμένη

en hō pasa oikodomē synarmologoumenē

in whom the whole building, being joined together,

21b αὔξει εἰς ναὸν ἅγιον

auxei eis naon hagion

grows into a holy temple

21c ἐν κυρίῳ,

en kyriō,

in the Lord,

22a ἐν ᾧ καὶ ὑμεῖς συνοικοδομεῖσθε

en hō kai hymeis synoikodomeisthe

in whom you are also being built together

22b εἰς κατοικητήριον τοῦ θεοῦ

*eis katoikē**tē**rion **tou** the**ou***

into a dwelling place of God

22c ἐν πνεύματι.

*en **pneu**mati.*

in the Spirit.

19a	**Ἄρα οὖν οὐκέτι ἐστὲ ξένοι καὶ πάροικοι,**		
	So then you are no longer strangers and aliens,		
Ἄρα ἄρα	so ***A**·ra*	---	particle
οὖν οὖν	then ***oun***	---	conj
οὐκέτι οὐκέτι	no longer *ou·**ke**·ti*	NEG	adv
ἐστὲ εἰμί	you (all) are *e·**ste***	PRES ACT IND 2ND PL	verb
ξένοι ξένος	strangers ***xe**·noi*	NOM PL MASC	adj
καὶ καί	and ***kai***	---	conj
πάροικοι πάροικος	aliens ***pa**·roi·koi*	NOM PL MASC	adj

19b	**ἀλλὰ ἐστὲ συνπολῖται τῶν ἁγίων καὶ οἰκεῖοι τοῦ θεοῦ,**		
	but you are co-citizens with the saints and members of the household of God,		
ἀλλὰ ἀλλά	but *al·**la***	---	conj
ἐστὲ εἰμί	you (all) are *e·**ste***	PRES ACT IND 2ND PL	verb
συνπολῖται συμπολίτης	co-citizens *syn·po·**li**·tai*	NOM PL MASC	noun

τῶν ὁ	with the ***tōn***	GEN PL MASC	article
ἁγίων ἅγιος	(with) saints *ha·**gi**·ōn*	GEN PL MASC	adj
καὶ καί	and ***kai***	---	conj
οἰκεῖοι οἰκεῖος	(members of the) household *oi·**kei**·oi*	NOM PL MASC	adj
τοῦ ὁ	of the ***tou***	GEN SG MASC	article
θεοῦ θεός	(of) God *the·**ou***	GEN SG MASC	noun

The reference to strangers (**ξένοι**) recalls 2:12, presenting the complete reversal of the alienation. The three terms used in this verse represent three ranked political levels in Greco-Roman society in ascending order of importance: strangers (**ξένοι**), resident aliens (**πάροικοι**), and citizens (**συνπολῖται**). So the gentile believers have moved from the most estranged position to the highest status—that of co-citizens with the saints. But beyond that, they have also been made members of God's household (**οἰκεῖοι**). The image is one of absolute inclusion.

20a **ἐποικοδομηθέντες ἐπὶ τῷ θεμελίῳ τῶν ἀποστόλων καὶ προφητῶν,**

built upon the foundation of the apostles and prophets,

ἐποικοδομηθέντες ἐποικοδομέω	built *e·poi·ko·do·mē·**then**·tes*	AOR PASS PTCP NOM PL MASC	verb
ἐπὶ ἐπί	upon *e·**pi***	---	prep
τῷ ὁ	the ***tō***	DAT SG MASC	article
θεμελίῳ θεμέλιος	foundation *the·me·**li**·ō*	DAT SG MASC	noun
τῶν ὁ	of the ***tōn***	GEN PL MASC	article
ἀποστόλων ἀπόστολος	(of) apostles *a·po·**sto**·lōn*	GEN PL MASC	noun
καὶ καί	and ***kai***	---	conj
προφητῶν προφήτης	(of) prophets *pro·phē·**tōn***	GEN PL MASC	noun

The apostles (**ἀποστόλων**) and prophets (**προφητῶν**) are listed in Eph 4:11 as two distinct and preeminent offices in the church. They are also those to whom the mystery of Christ has been revealed (Eph 3:5). The apostles are responsible for establishing the church firmly in the teaching of the gospel, while the prophets are individuals who, through the gift of prophecy, exercise an important leading role in the church. The gift of prophecy is ubiquitous in the New Testament (Luke 1:67; Acts 2:17–18; 19:6; 21:9; 1 Cor 11:4–5; 13:9; 14:1, 3–5, 20–25) and entailed a word or oracle from God revealed by the Holy Spirit through an individual.

20b **ὄντος ἀκρογωνιαίου αὐτοῦ Χριστοῦ Ἰησοῦ,**

Christ Jesus himself being the cornerstone,

ὄντος εἰμί	(he) being *on·tos*	PRES ACT PTCP GEN SG MASC	verb
ἀκρογωνιαίου ἀκρογωνιαῖος	cornerstone *a·kro·gō·ni·**ai**·ou*	GEN SG MASC	adj
αὐτοῦ αὐτός	himself *au·**tou***	3RD GEN SG	personal pron
Χριστοῦ Χριστός	Christ *Chri·**stou***	GEN SG MASC	noun
Ἰησοῦ Ἰησοῦς	Jesus *I·ē·**sou***	GEN SG MASC	noun

21a **ἐν ᾧ πᾶσα οἰκοδομὴ συναρμολογουμένη**

in whom the whole building, being joined together,

ἐν ἐν	in *en*	---	prep
ᾧ ὅς	whom ***hō***	DAT SG MASC	relative pron
πᾶσα πᾶς	whole ***pa**·sa*	NOM SG FEM	adj
οἰκοδομὴ οἰκοδομή	building *oi·ko·do·**mē***	NOM SG FEM	noun
συναρμολογουμένη συναρμολογέω	(it) being joined together *syn·ar·mo·lo·gou·**me**·nē*	PRES PASS PTCP NOM SG FEM	verb

The **οικ-** root in **ἐποικοδομηθέντες** ("built" [20a]) and **οἰκοδομὴ** ("building") keeps the "household" (**οἰκεῖοι**) image from 19b (cf. **κατοικητήριον** in v. 22), but Paul now adds architectural metaphors with his use of **θεμελίῳ** ("foundation" [20a]) and **ἀκρογωνιαίου** ("cornerstone" [20b]). The Jewish and gentile believers are together made into a building that has Christ as the cornerstone of its foundation, which is the teaching and ministry of the apostles and prophets. The image complements Paul's body metaphor (2:6; 4:15; 5:23). Christ is above the church as its head, and he is under the church, as the cornerstone of its foundation.

21b	**αὔξει εἰς ναὸν ἅγιον**		
	grows into a holy temple		
αὔξει αὔξω	(it) grows ***au***·*xei*	PRES ACT IND 3RD SG	verb
εἰς εἰς	into *eis*	---	prep
ναὸν ναός	temple *na*·***on***	ACC SG MASC	noun
ἅγιον ἅγιος	holy ***ha***·*gi*·*on*	ACC SG MASC	adj

The verb **αὔξει** ("grows") is in the present active and so indicates a continuous aspect: the building is growing. Furthermore, this is not just any building. It is **ναὸν ἅγιον** ("a holy temple") for God's dwelling. The word **ναός** refers to the place of God's habitation (cf. Acts 7:48; 14:24; 1 Cor 6:19), different from the more general **ἱερόν**, which typically identifies the entire area of the temple, which would include the "dividing wall" of 2:14. So while the dividing wall is broken down, a new reconfigured temple emerges out of the unity of Jews and gentiles, which is the new place for God's dwelling.

21c	**ἐν κυρίῳ,**		
	in the Lord,		
ἐν ἐν	in *en*	---	prep
κυρίῳ κύριος	Lord *ky*·***ri***·*ō*	DAT SG MASC	noun

22a	**ἐν ᾧ καὶ ὑμεῖς συνοικοδομεῖσθε**		
	in whom you are also being built together		
ἐν ἐν	in *en*	---	prep
ᾧ ὅς	whom ***hō***	DAT SG MASC	relative pron
καὶ καί	also ***kai***	---	conj
ὑμεῖς σύ	you (all) *hy*·***meis***	2ND NOM PL	pron
συνοικοδομεῖσθε συνοικοδομέω	(you all) are being built together *syn·oi·ko·do·**meis**·the*	PRES PASS IND 2ND PL	verb

Notice another set of **συν-** verbs, **συναρμολογουμένη** ("being joined together") from 21a and **συνοικοδομεῖσθε** ("being built together") here, which recalls the set of three **συν-** verbs we saw in 2:5–6. Union with Christ and union with one another are two key, interdependent realities in which the believers are to participate. Both verbs are architectural in nature: **συναρμολογέω** denotes the joining together of building structures, while **συνοικοδομέω** relates to the act of building.

22b	**εἰς κατοικητήριον τοῦ θεοῦ**		
	into a dwelling place of God		
εἰς εἰς	into *eis*	---	prep
κατοικητήριον κατοικητήριον	a dwelling place *kat·oi·kē·**tē**·ri·on*	ACC SG NEUT	noun
τοῦ ὁ	of the ***tou***	GEN SG MASC	article
θεοῦ θεός	(of) God *the*·***ou***	GEN SG MASC	noun

22c	**ἐν πνεύματι.**		
	in the Spirit.		
ἐν ἐν	in *en*	---	prep
πνεύματι πνεῦμα	Spirit ***pneu***·*ma·ti*	DAT SG NEUT	noun

 From Text to Sermon 

Main Exegetical Idea. Formerly estranged from the covenant and from the people of God, gentile believers are now reconciled to God and fully integrated into the people of God as part of one body and one holy temple made of Jews and gentiles.

Bridge to Theology. The central theological idea of the passage is an ecclesiological one: the full inclusion of gentiles as part of the covenant people of God. Notice that Paul recognizes the covenant identity of Israel as the people of God, associating them with the covenants of promise (2:12). The point, therefore, is not the obliteration or substitution of Israel as the covenant people but the absolute inclusion of gentiles in the covenant as God's people. Christ's redemptive sacrifice and believers' participation in Christ through the Spirit are the means by which this reconciliation happens (2:13, 18). The result of that inclusion, however, is not a simple appendage of gentiles to Israel, but rather, a new reality—a new corporate person made out of both Jews and gentiles, or, from another angle, a new corporate temple for God's dwelling through the Spirit. Although the central idea has to do with the history of salvation—particularly the inclusion of gentiles in God's people—unity also emerges as a central theological point. The two former enemies are made one, merging their different identities into a single people.

Possible Sermon Structure. As we saw in the previous passage (Eph 2:1–10), Paul's rhetoric moves from plight to solution (notice the similar construction: "you were once . . . but now . . ."), which the preacher can again use to structure a sermon. The solution section in 2:13–22 can be further divided according to Paul's metaphors. Thus:

1 The plight: alienation from the covenant (2:11–12)

2 God's solution: one new corporate identity in Christ (2:13–22)

- 2.1 One new body (2:14–16)
- 2.2 One new people (2:19)
- 2.3 One holy temple (2:14, 21–22)

In fact, the similarity between the previous passage and this (Eph 2:1–10 and 11–22) may even justify combining them into a two-part miniseries on plight and solution.

 ***Points of Application.*** Ecclesiology is often an underemphasized topic in churches, in part because of the heightened individualism common in Western culture—an individualism that sometimes finds its way into different parts of the world as well. Being "one in Christ" is more often a slogan than a reality on which we intentionally want to dwell. Therefore, the preacher has the challenge of setting the context for his/her audience so they can listen to Paul's words as members of a group rather than as individuals. The picture Paul paints is not one of individuals being included in the covenant, even if such an inclusion implies an individual response to the gospel. Rather, he uses the image of a body and a temple—whose identity is the corporate and unified joining together of the people of God. The point to drive home, therefore, is this corporate existence, the reality that we are not simply individuals saved by grace through Christ's sacrifice (2:1–10), but also, through the same sacrifice, we are made into one body with the church. An individualized and isolated Christian life is simply not an option.

Another point of application is a biblical-theological one: as gentiles, we are included in the covenants of promise and made co-citizens with Israel, the people of God. It is important to understand that we are participants in the story of Israel, included in the narrative of God's formation of his people. Therefore, the stories of the Old Testament do not merely serve as a reservoir of "moral values" designed to exemplify virtuous behavior for Christians to imitate. They are the very narrative in which we are included—our story—which shapes our identity. Therefore, being a Christian entails understanding and dwelling in that story, contemplating God's self-disclosure and relationship with his people through history, and acknowledging the climax of that story in Christ. The preacher will do well to retrace key points in that narrative to help congregants appropriate it for themselves, corporately.

The negative example of the Jews of Paul's day—"the so-called circumcision made by hands in the flesh" who call others the "uncircumcision" to alienate them—is itself a point of application. God blesses people through his people. He saves people by including them in his covenant people (cf. Gen 12:3). But when the people of God fail to be agents of reconciliation, they become agents of alienation. That stands as a warning for the church. Although the problem in Paul's audience is specifically of an ethnic nature, this passage constitutes an appropriate starting point to talk about other types of reconciliation, including racial and socioeconomic, that are so necessary today.

 ***Illustration Opportunities.*** Calling attention to the individualistic tendencies in Western society and at the same time the evident desire for connection is a good way to introduce the topic of humanity's alienation. In the movie *Castaway*, Tom Hanks plays the role of a FedEx executive named Chuck Noland, who finds himself stranded on a deserted island after a plane crash. Noland is portrayed as a resourceful and self-sufficient person, whose skills, in addition to the contents of many of the packages that also washed ashore, enable him to survive for four years by himself. But Noland's biggest need is connection. One of the boxes he opened contained a Wilson volleyball. Before long he has personified it: he talks to it and calls it by name (Wilson). At first, this is clearly a coping mechanism, but when he loses the ball in the middle of a storm, we can see in Noland's desperation that the relationship has become much more—a clear expression of his longing for connection. This can be a powerful story to illustrate the irony of how resourceful we have become as a society but how ultimately our resources cannot mask our need for belonging.

Another point that may be used as an illustration is the idea of the new collective "self." A positive illustration of corporate identity is the family, and the preacher may want to allude to family stories that capture the sense of one's identity as connected to a group. There may be other similar illustrations, like belonging to a team or a culture. The usefulness of these illustrations is to set the congregants' minds on a corporate mode and encourage them to hear the sermon as belonging to a body. But beware of the limitations of the illustration. What Paul is describing is an unprecedented and unrivaled reality. Illustrations can sometimes trivialize a mysterious and unique concept. The preacher should highlight that uniqueness.

To illustrate the covenant identity, you may resort to stories of family lineage. For example, my son, Matt, once asked me about our family history. I went on and on telling him about my Spanish ancestor who adopted a native Brazilian, and how our family (on my side) stemmed from that wonderful coming together of two different cultures. But then I had an insight and told him: "But son, the stories that I tell you every night—about how God created Adam and Eve, how he chose Abraham, Moses, David, Esther, Daniel—those are not just bedtime stories. They are your story!" Examples like that may help congregants understand what it means to own the identity of the covenant people of God.

Finally, Paul's use of political language in vv. 11–12 and 19–20 affords many illustrations. Refugees finding home in a country that is not their own, or children being adopted by parents from a different country or culture, may illustrate the full inclusion of a former alienated people into the body of Christ.

EPHESIANS 3:1–13

THE WISDOM OF GOD REVEALED THROUGH THE CHURCH

In 2:1–22 Paul expounded on two fundamental aspects of God's work in Christ on behalf of believers—salvation and reconciliation. These aspects are part of God's eternal plan unfolding in history according to his grace and careful administration. Now Paul weaves into his ecclesiological discourse a reflection on his own role in God's plan for the church. The reason for this reflection is so that the Ephesians, who are likely concerned with the apostle's situation, will be comforted in knowing that his sufferings are part of a greater purpose—the administration of the mystery of Christ. The apostle speaks of his role as a servant to whom this mystery has been revealed. This mystery is the incorporation of the gentiles in the covenant. Ultimately the purpose of his calling is also ecclesiological—that through the church the manifold wisdom of God will be made known.

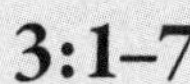

3:1–7

1a Τούτου χάριν ἐγὼ Παῦλος

Toutou charin egō Paulos

For this reason, I, Paul,

1b ὁ δέσμιος τοῦ χριστοῦ Ἰησοῦ

ho desmios tou christou Iēsou

the prisoner of Christ Jesus

1c ὑπὲρ ὑμῶν τῶν ἐθνῶν,—

hyper hymōn tōn ethnōn,—

on behalf of you gentiles—

2a εἴ γε ἠκούσατε τὴν οἰκονομίαν τῆς χάριτος τοῦ θεοῦ

ei ge ēkousate tēn oikonomian tēs charitos tou theou

If indeed you heard of the plan of the grace of God

2b τῆς δοθείσης μοι εἰς ὑμᾶς,

tēs dotheisēs moi eis hymas,

which was given to me for you

3a ὅτι κατὰ ἀποκάλυψιν ἐγνωρίσθη μοι τὸ μυστήριον,

hoti kata apokalypsin egnōristhē moi to mystērion,

that the mystery was made known to me according to the revelation,

3b καθὼς προέγραψα ἐν ὀλίγῳ,

kathōs proegrapsa en oligō,

as I have written briefly,

4a πρὸς ὃ δύνασθε ἀναγινώσκοντες

pros ho dynasthe anaginōskontes

so that when you read it, you might be able

4b νοῆσαι τὴν σύνεσίν μου ἐν τῷ μυστηρίῳ τοῦ χριστοῦ,

*noēsai **tēn synesin** mou en **tō** mystēriō **tou** christou,*

to know my insight into the mystery of Christ,

5a ὃ ἑτέραις γενεαῖς οὐκ ἐγνωρίσθη τοῖς υἱοῖς τῶν ἀνθρώπων

ho heterais geneais ouk egnōristhē tois huiois tōn anthrōpōn

which in other generations was not made known to the sons of men

5b ὡς νῦν ἀπεκαλύφθη

hōs nyn apekalyphthē

τοῖς ἁγίοις ἀποστόλοις αὐτοῦ καὶ προφήταις

tois hagiois apostolois autou kai prophētais

as it has now been revealed to his holy apostles and prophets

5c ἐν πνεύματι,

en pneumati,

by the Spirit,

6a εἶναι τὰ ἔθνη συνκληρονόμα

einai ta ethnē synklēronoma

Namely, that the gentiles are coheirs

6b καὶ σύνσωμα

kai sysōma

and co-members of the body,

6c καὶ συνμέτοχα τῆς ἐπαγγελίας

kai synmetocha tēs epangelias

and co-participants in the promise

6d ἐν Χριστῷ Ἰησοῦ

en Christō Iēsou

in Christ Jesus

6e διὰ τοῦ εὐαγγελίου,

*dia **tou** euangeliou,*

through the gospel,

7a οὗ ἐγενήθην διάκονος

***hou** egenēthēn diakonos*

of which I became a servant

7b κατὰ τὴν δωρεὰν τῆς χάριτος τοῦ θεοῦ

*kata **tēn** dōrean **tēs** charitos **tou** theou*

according to the gift of the grace of God

7c τῆς δοθείσης μοι

***tēs** dotheisēs moi*

which was given to me

7d κατὰ τὴν ἐνέργειαν τῆς δυνάμεως αὐτοῦ,

*kata **tēn** energeian **tēs** dynameōs autou,*

according to the working of his power.

1a	**Τούτου χάριν ἐγὼ Παῦλος**		
	For this reason, I, Paul,		
Τούτου οὗτος	this (reason) ***Tou**·tou*	GEN SG NEUT	demonstr pron
χάριν χάριν	for ***cha**·rin*	---	adv
ἐγὼ ἐγώ	I *e·**gō***	1ST NOM SG	pron
Παῦλος Παῦλος	Paul ***Pau**·los*	NOM SG MASC	noun

1b ὁ δέσμιος τοῦ χριστοῦ Ἰησοῦ

the prisoner of Christ Jesus

ὁ ὁ	the *ho*	NOM SG MASC	article
δέσμιος δέσμιος	prisoner ***des**·mi·os*	NOM SG MASC	noun
τοῦ ὁ	of the ***tou***	GEN SG MASC	article
χριστοῦ Χριστός	(of) Christ *chri·**stou***	GEN SG MASC	noun
Ἰησοῦ Ἰησοῦς	(of) Jesus *I·ē·**sou***	GEN SG MASC	noun

The use of the word **δέσμιος** ("prisoner") with the definite article (**ὁ**) makes this almost a title. Twice Paul uses this descriptor to identify himself (cf. 4:1). The addition of the possessive genitive **τοῦ χριστοῦ Ἰησοῦ** ("of Christ Jesus") is effectively a reframing of Paul's circumstances. He is not a prisoner of Rome but a prisoner of Christ.

1c ὑπὲρ ὑμῶν τῶν ἐθνῶν,—

on behalf of you gentiles—

ὑπὲρ ὑπέρ	on behalf of *hy·**per***	---	prep
ὑμῶν σύ	you (all) *hy·**mōn***	2ND GEN PL	pron
τῶν ὁ	the ***tōn***	GEN PL NEUT	article
ἐθνῶν ἔθνος	gentiles *eth·**nōn***	GEN PL NEUT	noun

2a εἴ γε ἠκούσατε τὴν οἰκονομίαν τῆς χάριτος τοῦ θεοῦ

If indeed you heard of the plan of the grace of God

εἴ εἰ	if ***ei***	---	cond
γε γέ	indeed *ge*	---	particle
ἠκούσατε ἀκούω	you (all) heard *ē·**kou**·sa·te*	AOR ACT IND 2ND PL	verb

τὴν ὁ	the ***tēn***	ACC SG FEM	article
οἰκονομίαν οἰκονομία	plan *oi·ko·no·**mi**·an*	ACC SG FEM	noun
τῆς ὁ	of the ***tēs***	GEN SG FEM	article
χάριτος χάρις	(of) grace ***cha**·ri·tos*	GEN SG FEM	noun
τοῦ ὁ	of the ***tou***	GEN SG MASC	article
θεοῦ θεός	(of) God *the·**ou***	GEN SG MASC	noun

The noun **τὴν οἰκονομίαν** was used previously to refer to God's careful administration or plan (cf. 1:10). Here, Paul is referring specifically to his own special role as a steward in the administration of God's grace.

2b **τῆς δοθείσης μοι εἰς ὑμᾶς,**

which was given to me for you

τῆς ὁ	which ***tēs***	GEN SG FEM	article
δοθείσης δίδωμι	(it) being/was given *do·**thei**·sēs*	AOR PASS PTCP GEN SG FEM	verb
μοι ἐγώ	to me *moi*	1ST DAT SG	pron
εἰς εἰς	for *eis*	---	prep
ὑμᾶς σύ	you (all) *hy·**mas***	2ND ACC PL	pron

3a **ὅτι κατὰ ἀποκάλυψιν ἐγνωρίσθη μοι τὸ μυστήριον,**

that the mystery was made known to me
according to the revelation,

ὅτι ὅτι	that ***ho**·ti*	---	conj
κατὰ κατά	according to *ka·**ta***	---	prep
ἀποκάλυψιν ἀποκάλυψις	revelation *a·po·**ka**·ly·psin*	ACC SG FEM	noun

ἐγνωρίσθη γνωρίζω	(it) was made known *e·gnō·**ris**·thē*	AOR PASS IND 3RD SG	verb
μοι ἐγώ	to me *moi*	1ST DAT SG	pron
τὸ ὁ	the ***to***	NOM SG NEUT	article
μυστήριον μυστήριον	mystery *my·**stē**·ri·on*	NOM SG NEUT	noun

The language of "making known" (**ἐγνωρίσθη**) refers to revelation. Paul will use the same word to refer to how God makes known his wisdom through the church. There is a connection here between the fact that this great mystery was revealed to "the very least of all saints" (3:8) and how the multiform wisdom of God is made known through the church. God makes himself and his plans known through unlikely vessels.

See comment on 1:9–10 regarding **τὸ μυστήριον** ("the mystery").

3b **καθὼς προέγραψα ἐν ὀλίγῳ,**

as I have written briefly,

καθὼς καθώς	as *ka·**thōs***	---	adv
προέγραψα προγράφω	I have written *pro·**e**·gra·psa*	AOR ACT IND 1ST SG	verb
ἐν ἐν	in *en*	---	prep
ὀλίγῳ ὀλίγος	brief *o·**li**·gō*	DAT SG MASC	adj

4a **πρὸς ὃ δύνασθε ἀναγινώσκοντες**

so that when you read it, you might be able

πρὸς πρός	toward ***pros***	---	prep
ὃ ὅς	which ***ho***	ACC SG NEUT	relative pron
δύνασθε δύναμαι	you (all) might be able ***dy**·nas·the*	PRES MID/PASS IND 2ND PL	verb
ἀναγινώσκοντες ἀναγινώσκω	when (you all) read it *a·na·gi·**nō**·skon·tes*	PRES ACT PTCP NOM PL MASC	verb

4b	**νοῆσαι τὴν σύνεσίν μου ἐν τῷ μυστηρίῳ τοῦ χριστοῦ,**

to know my insight into the mystery of Christ,

Greek	English	Parsing	Part of speech
νοῆσαι νοέω	to know *no·**ē**·sai*	AOR ACT INF	verb
τὴν ὁ	the ***tēn***	ACC SG FEM	article
σύνεσίν σύνεσις	insight ***syn**·e·**sin***	ACC SG FEM	noun
μου ἐγώ	of me/my *mou*	1ST GEN SG	pron
ἐν ἐν	into *en*	---	prep
τῷ ὁ	the ***tō***	DAT SG NEUT	article
μυστηρίῳ μυστήριον	mystery *my·stē·**ri**·ō*	DAT SG NEUT	noun
τοῦ ὁ	of the ***tou***	GEN SG MASC	article
χριστοῦ Χριστός	(of) Christ *chri·**stou***	GEN SG MASC	noun

5a	**ὃ ἑτέραις γενεαῖς οὐκ ἐγνωρίσθη τοῖς υἱοῖς τῶν ἀνθρώπων**

which in other generations was not made known to the sons of men

Greek	English	Parsing	Part of speech
ὃ ὅς	which ***ho***	NOM SG NEUT	relative pron
ἑτέραις ἕτερος	in other (ones) *he·**te**·rais*	DAT PL FEM	adj
γενεαῖς γενεά	(in) generations *ge·ne·**ais***	DAT PL FEM	noun
οὐκ οὐ	not *ouk*	---	particle
ἐγνωρίσθη γνωρίζω	(it) was made known *e·gnō·**ris**thē*	AOR PASS IND 3RD SG	verb
τοῖς ὁ	to the ***tois***	DAT PL MASC	article
υἱοῖς υἱός	(to) sons *hui·**ois***	DAT PL MASC	noun
τῶν ὁ	of the ***tōn***	GEN PL MASC	article
ἀνθρώπων ἄνθρωπος	(of) men *an·**thrō**·pōn*	GEN PL MASC	noun

As with the reference to the "fullness of time" in 1:9–10, the mystery that "was not made known" (**οὐκ ἐγνωρίσθη**) to "other generations" (**ὃ ἑτέραις γενεαῖς**) is explained in terms of God's careful dispensation at a certain point in time and to certain individuals.

5b **ὡς νῦν ἀπεκαλύφθη τοῖς ἁγίοις ἀποστόλοις αὐτοῦ καὶ προφήταις**

as it has now been revealed to his holy apostles and prophets

ὡς ὡς	as ***hōs***	---	adv
νῦν νῦν	now ***nyn***	---	adv
ἀπεκαλύφθη ἀποκαλύπτω	it has been revealed *a·pe·ka·**lyph**·thē*	AOR PASS IND 3RD SG	verb
τοῖς ὁ	to the ***tois***	DAT PL MASC	article
ἁγίοις ἅγιος	(to) holy *ha·**gi**·ois*	DAT PL MASC	adj
ἀποστόλοις ἀπόστολος	(to) apostles *a·po·**sto**·lois*	DAT PL MASC	noun
αὐτοῦ αὐτός	of him/his *au·**tou***	3RD GEN SG	personal pron
καὶ καί	and ***kai***	---	conj
προφήταις προφήτης	(to) prophets *pro·**phē**·tais*	DAT PL MASC	noun

5c **ἐν πνεύματι,**

by the Spirit,

ἐν ἐν	by *en*	---	prep
πνεύματι πνεῦμα	Spirit ***pneu**·ma·ti*	DAT SG NEUT	noun

6a	εἶναι τὰ ἔθνη συνκληρονόμα

Namely, that the gentiles are coheirs

εἶναι εἰμί	to be ***ei***·*nai*	PRES ACT INF	verb
τὰ ὁ	the ***ta***	ACC PL NEUT	article
ἔθνη ἔθνος	gentiles ***eth***·*nē*	ACC PL NEUT	noun
συνκληρονόμα συγκληρονόμος	coheirs *syn*·*klē*·*ro*·***no***·*ma*	ACC PL NEUT	adj

The mystery, once identified with the summing up of all things in Christ (1:9–10), now refers to the inclusion of the gentiles in the covenant. Paul presents these two elements—the supremacy of Christ and the unity of Jews and gentiles in one body—as two interrelated aspects of God's plan.

6b	καὶ σύνσωμα

and co-members of the body,

καὶ καί	and ***kai***	---	conj
σύνσωμα σύσσωμος	(co-members) of the body ***sy***·*sō*·*ma*	ACC PL NEUT	adj

6c	καὶ συνμέτοχα τῆς ἐπαγγελίας

and co-participants in the promise

καὶ καί	and ***kai***	---	conj
συνμέτοχα συμμέτοχος	co-participants *syn*·***me***·*to*·*cha*	ACC PL NEUT	adj
τῆς ὁ	in the ***tēs***	GEN SG FEM	article
ἐπαγγελίας ἐπαγγελία	(the) promise *e*·*pan*·*ge*·***li***·*as*	GEN SG FEM	noun

The triad of **συν-** words—**συνκληρονόμα** ("coheirs"), **σύνσωμα** ("co-members of the body"), and **συνμέτοχα** ("co-participants")—recalls 2:19, emphasizing the "togetherness" of Jews and gentiles and the unity of the church in one corporate body. The references to inheritance and participation in the promise once again include the gentiles in the covenant between God and his people.

6d	**ἐν Χριστῷ Ἰησοῦ**		
	in Christ Jesus		
ἐν ἐν	in *en*	---	prep
Χριστῷ Χριστός	Christ *Chri·stō*	DAT SG MASC	noun
Ἰησοῦ Ἰησοῦς	Jesus *I·ē·sou*	DAT SG MASC	noun

6e	**διὰ τοῦ εὐαγγελίου,**		
	through the gospel,		
διὰ διά	through *di·a*	---	prep
τοῦ ὁ	the *tou*	GEN SG NEUT	article
εὐαγγελίου εὐαγγέλιον	gospel *eu·an·ge·li·ou*	GEN SG NEUT	noun

7a	**οὗ ἐγενήθην διάκονος**		
	of which I became a servant		
οὗ ὅς	of which *hou*	GEN SG NEUT	relative pron
ἐγενήθην γίνομαι	I became *e·ge·nē·thēn*	AOR PASS IND 1ST SG	verb
διάκονος διάκονος	servant *di·a·ko·nos*	NOM SG MASC	noun

The word **διάκονος** ("servant/minister") is used for people in various contexts, such as a king's court servant, a household servant, or a deacon in a church. It denotes both humility and responsibility in service.

7b	**κατὰ τὴν δωρεὰν τῆς χάριτος τοῦ θεοῦ**		
	according to the gift of the grace of God		
κατὰ κατά	according to *ka·**ta***	---	prep
τὴν ὁ	the ***tēn***	ACC SG FEM	article
δωρεὰν δωρεά	gift *dō·re·**an***	ACC SG FEM	noun
τῆς ὁ	of the ***tēs***	GEN SG FEM	article
χάριτος χάρις	(of) grace ***cha**·ri·tos*	GEN SG FEM	noun
τοῦ ὁ	of the ***tou***	GEN SG MASC	article
θεοῦ θεός	(of) God *the·**ou***	GEN SG MASC	noun

7c	**τῆς δοθείσης μοι**		
	which was given to me		
τῆς ὁ	of the one/which ***tēs***	GEN SG FEM	article
δοθείσης δίδωμι	(it) being/was given *do·**thei**·sēs*	AOR PASS PTCP GEN SG FEM	verb
μοι ἐγώ	to me *moi*	1ST DAT SG	pron

7d	**κατὰ τὴν ἐνέργειαν τῆς δυνάμεως αὐτοῦ,**		
	according to the working of his power.		
κατὰ κατά	according to *ka·**ta***	---	prep
τὴν ὁ	the ***tēn***	ACC SG FEM	article
ἐνέργειαν ἐνέργεια	working *en·**er**·gei·an*	ACC SG FEM	noun
τῆς ὁ	of the ***tēs***	GEN SG FEM	article

δυνάμεως δύναμις	(of) power *dy·**na**·me·ōs*	GEN SG FEM	noun
αὐτοῦ αὐτός	of him/his *au·**tou***	3RD GEN SG	personal pron

3:8–13

8a ἐμοὶ τῷ ἐλαχιστοτέρῳ πάντων ἁγίων

emoi tō elachistoterō pantōn hagiōn

To me, the very least of all the saints,

8b ἐδόθη ἡ χάρις αὕτη—

edothē hē charis hautē—

this grace was given—

8c τοῖς ἔθνεσιν εὐαγγελίσασθαι

tois ethnesin euangelisasthai

τὸ ἀνεξιχνίαστον πλοῦτος τοῦ χριστοῦ,

to anexichniaston ploutos tou christou,

to proclaim to the gentiles the unsearchable riches of Christ

9a καὶ φωτίσαι τίς ἡ οἰκονομία τοῦ μυστηρίου

kai phōtisai tis hē oikonomia tou mystēriou

τοῦ ἀποκεκρυμμένου ἀπὸ τῶν αἰώνων ἐν τῷ θεῷ

tou apokekrymmenou apo tōn aiōnōn en tō theō

and to bring light [concerning] the plan of the mystery hidden for ages in God

9b τῷ τὰ πάντα κτίσαντι,

tō ta panta ktisanti,

who created all things

10a ἵνα γνωρισθῇ νῦν

hina gnōristhē nyn

So that now, [it] might be made known

10b ταῖς ἀρχαῖς καὶ ταῖς ἐξουσίαις

tais archais kai tais exousiais

to the rulers and authorities

10c ἐν τοῖς ἐπουρανίοις

*en **tois** epoura**ni**ois*

in the heavenly places,

10d διὰ τῆς ἐκκλησίας

*di**a** **tēs** ekklē**si**as*

through the church

10e ἡ πολυποίκιλος σοφία τοῦ θεοῦ,

*hē poly**poi**kilos so**phi**a **tou** the**ou**,*

the manifold wisdom of God

11a κατὰ πρόθεσιν τῶν αἰώνων

*ka**ta** **pro**thesin **tōn** ai**ō**nōn*

according to the eternal purpose

11b ἣν ἐποίησεν ἐν τῷ χριστῷ Ἰησοῦ τῷ κυρίῳ ἡμῶν,

***hēn** e**poi**ēsen en **tō** chris**tō** Iē**sou** **tō** ky**ri**ō hē**mōn**,*

which he accomplished in Christ Jesus our Lord,

12a ἐν ᾧ ἔχομεν τὴν παρρησίαν καὶ προσαγωγὴν

*en **hō** **e**chomen **tēn** parrhē**si**an **kai** prosagō**gēn***

In whom we have boldness and access

12b ἐν πεποιθήσει

*en pepoi**thē**sai*

in confidence

12c διὰ τῆς πίστεως αὐτοῦ.

*di**a** **tēs** **pis**teōs au**tou**.*

through faith in him.

13a Διὸ αἰτοῦμαι μὴ ἐνκακεῖν

Dio aitoumai mē enkakein

ἐν ταῖς θλίψεσίν μου ὑπὲρ ὑμῶν,

en tais thlipsesin mou hyper hymōn,

Therefore I ask you not to be discouraged because of my afflictions on your behalf,

13b ἥτις ἐστὶν δόξα ὑμῶν.

hētis estin doxa hymōn.

which is your glory.

8a **ἐμοὶ τῷ ἐλαχιστοτέρῳ πάντων ἁγίων**

To me, the very least of all the saints,

ἐμοὶ ἐγώ	to me *e·moi*	1ST DAT SG	pron
τῷ ὁ	(to) the *tō*	DAT SG MASC	article
ἐλαχιστοτέρῳ ἐλαχιστότερος	(to) very least *e·la·chi·sto·te·rō*	DAT SG MASC	adj
πάντων πᾶς	of all *pan·tōn*	GEN PL MASC	adj
ἁγίων ἅγιος	(of) saints *ha·gi·ōn*	GEN PL MASC	adj

Paul uses an adjective in the superlative to refer to his status: the least (**τῷ ἐλαχιστοτέρῳ**) of all the saints (**πάντων ἁγίων**). Although humility is perceived as a virtue in the Christian tradition, that was not the case in the Greco-Roman world. Therefore, this kind of statement would not have been expected from someone of Paul's stature in the culture. This is not some sort of modest posturing on the part of the apostle. Although the mystery is revealed to him in a special manner, Paul does not see this as a merited privilege, but as a gracious and sovereign gift of God.

8b ἐδόθη ἡ χάρις αὕτη—

this grace was given—

ἐδόθη δίδωμι	(it) was given *e·**do**·thē*	AOR PASS IND 3RD SG	verb
ἡ ὁ	the ***hē***	NOM SG FEM	article
χάρις χάρις	grace ***cha**·ris*	NOM SG FEM	noun
αὕτη οὗτος	this ***hau**·tē*	NOM SG FEM	demonstr pron

8c τοῖς ἔθνεσιν εὐαγγελίσασθαι τὸ ἀνεξιχνίαστον πλοῦτος τοῦ χριστοῦ,

to proclaim to the gentiles the unsearchable riches of Christ

τοῖς ὁ	to the ***tois***	DAT PL NEUT	article
ἔθνεσιν ἔθνος	(to) gentiles ***eth**·ne·sin*	DAT PL NEUT	noun
εὐαγγελίσασθαι εὐαγγελίζω	to proclaim *eu·an·ge·**li**·sas·thai*	AOR MID INF	verb
τὸ ὁ	the ***to***	ACC SG NEUT	article
ἀνεξιχνίαστον ἀνεξιχνίαστος	unsearchable *a·ne·xich·**ni**·a·ston*	ACC SG NEUT	adj
πλοῦτος πλοῦτος	riches ***plou**·tos*	ACC SG NEUT	noun
τοῦ ὁ	of the ***tou***	GEN SG MASC	article
χριστοῦ Χριστός	(of) Christ *chri·**stou***	GEN SG MASC	noun

The word **εὐαγγελίσασθαι** ("preach") is used in the Greco-Roman world to refer to the proclamation of good news, such as when emperors would broadcast their military conquests and accomplishments. In Isa 40:9 in the Septuagint, it is used to refer to the announcement of YHWH's intervention in the deliverance of his people. Mark the evangelist begins his account of Jesus' life, death, and resurrection by identifying his narrative as **Ἀρχὴ τοῦ *εὐαγγελίου* Ἰησοῦ χριστοῦ** ("the beginning of the *gospel* of Jesus Christ"). The verb became a technical term in Christian tradition to refer to the proclamation of the Christ event.

9a	**καὶ φωτίσαι τίς ἡ οἰκονομία τοῦ μυστηρίου τοῦ ἀποκεκρυμμένου ἀπὸ τῶν αἰώνων ἐν τῷ θεῷ**

and to bring light [concerning] the plan of the mystery hidden for ages in God

καὶ καί	and ***kai***	---	conj
φωτίσαι φωτίζω	to bring light *phō·**ti**·sai*	AOR ACT INF	verb
τίς τίς~2	what ***tis***	NOM SG FEM	interr pron
ἡ ὁ	the *hē*	NOM SG FEM	article
οἰκονομία οἰκονομία	plan *oi·ko·no·**mi**·a*	NOM SG FEM	noun
τοῦ ὁ	of the ***tou***	GEN SG NEUT	article
μυστηρίου μυστήριον	(of) mystery *my·stē·**ri**·ou*	GEN SG NEUT	noun
τοῦ ὁ	(of) the ***tou***	GEN SG NEUT	article
ἀποκεκρυμμένου ἀποκρύπτω	(of) (one) hidden *a·po·ke·krym·**me**·nou*	PERF PASS PTCP GEN SG NEUT	verb
ἀπὸ ἀπό	for *a·**po***	---	prep
τῶν ὁ	the ***tōn***	GEN PL MASC	article
αἰώνων αἰών	ages *ai·**ō**·nōn*	GEN PL MASC	noun
ἐν ἐν	in *en*	---	prep
τῷ ὁ	the ***tō***	DAT SG MASC	article
θεῷ θεός	God *the·**ō***	DAT SG MASC	noun

The purpose of Paul's stewardship is to shine a light (**φωτίσαι**) on God's plan. The theme of "light" also shows up in 1:18 and 5:8–20.

9b	**τῷ τὰ πάντα κτίσαντι,**

who created all things

τῷ ὁ	who ***tō***	DAT SG MASC	article

τὰ ὁ	the *ta*	ACC PL NEUT	article
πάντα πᾶς	all (things) ***pan***·*ta*	ACC PL NEUT	adj
κτίσαντι κτίζω	created ***kti***·*san*·*ti*	AOR ACT PTCP DAT SG MASC	verb

10a ἵνα γνωρισθῇ νῦν

So that now, [it] might be made known

ἵνα ἵνα	so that ***hi***·*na*	---	conj
γνωρισθῇ γνωρίζω	(it) might be made known *gnō*·*ris*·***thē***	AOR PASS SUBJ 3RD SG	verb
νῦν νῦν	now ***nyn***	---	adv

The next few verses (3:10–12) focus on the theme of the church as the means by which God reveals himself. We saw the same theme in 1:15–23: the church is the expression of Christ's supremacy over every ruler and authority (1:21–22), and here the church is the vehicle through which God's wisdom is made known to rulers and authorities. The passages inform one another.

See comments on 3:3–5 above for a discussion of **γνωρισθῇ** ("might be made known").

10b ταῖς ἀρχαῖς καὶ ταῖς ἐξουσίαις

to the rulers and authorities

ταῖς ὁ	to the ***tais***	DAT PL FEM	article
ἀρχαῖς ἀρχή	(to) rulers *ar*·***chais***	DAT PL FEM	noun
καὶ καί	and ***kai***	---	conj
ταῖς ὁ	(to) the ***tais***	DAT PL FEM	article
ἐξουσίαις ἐξουσία	(to) authorities *e*·*xou*·***si***·*ais*	DAT PL FEM	noun

10c ἐν τοῖς ἐπουρανίοις

in the heavenly places,

ἐν ἐν	in *en*	---	prep
τοῖς ὁ	the ***tois***	DAT PL NEUT	article
ἐπουρανίοις ἐπουράνιος	heavenly (places) *e·pou·ra·**ni**·ois*	DAT PL NEUT	adj

10d διὰ τῆς ἐκκλησίας

through the church

διὰ διά	through *di·**a***	---	prep
τῆς ὁ	the ***tēs***	GEN SG FEM	article
ἐκκλησίας ἐκκλησία	church *ek·klē·**si**·as*	GEN SG FEM	noun

The word order in Greek emphasizes first (v. 10b) to whom the wisdom is made known—**ταῖς ἀρχαῖς καὶ ταῖς ἐξουσίαις** ("rulers and authorities")—and then (v. 10d) through whom—**διὰ τῆς ἐκκλησίας** ("the church"). The statement is consistent with Paul's description of the church as sitting together with Christ in the heavenly places (2:6) far above rulers and authorities (1:20–21). That the church is the instrument by which God's wisdom is revealed to the authorities is one of the most remarkable affirmations of Paul in the letter.

10e ἡ πολυποίκιλος σοφία τοῦ θεοῦ,

the manifold wisdom of God

ἡ ὁ	the *hē*	NOM SG FEM	article
πολυποίκιλος πολυποίκιλος	manifold *po·ly·**poi**·ki·los*	NOM SG FEM	adj
σοφία σοφία	wisdom *so·**phi**·a*	NOM SG FEM	noun
τοῦ ὁ	of the ***tou***	GEN SG MASC	article

θεοῦ θεός	(of) God *the·**ou***	GEN SG MASC	noun

The adjective **πολυποίκιλος**, translated here as "manifold," refers to something with many colors or stripes. It is used to refer to artisanal work, such as embroidering or ornaments. It can also refer to the complexity of a subject. The complex woven fabric of God's wisdom is revealed through the church.

11a **κατὰ πρόθεσιν τῶν αἰώνων**

according to the eternal purpose

κατὰ κατά	according to *ka·**ta***	---	prep
πρόθεσιν πρόθεσις	purpose ***pro**·the·sin*	ACC SG FEM	noun
τῶν ὁ	of the ***tōn***	GEN PL MASC	article
αἰώνων αἰών	(of) the ages/eternal *ai·**ō**·nōn*	GEN PL MASC	noun

11b **ἣν ἐποίησεν ἐν τῷ χριστῷ Ἰησοῦ τῷ κυρίῳ ἡμῶν,**

which he accomplished in Christ Jesus our Lord,

ἣν ὅς	which ***hēn***	ACC SG FEM	relative pron
ἐποίησεν ποιέω	he accomplished *e·**poi**·ē·sen*	AOR ACT IND 3RD SG	verb
ἐν ἐν	in *en*	---	prep
τῷ ὁ	the ***tō***	DAT SG MASC	article
χριστῷ Χριστός	Christ *chri·**stō***	DAT SG MASC	noun
Ἰησοῦ Ἰησοῦς	Jesus *I·ē·**sou***	DAT SG MASC	noun
τῷ ὁ	the ***tō***	DAT SG MASC	article
κυρίῳ κύριος	Lord *ky·**ri**·ō*	DAT SG MASC	noun

ἡμῶν ἐγώ	of us/our *hē·**mōn***	1ST GEN PL	pron

12a	**ἐν ᾧ ἔχομεν τὴν παρρησίαν καὶ προσαγωγὴν**
	In whom we have boldness and access

ἐν ἐν	in *en*	---	prep
ᾧ ὅς	whom ***hō***	DAT SG MASC	relative pron
ἔχομεν ἔχω	we have ***e**·cho·men*	PRES ACT IND 1ST PL	verb
τὴν ὁ	the ***tēn***	ACC SG FEM	article
παρρησίαν παρρησία	boldness *par·rhē·**si**·an*	ACC SG FEM	noun
καὶ καί	and ***kai***	---	conj
προσαγωγὴν προσαγωγή	access *pros·a·gō·**gēn***	ACC SG FEM	noun

12b	**ἐν πεποιθήσει**
	in confidence

ἐν ἐν	in *en*	---	prep
πεποιθήσει πεποίθησις	confidence *pe·poi·**thē**·sai*	DAT SG FEM	noun

12c	**διὰ τῆς πίστεως αὐτοῦ.**
	through faith in him.

διὰ διά	through *di·**a***	---	prep
τῆς ὁ	the ***tēs***	GEN SG FEM	article
πίστεως πίστις	faith ***pi**·ste·ōs*	GEN SG FEM	noun
αὐτοῦ αὐτός	in him *au·**tou***	3RD GEN SG	personal pron

The phrase **διὰ τῆς πίστεως αὐτοῦ** may be translated as an objective genitive ("faith in Christ") or a subjective genitive ("faithfulness of Christ"). Both make sense in context, and as in other instances, Paul does not spell it out, perhaps because both meanings may be in view. However, in light of 3:17, where the objective sense is clearer, that is likely the primary meaning here as well.

13a **Διὸ αἰτοῦμαι μὴ ἐνκακεῖν ἐν ταῖς θλίψεσίν μου ὑπὲρ ὑμῶν,**

Therefore I ask you not to be discouraged because of my afflictions on your behalf,

Διὸ διό	therefore *Di·**o***	---	conj
αἰτοῦμαι αἰτέω	I ask you (all) *ai·**tou**·mai*	PRES MID IND 1ST SG	verb
μὴ μή	not ***mē***	---	particle
ἐνκακεῖν ἐκκακέω	to be discouraged *en·ka·**kein***	PRES ACT INF	verb
ἐν ἐν	because of *en*	---	prep
ταῖς ὁ	the ***tais***	DAT PL FEM	article
θλίψεσίν θλῖψις	afflictions ***thli**·pse·sin*	DAT PL FEM	noun
μου ἐγώ	of me/my *mou*	1ST GEN SG	pron
ὑπὲρ ὑπέρ	on behalf of *hy·**per***	---	prep
ὑμῶν σύ	of you (all) *hy·**mōn***	2ND GEN PL	pron

13b **ἥτις ἐστὶν δόξα ὑμῶν.**

which is your glory.

ἥτις ὅστις	which ***hē**·tis*	NOM SG FEM	relative pron
ἐστὶν εἰμί	is *e·**stin***	PRES ACT IND 3RD SG	verb

δόξα δόξα	glory ***do***·*xa*	NOM SG FEM	noun
ὑμῶν σύ	of you (all)/your *hy*·***mōn***	2ND GEN PL	pron

From Text to Sermon

Main Exegetical Ideas. Paul is the faithful and humble steward of the mystery of Christ. This mystery is that gentiles are members of the body of Christ, through which the manifold wisdom of God is made known to rulers and authorities.

Bridge to Theology. Paul's description of his ministry emphasizes his understanding of the role he is to play in God's plan. The reason he draws attention to himself is seen in v. 13—that the Ephesians would not lose heart over his sufferings but would know, as Paul himself clearly does, that his sufferings are part of God's unfailing plan for the benefit of the church. This is a window into Paul's theology of suffering, which is also seen in texts like Phil 1:12–26 and 2 Cor 4:1–18. Paul understands his identity, ministry, and suffering in light of the mystery of Christ. He is but a humble servant and a steward of the gospel who finds contentment and purpose in playing his role in God's eternal plan.

Paul's description of his ministry culminates in the ecclesiological purpose statement of 3:10—the rhetorical center of the passage (3:1–13). The mystery of Christ, which was conceived in eternity, envisions the full inclusion of gentiles in the one body of Christ so that through the church the wisdom of God will be revealed. Notice the Trinitarian dynamics of the mystery: planned by God the Father, accomplished in Christ the Son, and revealed by the Spirit.

As pointed out in the commentary, there is likely a link between Paul's view of his calling as a humble servant to whom the mystery of Christ has been revealed and the church as the vehicle of God's revelation of his wisdom. This is how God reveals himself: through flawed instruments to magnify his power (cf. 1 Cor 1:26–29; 2 Cor 4:7)

Possible Sermon Structures. There are two main focal points in this passage: Paul's ministry and the mystery of Christ. These are not rhetorically isolated but interwoven. There are possibly two sermons in this passage:

1 Paul's ministry and the purpose of his suffering

- 1.1 A prisoner (3:1)
- 1.2 A steward (3:2)
- 1.3 A humble servant (3:7–8)
- 1.4 A preacher of good news (3:8–9)

- 2 The mystery of Christ
  - 2.1 The nature of the mystery:
    - 2.1.1 Eternally planned by God (3:11)
    - 2.1.2 Accomplished in Christ (3:11)
    - 2.1.3 Revealed by the Spirit (3:3–5, 9)
  - 2.2 The content of the mystery: the united body of Christ (3:6)
  - 2.3 The purpose of the mystery: to reveal God's wisdom (3:10)

 ***Points of Application.*** The first point of focus of this passage—Paul's ministry—provides a great resource for Bible studies aimed at pastors and Christian leaders since Paul positions his vocation in the context of God's eternal plan. This can be a powerful reminder for those who are called to ministry, that they are but stewards and servants of God in the revelation of his plan. Obviously, Paul's ministry was one of a kind, but his posture is a model to be imitated.

A second point of application coming from this first aspect has to do with suffering. Paul's attitude in the face of adversity is informed by his understanding of God's plan. The apostle knows that God is at work in his church and that a greater purpose is in view: that God's wisdom will be fully revealed through his people. This understanding makes sense of his suffering. Similarly, our daily challenges have to be situated in the context of God's eternal plan.

Finally, Paul's statement that the united body of Christ becomes the very means by which God reveals his manifold wisdom is a remarkable affirmation. That God would choose the church, made of flawed human beings, to display his multiform wisdom to the principalities and powers is both a humbling and inspiring reality. Notice that this high calling of the church is introduced by Paul's own calling as the "very least of all the saints." In the case of both the apostle and the church, God chooses unlikely people to carry out his sovereign plan.

 ***Illustration Opportunities.*** The remarkable ecclesiological point Paul makes in 3:10 is worth exploring with the congregation. There is a fictional story about a genius—arguably the most remarkable mind ever to have existed—who was contacted by a reporter for an interview. The genius agreed and a date was set. When the day comes, the reporter, excited with the opportunity, knocks on the door of the house of the genius and is welcomed by his helper. The helper then sadly informs the reporter

that between the time they arranged the interview and that day, the genius had suffered an accident that rendered his entire body paralyzed. Discouraged, the reporter asks the helper if there is any way to interview him, to which the helper answers: "his mind is still there, but his body cannot express his mind." It is significant that God has determined that his wisdom would be revealed by the body of Christ and that there is no alternative plan for it.

EPHESIANS 3:14–21

STRENGTHENED BY THE SPIRIT, INDWELT BY CHRIST, FILLED WITH THE FULLNESS OF GOD

Paul closes his theological section (1:1–3:21) in the same way he began, but in reverse order. He began with a blessing (1:3–14) followed by a prayer (1:15–23), and he now closes with a prayer (3:14–19) followed by a doxology (3:20–21). These bookending sections frame the whole theological discourse in doxology. The deep realities Paul discusses—God's eternal plan to sum up all things in Christ and to reveal his wisdom through his church—are enveloped in praise to the God who works mightily in the church.

3:14–19

14a Τούτου χάριν κάμπτω τὰ γόνατά μου

Toutou charin kampto ta gonata mou

For this reason, I bow my knees

14b πρὸς τὸν πατέρα,

pros ton patera,

before the Father,

15a ἐξ οὗ πᾶσα πατριὰ ἐν οὐρανοῖς καὶ ἐπὶ γῆς ὀνομάζεται,

ex hou pasa patria en ouranois kai epi gēs onomazetai,

from whom every family in heaven and on earth is named,

16a ἵνα δῷ ὑμῖν

hina dō hymin

so that he should give you,

16b κατὰ τὸ πλοῦτος τῆς δόξης αὐτοῦ

kata to ploutos tēs doxēs autou

according to the riches of his glory,

16c δυνάμει κραταιωθῆναι διὰ τοῦ πνεύματος αὐτοῦ

dynamei krataiōthēnai dia tou pneumatos autou

to be strengthened with power through his Spirit,

16d εἰς τὸν ἔσω ἄνθρωπον,

eis ton esō anthrōpon,

in [your] inner person

17a κατοικῆσαι τὸν χριστὸν διὰ τῆς πίστεως

katoikēsai ton christon dia tēs pisteōs

ἐν ταῖς καρδίαις ὑμῶν,

en tais kardiais hymōn,

[and] for Christ to dwell in your hearts through faith,

17b ἐν ἀγάπῃ ἐρριζωμένοι καὶ τεθεμελιωμένοι,

*en a**ga**pē errhizō**me**noi **kai** tethemeliō**me**noi,*

having been rooted and founded in love.

18a ἵνα ἐξισχύσητε καταλαβέσθαι

***hi**na exis**chy**sēte katala**bes**thai*

So that you might be strengthened to grasp

18b σὺν πᾶσιν τοῖς ἁγίοις

***syn pa**sin **tois** ha**gi**ois*

with all the saints

18c τί τὸ πλάτος καὶ μῆκος καὶ ὕψος καὶ βάθος,

***ti to pla**tos **kai mē**kos **kai hy**psos **kai ba**thos,*

what is the breadth and length and height and depth,

19a γνῶναί τε τὴν ὑπερβάλλουσαν τῆς γνώσεως

***gnō**nai te **tēn** hyper**bal**lousan **tēs gnō**seōs*

ἀγάπην τοῦ χριστοῦ,

*a**ga**pēn **tou** chris**tou**,*

and to know the love of Christ which surpasses knowledge,

19b ἵνα πληρωθῆτε εἰς πᾶν τὸ πλήρωμα τοῦ θεοῦ.

***hi**na plērō**thē**te eis **pan to plē**rōma **tou** the**ou**.*

so that you may be filled with all the fullness of God.

14a	**Τούτου χάριν κάμπτω τὰ γόνατά μου**		
	For this reason, I bow my knees		
Τούτου οὗτος	this (reason) *Tou·tou*	GEN SG NEUT	demonstr pron
χάριν χάριν	for *cha·rin*	---	adv

κάμπτω κάμπτω	I bow ***kam***·*pto*	PRES ACT IND 1ST SG	verb
τὰ ὁ	the ***ta***	ACC PL NEUT	article
γόνατά γόνυ	knees ***go***·*na*·***ta***	ACC PL NEUT	noun
μου ἐγώ	of me/my *mou*	1ST GEN SG	pron

This is Paul's second prayer, which bookends the core of Paul's discourse with the first prayer in 1:15–23.

14b **πρὸς τὸν πατέρα,**

before the Father,

πρὸς πρός	before ***pros***	---	prep
τὸν ὁ	the ***ton***	ACC SG MASC	article
πατέρα πατήρ	father *pa*·***te***·*ra*	ACC SG MASC	noun

15a **ἐξ οὗ πᾶσα πατριὰ ἐν οὐρανοῖς καὶ ἐπὶ γῆς ὀνομάζεται,**

from whom every family in heaven and on earth is named,

ἐξ ἐκ	from *ex*	---	prep
οὗ ὅς	whom ***hou***	GEN SG MASC	relative pron
πᾶσα πᾶς	every ***pa***·*sa*	NOM SG FEM	adj
πατριὰ πατριά	family *pa*·***tri***·*a*	NOM SG FEM	noun
ἐν ἐν	in *en*	---	prep
οὐρανοῖς οὐρανός	heaven *ou*·*ra*·***nois***	DAT PL MASC	noun
καὶ καί	and ***kai***	---	conj
ἐπὶ ἐπί	on *e*·***pi***	---	prep

γῆς γῆ	earth *gēs*	GEN SG FEM	noun
ὀνομάζεται ὀνομάζω	(it) is named *o·no·**ma**·ze·tai*	PRES PASS IND 3RD SG	verb

The words **πατέρα** ("father") and **πατριὰ** ("family") sound similar and are semantically related. Here, the terms work together to portray God as the head of the household, carrying out his careful administration (**οἰκονομία** [1:10]) for its benefit. God's absolute sovereignty oversees a well-ordered reality in which all beings, earthly and heavenly, derive their existence from him and are subject to him.

16a **ἵνα δῷ ὑμῖν**

so that he should give you,

ἵνα ἵνα	so that *hi·na*	---	conj
δῷ δίδωμι	he should give *dō*	AOR ACT SUBJ 3RD SG	verb
ὑμῖν σύ	to you (all) *hy·**min***	2ND DAT PL	pron

16b **κατὰ τὸ πλοῦτος τῆς δόξης αὐτοῦ**

according to the riches of his glory,

κατὰ κατά	according to *ka·**ta***	---	prep
τὸ ὁ	the ***to***	ACC SG NEUT	article
πλοῦτος πλοῦτος	riches ***plou**·tos*	ACC SG NEUT	noun
τῆς ὁ	of the ***tēs***	GEN SG FEM	article
δόξης δόξα	(of) glory ***do**·xēs*	GEN SG FEM	noun
αὐτοῦ αὐτός	of him/his *au·**tou***	3RD GEN SG	personal pron

16c **δυνάμει κραταιωθῆναι διὰ τοῦ πνεύματος αὐτοῦ**

to be strengthened with power through his Spirit,

δυνάμει δύναμις	with power *dy·**na**·mei*	DAT SG FEM	noun
κραταιωθῆναι κραταιόω	to be strengthened *kra·tai·ō·**thē**·nai*	AOR PASS INF	verb
διὰ διά	through *di·**a***	---	prep
τοῦ ὁ	the ***tou***	GEN SG NEUT	article
πνεύματος πνεῦμα	Spirit ***pneu**·ma·tos*	GEN SG NEUT	noun
αὐτοῦ αὐτός	of him/his *au·**tou***	3RD GEN SG	personal pron

16d **εἰς τὸν ἔσω ἄνθρωπον,**

in [your] inner person

εἰς εἰς	in *eis*	---	prep
τὸν ὁ	the ***ton***	ACC SG MASC	article
ἔσω ἔσω	inner ***e**·sō*	---	adv
ἄνθρωπον ἄνθρωπος	person ***an**·thrō·pon*	ACC SG MASC	noun

The possessive pronoun “your” is not in the Greek text, but it is implied through the parallelism with v. 17a, where the pronoun is present.

17a **κατοικῆσαι τὸν χριστὸν διὰ τῆς πίστεως ἐν ταῖς καρδίαις ὑμῶν,**

[and] for Christ to dwell in your hearts through faith,

κατοικῆσαι κατοικέω	to dwell *ka·toi·**kē**·sai*	AOR ACT INF	verb
τὸν ὁ	the ***ton***	ACC SG MASC	article
χριστὸν Χριστός	Christ *chri·**ston***	ACC SG MASC	noun

διὰ διά	through *di·**a***	---	prep
τῆς ὁ	the ***tēs***	GEN SG FEM	article
πίστεως πίστις	faith ***pi**·ste·ōs*	GEN SG FEM	noun
ἐν ἐν	in *en*	---	prep
ταῖς ὁ	the ***tais***	DAT PL FEM	article
καρδίαις καρδία	hearts *kar·**di**·ais*	DAT PL FEM	noun
ὑμῶν σύ	of you (all)/your *hy·**mōn***	2ND GEN PL	pron

The infinitives in v. 16c and v. 17a constitute the two prayer requests: that the believers will be strengthened (**κραταιωθῆναι**) and that Christ will dwell (**κατοικῆσαι**) in their hearts (**ἐν ταῖς καρδίαις ὑμῶν**). The two requests, however, are in logical sequence. They are to be strengthened in their inner self so that Christ will dwell in their hearts. The verb **κατοικέω** ("dwell") connects with both the household imagery (notice the **οικ**- root) and with the temple metaphor in 2:22, where Paul refers to the church as God's **κατοικητήριον** ("dwelling place").

17b **ἐν ἀγάπῃ ἐρριζωμένοι καὶ τεθεμελιωμένοι,**

having been rooted and founded in love.

ἐν ἐν	in *en*	---	prep
ἀγάπῃ ἀγάπη	love *a·**ga**·pē*	DAT SG FEM	noun
ἐρριζωμένοι ῥιζόω	(you all) having been rooted *er·rhi·zō·**me**·noi*	PERF PASS PTCP NOM PL MASC	verb
καὶ καί	and ***kai***	---	conj
τεθεμελιωμένοι θεμελιόω	(you all) having been founded *te·the·me·li·ō·**me**·noi*	PERF PASS PTCP NOM PL MASC	verb

The prepositional phrase **ἐν ἀγάπῃ** ("in love") could be modifying **κατοικῆσαι** ("dwell") or **ἐρριζωμένοι καὶ τεθεμελιωμένοι** ("being rooted and founded"). The latter is more likely given its proximity to the participles, indicating their mode.

While the syntax is difficult, it is better to see the participles **ἐρριζωμένοι καὶ τεθεμελιωμένοι** connected to the infinitive **κατοικῆσαι** ("to dwell"). The participle **τεθεμελιωμένοι** ("having been founded") has architectural connotations, which go with the image of "dwelling." The participles are in the perfect tense: because they have been rooted and founded in love, Paul prays that Christ will dwell in their hearts.

18a **ἵνα ἐξισχύσητε καταλαβέσθαι**

So that you might be strengthened to grasp

ἵνα ἵνα	so that *__hi__·na*	---	conj
ἐξισχύσητε ἐξισχύω	you (all) might be strengthened *e·xis·__chy__·sē·te*	AOR ACT SUBJ 2ND PL	verb
καταλαβέσθαι καταλαμβάνω	to grasp *ka·ta·la·__bes__·thai*	AOR MID INF	verb

18b **σὺν πᾶσιν τοῖς ἁγίοις**

with all the saints

σὺν σύν	with ***syn***	---	prep
πᾶσιν πᾶς	all *__pa__·sin*	DAT PL MASC	adj
τοῖς ὁ	the ***tois***	DAT PL MASC	article
ἁγίοις ἅγιος	saints *ha·__gi__·ois*	DAT PL MASC	adj

18c **τί τὸ πλάτος καὶ μῆκος καὶ ὕψος καὶ βάθος,**

what is the breadth and length and height and depth,

τί τίς~2	what ***ti***	NOM SG NEUT	interr pron
τὸ ὁ	the ***to***	NOM SG NEUT	article

πλάτος πλάτος	breadth *pla·tos*	NOM SG NEUT	noun
καὶ καί	and *kai*	---	conj
μῆκος μῆκος	length *mē·kos*	NOM SG NEUT	noun
καὶ καί	and *kai*	---	conj
ὕψος ὕψος	height *hy·psos*	NOM SG NEUT	noun
καὶ καί	and *kai*	---	conj
βάθος βάθος	depth *ba·thos*	NOM SG NEUT	noun

Along with the reference to fullness (**πλήρωμα**) below in v. 19b, the dimensions **πλάτος καὶ μῆκος καὶ ὕψος καὶ βάθος** ("breadth and length and height and depth") contribute to an image of completeness. But to what do these dimensions refer? While there is a plethora of suggestions for what this referent might be, contextually, the closest is the love of Christ in the next sentence. Therefore, the believers are to grasp with all the saints the full reality of the love of Christ.

19a **γνῶναί τε τὴν ὑπερβάλλουσαν τῆς γνώσεως ἀγάπην τοῦ χριστοῦ,**

and to know the love of Christ which surpasses knowledge,

γνῶναί γινώσκω	to know *gnō·nai*	AOR ACT INF	verb
τε τέ	and *te*	---	particle
τὴν ὁ	the *tēn*	ACC SG FEM	article
ὑπερβάλλουσαν ὑπερβάλλω	(one which) surpasses *hy·per·bal·lou·san*	PRES ACT PTCP ACC SG FEM	verb
τῆς ὁ	the *tēs*	GEN SG FEM	article
γνώσεως γνῶσις	knowledge *gnō·se·ōs*	GEN SG FEM	noun
ἀγάπην ἀγάπη	love *a·ga·pēn*	ACC SG FEM	noun
τοῦ ὁ	of the *tou*	GEN SG MASC	article

χριστοῦ Χριστός	(of) Christ *chri·**stou***	GEN SG MASC	noun

Paul uses cognitive language here in a deliberately contrastive way—"to know the knowledge-surpassing love of Christ." The love of Christ, therefore, is not to be grasped simply on a cognitive level but through a kind of knowledge that goes beyond cognition—one that involves relationship and experience. That this is to be done "with all the saints" indicates that the experience of this love is communal. We experience Christ's love with the body of Christ.

19b **ἵνα πληρωθῆτε εἰς πᾶν τὸ πλήρωμα τοῦ θεοῦ.**

so that you may be filled with all the fullness of God.

ἵνα ἵνα	so that ***hi**·na*	---	conj
πληρωθῆτε πληρόω	you (all) may be filled *plē·rō·**thē**·te*	AOR PASS SUBJ 2ND PL	verb
εἰς εἰς	with *eis*	---	prep
πᾶν πᾶς	all ***pan***	ACC SG NEUT	adj
τὸ ὁ	the ***to***	ACC SG NEUT	article
πλήρωμα πλήρωμα	fullness ***plē**·rō·ma*	ACC SG NEUT	noun
τοῦ ὁ	of the ***tou***	GEN SG MASC	article
θεοῦ θεός	(of) God *the·**ou***	GEN SG MASC	noun

3:20–21

20a Τῷ δὲ δυναμένῳ ὑπὲρ πάντα ποιῆσαι

Tō de dynamenō hyper panta poiēsai

ὑπερεκπερισσοῦ ὧν αἰτούμεθα ἢ νοοῦμεν

hyperekperissou hōn aitoumetha ē nooumen

Now to the one who is able to do
far beyond all things we ask or think

20b κατὰ τὴν δύναμιν τὴν ἐνεργουμένην ἐν ἡμῖν,

kata tēn dynamin tēn energoumenēn en hēmin,

according to the power that is working in us,

21a αὐτῷ ἡ δόξα

autō hē doxa

to him be glory

21b ἐν τῇ ἐκκλησίᾳ

en tē ekklēsia

in the church

21c καὶ ἐν Χριστῷ Ἰησοῦ

kai en Christō Iēsou

and in Christ Jesus

21d εἰς πάσας τὰς γενεὰς τοῦ αἰῶνος τῶν αἰώνων·

eis pasas tas geneas tou aiōnos tōn aiōnōn;

into all generations forever and ever.

21e ἀμήν.

amēn.

Amen.

20a	**Τῷ δὲ δυναμένῳ ὑπὲρ πάντα ποιῆσαι ὑπερεκπερισσοῦ ὧν αἰτούμεθα ἢ νοοῦμεν**

Now to the one who is able to do far beyond all things we ask or think

Τῷ ὁ	to the ***Tō***	DAT SG MASC	article
δὲ δέ	now ***de***	---	conj
δυναμένῳ δύναμαι	(to) one who is able *dy·na·**me**·nō*	PRES MID/PASS PTCP DAT SG MASC	verb
ὑπὲρ ὑπέρ	over *hy·**per***	---	prep
πάντα πᾶς	all (things) ***pan**·ta*	ACC PL NEUT	adj
ποιῆσαι ποιέω	to do *poi·**ē**·sai*	AOR ACT INF	verb
ὑπερεκπερισσοῦ ὑπερεκπερισσοῦ	far beyond *hy·per·ek·pe·ris·**sou***	---	adv
ὧν ὅς	which ***hōn***	GEN PL NEUT	relative pron
αἰτούμεθα αἰτέω	we ask *ai·**tou**·me·tha*	PRES MID IND 1ST PL	verb
ἢ ἤ	or ***ē***	---	particle
νοοῦμεν νοέω	(we) think *no·**ou**·men*	PRES ACT IND 1ST PL	verb

20b	**κατὰ τὴν δύναμιν τὴν ἐνεργουμένην ἐν ἡμῖν,**

according to the power that is working in us,

κατὰ κατά	according to *ka·**ta***	---	prep
τὴν ὁ	the ***tēn***	ACC SG FEM	article
δύναμιν δύναμις	power ***dy**·na·min*	ACC SG FEM	noun
τὴν ὁ	that ***tēn***	ACC SG FEM	article
ἐνεργουμένην ἐνεργέω	(it) is working *en·er·gou·**me**·nēn*	PRES MID PTCP ACC SG FEM	verb
ἐν ἐν	in *en*	---	prep

ἡμῖν ἐγώ	us *hē·**min***	1ST DAT PL	pron

The theme of power is featured throughout this first section of the letter through words such as **ἐνέργεια/ἐνεργέω** (Eph 1:11, 19–20; 3:7) and **δύναμις** (Eph 1:19; 3:7, 16). From start to finish, it is God's power that energizes the church and guarantees that his purposes for her will be fulfilled.

21a **αὐτῷ ἡ δόξα**

to him be glory

αὐτῷ αὐτός	to him *au·**tō***	3RD DAT SG	personal pron
ἡ ὁ	the *hē*	NOM SG FEM	article
δόξα δόξα	glory ***do**·xa*	NOM SG FEM	noun

The theme of glory (**δόξα**) is also prominent in the first part of Ephesians (Eph 1:6, 12, 14, 17–18; 3:13, 16), especially in the refrain "for the praise of his glory." God's glory is the ultimate purpose of his actions on behalf of the church.

21b **ἐν τῇ ἐκκλησίᾳ**

in the church

ἐν ἐν	in *en*	---	prep
τῇ ὁ	the *tē*	DAT SG FEM	article
ἐκκλησίᾳ ἐκκλησία	church *ek·klē·**si**·a*	DAT SG FEM	noun

21c **καὶ ἐν Χριστῷ Ἰησοῦ**

and in Christ Jesus

καὶ καί	and ***kai***	---	conj

ἐν ἐν	in *en*	---	prep
Χριστῷ Χριστός	Christ *Chri·**stō***	DAT SG MASC	noun
Ἰησοῦ Ἰησοῦς	Jesus *I·ē·**sou***	DAT SG MASC	noun

21d **εἰς πάσας τὰς γενεὰς τοῦ αἰῶνος τῶν αἰώνων·**

into all generations forever and ever.

εἰς εἰς	into *eis*	---	prep
πάσας πᾶς	all ***pa**·sas*	ACC PL FEM	adj
τὰς ὁ	the ***tas***	ACC PL FEM	article
γενεὰς γενεά	generations *ge·ne·**as***	ACC PL FEM	noun
τοῦ ὁ	of the ***tou***	GEN SG MASC	article
αἰῶνος αἰών	(of) age/forever *ai·**ō**·nos*	GEN SG MASC	noun
τῶν ὁ	of the ***tōn***	GEN PL MASC	article
αἰώνων αἰών	(of) age/forever *ai·**ō**·nōn*	GEN PL MASC	noun

21e **ἀμήν.**

Amen.

ἀμήν ἀμήν	amen *a·**mēn***	HEB	transliteration

Along with the opening bookend in Eph 1:3–14, the doxology here in 3:20–21 serves as the closing bookend to the first major section of the letter.

From Text to Sermon

Main Exegetical Ideas. Strengthened by the Spirit and having Christ dwelling in their hearts, the believers must grasp the love of Christ and be filled with the fullness of God.

Bridge to Theology. This passage pulls together several theological threads from the entire first section of Ephesians. First, Paul's prayer that the Ephesians be strengthened with power alludes to the numerous references to God's power at work in the church (Eph. 1:19; 3:7, 20; 6:10). The same power now strengthens individual believers in their inner selves through the Spirit, making it possible for them to be indwelt by Christ.

Second, participation in Christ, expressed throughout the letter as being "in Christ," is now conveyed in a different way: Christ dwells in the believers' hearts. This is, therefore, full participation—Christ in the believer and the believer in Christ.

Finally, the love of God, which is the means of God's redemption and adoption of sinners (1:14–15; 2:4–5), is now expressed in the love of Christ, which is the ultimate object of the believer's knowledge (3:19), being also the foundation of such knowledge (3:17).

Possible Sermon Structure. The passage can be structured around the verbs that carry its main theological ideas. Thus,

1 The reality of the Christian life (3:14–17)
- 1.1 Belonging to God (3:14–15)
- 1.2 Strengthened by the Spirit (3:16)
- 1.3 Indwelt by Christ (3:17a)
- 1.4 Grounded in love (3:17b)

2 The goal of the Christian life (3:18–19)
- 2.1 Knowing fully the love of Christ (3:18–19a)
- 2.2 Being filled with the fullness of God (3:19b)

Points of Application. The passage can be very elusive on its own. It requires that the preacher unpack the theological ideas in light of either the letter as a whole or, at least, the section from 1:1–3:21. Two main focal points of application are the dwelling of Christ in the believer and the experience of the love of Christ. What does the knowledge of Christ's dwelling in our hearts produce in us? How do we experience the love of Christ in our lives? Here, the preacher can emphasize the magnitude of Christ's love for us, which—even though it cannot be measured—can still be experienced in its fullness through the Spirit. It is also important to underscore that the experience of this love is not simply private and personal but something of which we take hold "with all the saints." The church, both the universal and the local church, is the environment or reality where the love of Christ is known and experienced.

Illustration Opportunities. The fact that Paul refers to Christ's dwelling in one's heart may render plenty of illustration opportunities. For example, there is a difference between one who dwells in a house as a guest, a resident, and an owner of a house. What does it mean for Christ to dwell in us?

In addition, any illustrations of how the love of Christ is experienced in the church will help to strengthen the point of how we grasp his love in fellowship with the saints. To be sure, there is a bigger picture in which the love of Christ is experienced mysteriously in the reality of the universal church, but there are also small ways in which such love is made known in caring for one another and doing life together.

Suppose an outsider wants to learn about the father of a family. She might do so by interviewing his children. In the process, she will inevitably discover that different children have different knowledge of the father, which is built upon their unique relationship with him. In a sense, the father's character will be more completely known through understanding his children and how they relate to him. Similarly, there are aspects of our relationship with God that are unique, given the way we experience fellowship with God personally. Therefore, in getting to know each other and the way each of us relates to the Father, we gain further knowledge of who the Father is and can therefore experience his love more fully.

KEEPING THE UNITY OF THE SPIRIT IN THE BOND OF PEACE

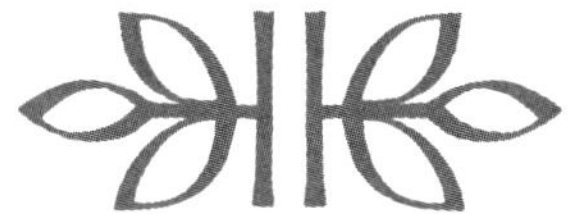

Chapter 4 begins what some have identified as the ethical section of Ephesians (4:1–6:20), which comes as a fitting application of the theological section (1:1–3:21). One should refrain from seeing in these distinctions too strict a separation between theology and ethics, since there is enough overlap between these categories in the two sections. However, it is clear that Paul moves from an exposition of the identity and calling of the church to a more pastoral admonition on Christian unity and conduct. This can be readily perceived by paying attention to the mood of the verbs. While in the first section we find only one imperative verb, in the second we find forty. These sections, however, are profoundly interrelated, sharing themes and vocabulary extensively. The ethical section should be seen as the necessary conclusion of Paul's profound theological exposition. It can be divided into two major subsections: 4:1–16—admonitions on Christian unity—and 4:17–20—admonitions on Christian conduct.

4:1–6

1a Παρακαλῶ οὖν ὑμᾶς

*Paraka**lō** **oun** hy**mas***

Therefore I urge you

1b ἐγὼ ὁ δέσμιος ἐν κυρίῳ

*e**gō** ho **des**mos en ky**ri**ō*

I, the prisoner in the Lord,

1c ἀξίως περιπατῆσαι τῆς κλήσεως

*a**xi**ōs peripa**tē**sai **tēs** **klē**seōs*

to walk in a manner worthy of the calling

1d ἧς ἐκλήθητε,

***hēs** e**klē**thēte,*

to which you have been called.

2a μετὰ πάσης ταπεινοφροσύνης καὶ πραΰτητος,

*me**ta** **pa**sēs tapeinophro**sy**nēs **kai** pra**u**tētos,*

With all humility and gentleness,

2b μετὰ μακροθυμίας,

*me**ta** makrothy**mi**as*

with patience,

2c ἀνεχόμενοι ἀλλήλων ἐν ἀγάπῃ,

*ane**cho**menoi al**lē**lōn en a**ga**pē,*

bearing with one another in love,

3a σπουδάζοντες τηρεῖν τὴν ἑνότητα τοῦ πνεύματος

*spou**da**zontes tē**rein** **tēn** he**no**tēta **tou** **pneu**matos*

making every effort to keep the unity of the Spirit

3b ἐν τῷ συνδέσμῳ τῆς εἰρήνης·

en tō syndesmō tēs eirēnēs.

in the bond of peace.

4a ἓν σῶμα

hen sōma

One body

4b καὶ ἓν πνεῦμα,

kai hen pneuma

and one Spirit,

4c καθὼς καὶ ἐκλήθητε ἐν μιᾷ ἐλπίδι τῆς κλήσεως ὑμῶν·

kathōs kai eklēthēte en mia elpidi tēs klēseōs hymōn;

just as you were also called into the one hope of your calling.

5a εἷς κύριος,

heis kyrios,

One Lord,

5b μία πίστις,

mia pistis,

one faith,

5c ἓν βάπτισμα·

hen baptisma;

one baptism,

6a εἷς θεὸς καὶ πατὴρ πάντων,

heis theos kai patēr pantōn,

one God and Father of all,

6b ὁ ἐπὶ πάντων

ho epi pantōn

who is over all

6c καὶ διὰ πάντων

kai dia pantōn

and through all

6d καὶ ἐν πᾶσιν.

kai en pasin.

and in all.

1a	**Παρακαλῶ οὖν ὑμᾶς**		
	Therefore I urge you		
Παρακαλῶ παρακαλέω	I urge *Pa·ra·ka·lō*	PRES ACT IND 1ST SG	verb
οὖν οὖν	therefore *oun*	---	conj
ὑμᾶς σύ	you (all) *hy·mas*	2ND ACC PL	pron

The word **παρακαλῶ** ("I urge") expresses an appeal or admonishment. It is used in admonitions among friends, but may also carry an authoritative tone (e.g., 1 Cor 1:10). Since Paul has just described his role as an "administrator" in the household of God (3:1–13), his appeal here is to be received as an authoritative exhortation.

Οὖν ("therefore") is an inferential conjunction, introducing a logical conclusion or application. It appears seven times in the letter, six of them in chs. 4–6.

1b	**ἐγὼ ὁ δέσμιος ἐν κυρίῳ**		
	I, the prisoner in the Lord,		
ἐγὼ ἐγώ	I *e·gō*	1ST NOM SG	pron
ὁ ὁ	the *ho*	NOM SG MASC	article

δέσμιος δέσμιος	prisoner *des·mi·os*	NOM SG MASC	noun
ἐν ἐν	in *en*	---	prep
κυρίῳ κύριος	Lord *ky·ri·ō*	DAT SG MASC	noun

A similar expression to this one is employed in 3:1. While in the first instance, Paul appeals to his condition as a prisoner to emphasize his role as a servant of Christ, here he employs it to add weight to his admonition. He is suffering for Christ and for the church, so his words should be heeded.

1c **ἀξίως περιπατῆσαι τῆς κλήσεως**

to walk in a manner worthy of the calling

ἀξίως ἀξίως	(in a manner) worthy *a·xi·ōs*	---	adv
περιπατῆσαι περιπατέω	to walk *pe·ri·pa·tē·sai*	AOR ACT INF	verb
τῆς ὁ	of the *tēs*	GEN SG FEM	article
κλήσεως κλῆσις	(of) calling *klē·se·ōs*	GEN SG FEM	noun

The object of the appeal in v. 1a is **περιπατῆσαι** ("walk"). The verb has ethical connotations and recalls both the description in Eph 2:2 of the conduct of the formerly pagan audience and the mention in 2:10 of their expected conduct in the new creation. Paul urges them to live according to the reality God has already prepared for them.

1d **ἧς ἐκλήθητε,**

to which you have been called.

ἧς ὅς	to which *hēs*	GEN SG FEM	relative pron
ἐκλήθητε καλέω	you (all) have been called *e·klē·thē·te*	AOR PASS IND 2ND PL	verb

The theme of "calling" (**τῆς κλήσεως** in 1c and **ἧς ἐκλήθητε** here) is part of a cluster of themes prominent in Ephesians that refer to God's election of believers (Eph 1:1, 4, 11, 13, 18; 4:1, 4, 30). Now, fittingly, Paul uses the same language to remind them that the conduct they are expected to exhibit should be consistent with their calling. The essential idea is "become what you are called to be." The narrative of election originates in the story of Israel, who were called out of Egypt and given God's law to live in covenantal relationship with him and each other (cf. Deut 4:37–40). Significantly, the concept of calling that was articulated in reference to God in terms of election and vocation is now expressed in relation to the unity of the body. We are called to live holy lives before God and also to live in unity with one another. Holiness and unity are both part of our election.

2a **μετὰ πάσης ταπεινοφροσύνης καὶ πραΰτητος,**

With all humility and gentleness,

μετὰ μετά	with *me*·***ta***	---	prep
πάσης πᾶς	all ***pa***·*sēs*	GEN SG FEM	adj
ταπεινοφροσύνης ταπεινοφροσύνη	humility *ta*·*pei*·*no*·*phro*·***sy***·*nēs*	GEN SG FEM	noun
καὶ καί	and ***kai***	---	conj
πραΰτητος πραΰτης	gentleness *pra*·***u***·*tē*·*tos*	GEN SG FEM	noun

2b **μετὰ μακροθυμίας,**

with patience,

μετὰ μετά	with *me*·***ta***	---	prep
μακροθυμίας μακροθυμία	patience *ma*·*kro*·*thy*·***mi***·*as*	GEN SG FEM	noun

2c **ἀνεχόμενοι ἀλλήλων ἐν ἀγάπῃ,**

bearing with one another in love,

ἀνεχόμενοι ἀνέχομαι	(you all) bearing *an*·*e*·***cho***·*me*·*noi*	PRES MID/PASS PTCP NOM PL MASC	verb
ἀλλήλων ἀλλήλων	with one another *al*·***lē***·*lōn*	GEN PL MASC	reciprocal pron

ἐν ἐν	in *en*	---	prep
ἀγάπη ἀγάπη	love *a·**ga**·pē*	DAT SG FEM	noun

3a **σπουδάζοντες τηρεῖν τὴν ἑνότητα τοῦ πνεύματος**

making every effort to keep the unity of the Spirit

σπουδάζοντες σπουδάζω	(you all) making every effort *spou·**da**·zon·tes*	PRES ACT PTCP NOM PL MASC	verb
τηρεῖν τηρέω	to keep *tē·**rein***	PRES ACT INF	verb
τὴν ὁ	the ***tēn***	ACC SG FEM	article
ἑνότητα ἑνότης	unity *he·**no**·tē·ta*	ACC SG FEM	noun
τοῦ ὁ	of the ***tou***	GEN SG NEUT	article
πνεύματος πνεῦμα	(of) Spirit ***pneu**·ma·tos*	GEN SG NEUT	noun

In vv. 2–3, Paul outlines three virtues to be nurtured—humility (**ταπεινοφροσύνης**, v. 2a), gentleness (**πραΰτητος**, v. 2a) and patience (**μακροθυμίας**, v. 2b)—and two intentional actions—"bearing with one another" (**ἀνεχόμενοι ἀλλήλων**, v. 2c) and "striving to keep the unity of the spirit" (**σπουδάζοντες τηρεῖν τὴν ἑνότητα τοῦ πνεύματος**, v. 3a). The two intentional actions are expressed with present participles denoting ongoing effort. The verb for "bearing" (**ἀνεχόμενοι**) is particularly important. It has the sense of intentional endurance in a difficult situation. The verb is used to express Jesus' complaints about having to "bear with" unbelieving people (Matt 17:17). Paul has in mind the particularly difficult situations in which Christians find themselves in their relationships with one another.

The subjective genitive **τοῦ πνεύματος** ("of the Spirit") indicates that it is the Spirit who produces unity; nevertheless, maintaining that unity requires our every effort (**σπουδάζοντες**).

3b	**ἐν τῷ συνδέσμῳ τῆς εἰρήνης·**

in the bond of peace

ἐν ἐν	in *en*	---	prep
τῷ ὁ	the *tō*	DAT SG MASC	article
συνδέσμῳ σύνδεσμος	bond *syn·**des**·mō*	DAT SG MASC	noun
τῆς ὁ	of the ***tēs***	GEN SG FEM	article
εἰρήνης εἰρήνη	(of) peace *ei·**rē**·nēs*	GEN SG FEM	noun

The noun **σύνδεσμος** means "fastener" or "binder." It is used in Col 2:19 to identify ligaments that hold joints together in the body. Paul will talk about unity using anatomical metaphors later (4:16). The verb **συνδέω**, associated with the noun **σύνδεσμος**, denotes the idea of binding with chains. Since Paul has identified himself as the **δέσμιος** in the Lord, it is possible that his word choice is informed by his own condition. In this case, the image would convey the idea of believers being "chained" to one another in unity.

4a	**ἓν σῶμα**

One body

ἓν εἷς	one ***hen***	NOM SG NEUT	adj
σῶμα σῶμα	body ***sō**·ma*	NOM SG NEUT	noun

The adjective **ἓν** ("one") appears seven times in this passage marking seven statements of unity. The formulaic nature of the statements might point to a symbolic usage of numbers, indicating perfect unity. In addition, their slogan-like nature (note the absence of main verbs) might indicate an early Christian creed, now modified by Paul.

4b	**καὶ ἓν πνεῦμα,**		
	and one Spirit,		

καὶ καί	and ***kai***	---	conj
ἓν εἷς	one ***hen***	NOM SG NEUT	adj
πνεῦμα πνεῦμα	Spirit ***pneu*·*ma***	NOM SG NEUT	noun

In Paul's ecclesiology, it is the Spirit that makes the body of Christ. We are one body because we share in the one Spirit (cf. 1 Cor 12:12–13).

4c	**καθὼς καὶ ἐκλήθητε ἐν μιᾷ ἐλπίδι τῆς κλήσεως ὑμῶν·**		
	just as you were also called into the one hope of your calling.		

καθὼς καθώς	just as *ka*·***thōs***	---	adv
καὶ καί	also ***kai***	---	conj
ἐκλήθητε καλέω	you (all) were called *e*·***klē***·*thē*·*te*	AOR PASS IND 2ND PL	verb
ἐν ἐν	into *en*	---	prep
μιᾷ εἷς	one *mi*·***a***	DAT SG FEM	adj
ἐλπίδι ἐλπίς	hope *el*·***pi***·*di*	DAT SG FEM	noun
τῆς ὁ	of the ***tēs***	GEN SG FEM	article
κλήσεως κλῆσις	(of) calling ***klē***·*se*·*ōs*	GEN SG FEM	noun
ὑμῶν σύ	of you (all)/your *hy*·***mōn***	2ND GEN PL	pron

The reference to hope (**ἐλπίδι**) adds an eschatological orientation to unity. Sharing the same hope is a fundamental part of what makes the church one body.

5a	**εἷς κύριος,**		
	One Lord,		
εἷς εἷς	one ***heis***	NOM SG MASC	adj
κύριος κύριος	Lord ***ky***·*ri*·*os*	NOM SG MASC	noun

5b	**μία πίστις,**		
	one faith,		
μία εἷς	one ***mi***·*a*	NOM SG FEM	adj
πίστις πίστις	faith ***pi***·*stis*	NOM SG FEM	noun

5c	**ἓν βάπτισμα·**		
	one baptism,		
ἓν εἷς	one ***hen***	NOM SG NEUT	adj
βάπτισμα βάπτισμα	baptism ***bap***·*tis*·*ma*	NOM SG NEUT	noun

Note the careful rhetorical construction with one noun of each gender—masculine: **εἷς κύριος** ("one Lord"); feminine: **μία πίστις** ("one faith"); and neuter: **ἓν βάπτισμα** ("one baptism"). The words "believing" and "baptism" are used together on several occasions in Acts where faith in the Lord ("Jesus Christ," "Lord," or "God") is expressed in baptism (8:12–13; 16:33–34; 18:8; 19:5). The unity envisioned in these statements is derived from their christological foundation. The faith is one and the baptism is one because the Lord is one. There were instances of factions in the early church formed on the basis of baptism (cf. 1 Cor 1:10–17). This statement might have been a correction to such a trend.

6a	**εἷς θεὸς καὶ πατὴρ πάντων,**

one God and Father of all,

εἷς εἷς	one ***heis***	NOM SG MASC	adj
θεὸς θεός	God *the*·***os***	NOM SG MASC	noun
καὶ καί	and ***kai***	---	conj
πατὴρ πατήρ	father *pa*·***tēr***	NOM SG MASC	noun
πάντων πᾶς	of all ***pan***·*tōn*	GEN PL MASC	adj

The reference to God as Father (**πατὴρ**) recalls the image of the household of God, which is introduced in 2:19.

6b	**ὁ ἐπὶ πάντων**

who is over all

ὁ ὁ	who *ho*	NOM SG MASC	article
ἐπὶ ἐπί	over *e*·***pi***	---	prep
πάντων πᾶς	all ***pan***·*tōn*	GEN PL MASC	adj

6c	**καὶ διὰ πάντων**

and through all

καὶ καί	and ***kai***	---	conj
διὰ διά	through *di*·***a***	---	prep
πάντων πᾶς	all ***pan***·*tōn*	GEN PL MASC	adj

6d	**καὶ ἐν πᾶσιν.**		
	and in all.		
καὶ καί	and ***kai***	---	conj
ἐν ἐν	in *en*	---	prep
πᾶσιν πᾶς	all ***pa*** · *sin*	DAT PL MASC	adj

The quadruple repetition of "all" (**πᾶς**)—in v. 6a with an implied preposition ("of all"), in v. 6b with **ἐπὶ** ("above"), in v. 6c with **διὰ** ("through"), and in v. 6d with **ἐν** ("in")—conveys completeness and recalls 1:23 where Christ "fills all in all." Now God stands above, through, and in the church.

From Text to Sermon

- ***Main Exegetical Idea.*** Because we were called to one body and one Spirit, believers should strive to maintain unity with one another.

- ***Bridge to Theology.*** This passage inaugurates the ethical section of the letter, and the first aspect Paul addresses is unity. Paul's approach is both practical and theological here. He talks about the need to maintain unity, emphasizing the virtues, the effort, and the intentionality necessary to do so. But he also grounds his practical command in the actions of the triune God. Therefore, there are two sides to unity. On the one hand, unity is promoted by the Spirit and can only be a reality in the church because of the work of Christ, who killed the hostility and created in himself "one new collective person" (2:14–16). But on the other hand, unity requires an active participation on the part of each individual, and it takes humility, gentleness, patience, and effort. Because of the reality created through Christ's work, we can be hopeful that our efforts will attain the goal established by God himself.

  Furthermore, this text helps to highlight the ecclesiological nature of baptism. Too often, we see baptism as a personal commitment between the believer and God, which is certainly true. But here Paul emphasizes the corporate reality that baptism inaugurates. We are baptized as an expression of the one faith we share with all the saints. We are baptized into one body.

- ***Possible Sermon Structure.*** This passage is clearly structured around the command to keep unity and the grounds for that command. It may be outlined thus:

  1 The hard work of unity
    - 1.1 Humility, gentleness, and patience (4:2)
    - 1.2 Bearing with one another (4:2)
    - 1.3 Striving to keep unity (4:3)

  2 The grounds of unity
    - 2.1 The unity of the body created by the Spirit (4:4)
    - 2.2 The unity of faith in the one Lord Jesus Christ (4:5)
    - 2.3 The unity of the many under the one God and Father (4:6)

 ***Points of Application.*** This would be a pivotal moment in a sermon series on Ephesians. The deep and sometimes mysterious reality Paul described in the first section of the letter finds its concrete and practical expression in 4:1–6:24. This is a point of application in itself. The deep theological truths we know and confess should not be merely confessional statements; they have concrete implications and practical expressions.

Unity is the main point of application. Unity is the fundamental reality in which the church must live. The sevenfold unity statements in this passage (see commentary) come as a strong affirmation of how important it is for the believers to maintain the bond of peace with one another. This is undoubtedly the biggest challenge in the body of Christ, which can be seen in the history of divisiveness and schisms in the church both on local and institutional levels. The preacher will do well to emphasize how this unity is already made possible by the actions of the triune God, but also how intentional we have to be in order to live into the reality that God has accomplished for us.

 ***Illustration Opportunities.*** There are many possible illustrations of unity. One of my favorites is the murmuration of starlings. Many birds travel in flocks, but the level of coordination of starlings is unparalleled in nature. Up to 750,000 individual birds can form beautiful patterns in the sky, moving with astounding synchronicity. Starlings are able to move together because of a mechanism known as "scale-free behavioral correlation," which allows each bird to interact with approximately seven nearby birds, causing the whole murmuration to move together in a beautiful dance. According to Haiken,

> Although each bird is interacting with its nearby neighbors, every bird's movement affects and is affected by the entire group, allowing information to travel across the flock at a constant speed. The result is collective decision making so agile that a signal to turn, usually initiated by a bird on the outskirts, can flash through a flock of 400 birds in half a second—a speed of 90 miles per hour. (Haiken 2021)

Besides the sheer beauty, the movement confuses predators and protects the stragglers in the group. Although they are many, they move as one.

EPHESIANS 4:7–16

THE GIFT OF CHRIST FOR THE EDIFICATION OF THE CHURCH

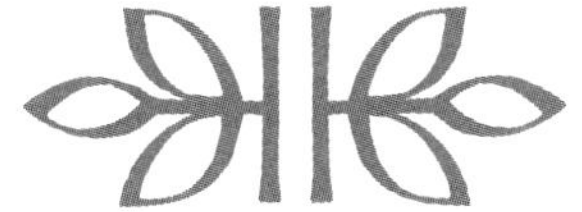

The emphasis on the unity of the church leads Paul to explore the precise dynamics of growth and maturity that a unified church is meant to experience. Paul focuses on how both the individual parts of the body and the body as a whole contribute to the formation of a "mature collective person" in Christ. On the individual level, each member grows in the body as they benefit from the specific ministries given to the church. On the corporate level, the whole body, connected to the head—namely, Christ—promotes its own growth in love.

4:7–10

7a Ἑνὶ δὲ ἑκάστῳ ἡμῶν ἐδόθη ἡ χάρις

Heni de hekastō hēmōn edothē hē charis

But grace was given to each one of us

7b κατὰ τὸ μέτρον τῆς δωρεᾶς τοῦ χριστοῦ.

kata to metron tēs dōreas tou christou.

according to the measure of the gift of Christ.

8a διὸ λέγει

dio legei

Therefore it says:

8b Ἀναβὰς εἰς ὕψος

Anabas eis hypsos

"When he ascended on high

8c ᾐχμαλώτευσεν αἰχμαλωσίαν,

ēchmalōteusen aichmalōsian,

he took captivity captive,

8d ἔδωκεν δόματα τοῖς ἀνθρώποις.

edōken domata tois anthrōpois.

he gave gifts to [his] people."

9a τὸ δέ Ἀνέβη τί ἐστιν

to de Anebē ti estin

Now what does "he ascended" mean,

9b εἰ μὴ ὅτι καὶ κατέβη

ei mē hoti kai katebē

but that he also descended

9c εἰς τὰ κατώτερα μέρη τῆς γῆς;

*eis **ta** katōtera **merē tēs gēs**?*

into the lower parts of the earth?

10a ὁ καταβὰς αὐτός ἐστιν καὶ ὁ ἀναβὰς

*ho kata**bas** **autos** estin **kai** ho ana**bas***

The one who descended is also the one who ascended

10b ὑπεράνω πάντων τῶν οὐρανῶν,

*hyper**a**nō **pan**tōn **tōn** ura**nōn**,*

far above all the heavens,

10c ἵνα πληρώσῃ τὰ πάντα.

***hi**na plē**rō**sē **ta pan**ta.*

so that he might fill all things.

7a	**Ἑνὶ δὲ ἑκάστῳ ἡμῶν ἐδόθη ἡ χάρις**		
	But grace was given to each one of us		
Ἑνὶ εἷς	to one *He·**ni***	DAT SG MASC	adj
δὲ δέ	but ***de***	---	conj
ἑκάστῳ ἕκαστος	(to) each *he·**ka**·stō*	DAT SG MASC	adj
ἡμῶν ἐγώ	of us *hē·**mōn***	1ST GEN PL	pron
ἐδόθη δίδωμι	(it) was given *e·**do**·thē*	AOR PASS IND 3RD SG	verb
ἡ ὁ	the *hē*	NOM SG FEM	article
χάρις χάρις	grace ***cha**·ris*	NOM SG FEM	noun

The reference to Ἑνὶ . . . ἑκάστῳ ἡμῶν ("each one of us") contrasts with the "all" in the previous verse by means of the word **δέ** ("but"). This balances out Paul's corporate emphasis present throughout Ephesians. Even though the governing concept in the letter, given its emphasis on unity, is the corporate identity of the church, the apostle situates each individual within the larger body as an effective member receiving grace.

7b	**κατὰ τὸ μέτρον τῆς δωρεᾶς τοῦ χριστοῦ.**
	according to the measure of the gift of Christ

Greek	English	Parsing	Part of speech
κατὰ κατά	according to *ka·**ta***	---	prep
τὸ ὁ	the ***to***	ACC SG NEUT	article
μέτρον μέτρον	measure ***me**·tron*	ACC SG NEUT	noun
τῆς ὁ	of the ***tēs***	GEN SG FEM	article
δωρεᾶς δωρεά	(of) gift *dō·re·**as***	GEN SG FEM	noun
τοῦ ὁ	of the ***tou***	GEN SG MASC	article
χριστοῦ Χριστός	(of) Christ *chri·**stou***	GEN SG MASC	noun

The references to **χάρις** ("grace" [v. 7a]) and **δωρεᾶς** ("gift") evoke 2:8, where God's grace is the means of salvation. The same grace now equips the church. The grace of God is experienced by the church according to the measure of Christ's gift. Paul will soon identify this gift as those ministries given for the edification of the body (cf. **ἔδωκεν** ["he gave"] in 4:11). So here the apostle specifies the way in which the grace of God is to be experienced by "each one"—namely, through the ministries which promote the edification of the body.

8a	**διὸ λέγει**
	Therefore it says:

Greek	English	Parsing	Part of speech
διὸ διό	therefore *di·**o***	---	conj
λέγει λέγω	it says ***le**·gei*	PRES ACT IND 3RD SG	verb

Ephesians 4:8 is a citation of Ps 68:18 and is offered as a biblical framework for the explanation of the gift. Paul changes the Septuagint wording of the psalm most notably by using the verb **ἔδωκεν** ("give" [v. 8d]) in place of the verb **ἔλαβες** ("receive"). The context of the psalm, however, affords such a change. YHWH is portrayed as overthrowing his enemies, giving the spoils of war to his people, and then being honored as he receives gifts from men. Several actions in the psalm reflect the benevolence of YHWH, which is the focus of Paul in Ephesians (cf. 1:3). Paul applies the text, which originally relates to YHWH, to Christ, indicating his high view of Christ. His choice of the psalm has to do with his view of the exaltation of Christ, which is the basis for Christ's benevolent giving of gifts to the church.

8b	**Ἀναβὰς εἰς ὕψος**		
	"When he ascended on high		
Ἀναβὰς ἀναβαίνω	when he ascended *A·na·**bas***	AOR ACT PTCP NOM SG MASC	verb
εἰς εἰς	on *eis*	---	prep
ὕψος ὕψος	high ***hy**·psos*	ACC SG NEUT	noun

8c	**ᾐχμαλώτευσεν αἰχμαλωσίαν,**		
	he took captivity captive,		
ᾐχμαλώτευσεν αἰχμαλωτεύω	he took captive *ēch·ma·**lō**·teu·sen*	AOR ACT IND 3RD SG	verb
αἰχμαλωσίαν αἰχμαλωσία	captivity *aich·ma·lō·**si**·an*	ACC SG FEM	noun

8d	**ἔδωκεν δόματα τοῖς ἀνθρώποις.**		
	he gave gifts to [his] people."		
ἔδωκεν δίδωμι	he gave ***e**·dō·ken*	AOR ACT IND 3RD SG	verb
δόματα δόμα	gifts ***do**·ma·ta*	ACC PL NEUT	noun

τοῖς ὁ	to the ***tois***	DAT PL MASC	article
ἀνθρώποις ἄνθρωπος	(to) men *an·**thrō**·pois*	DAT PL MASC	noun

9a **τὸ δέ Ἀνέβη τί ἐστιν**

Now what does "he ascended" mean,

τὸ ὁ	the ***to***	NOM SG NEUT	article
δέ δέ	now ***de***	---	conj
Ἀνέβη ἀναβαίνω	he ascended *A·**ne**·bē*	AOR ACT IND 3RD SG	verb
τί τίς~2	what ***ti***	NOM SG NEUT	interr pron
ἐστιν εἰμί	is *e·stin*	PRES ACT IND 3RD SG	verb

9b **εἰ μὴ ὅτι καὶ κατέβη**

but that he also descended

εἰ εἰ	if *ei*	---	cond
μὴ μή	not ***mē***	---	particle
ὅτι ὅτι	that ***ho**·ti*	---	conj
καὶ καί	also ***kai***	---	conj
κατέβη καταβαίνω	he descended *ka·**te**·bē*	AOR ACT IND 3RD SG	verb

9c **εἰς τὰ κατώτερα μέρη τῆς γῆς;**

into the lower parts of the earth?

εἰς εἰς	into *eis*	---	prep

τὰ ὁ	the *ta*	ACC PL NEUT	article
κατώτερα κατώτερος	lower *ka·tō·te·ra*	ACC PL NEUT	adj
μέρη μέρος	parts *me·rē*	ACC PL NEUT	noun
τῆς ὁ	of the *tēs*	GEN SG FEM	article
γῆς γῆ	(of) earth *gēs*	GEN SG FEM	noun

Paul picks up on the image of the ascension and connects it with Christ's descent (**κατέβη**). The reference to **τὰ κατώτερα μέρη τῆς γῆς** ("the lower parts of the earth") may point to the incarnation, to Christ's burial, or, more likely, to Christ's descent into the underworld, a tradition attested elsewhere in the New Testament (Acts 2:27; 1 Pet 4:6; Rev 1:18).

10a **ὁ καταβὰς αὐτός ἐστιν καὶ ὁ ἀναβὰς**

The one who descended is also the one who ascended

ὁ ὁ	the *ho*	NOM SG MASC	article
καταβὰς καταβαίνω	one who descended *ka·ta·bas*	AOR ACT PTCP NOM SG MASC	verb
αὐτός αὐτός	he *au·tos*	3RD NOM SG	personal pron
ἐστιν εἰμί	is *e·stin*	PRES ACT IND 3RD SG	verb
καὶ καί	also *kai*	---	conj
ὁ ὁ	the *ho*	NOM SG MASC	article
ἀναβὰς ἀναβαίνω	one who ascended *a·na·bas*	AOR ACT PTCP NOM SG MASC	verb

10b **ὑπεράνω πάντων τῶν οὐρανῶν,**

far above all the heavens,

ὑπεράνω ὑπεράνω	far above *hy·pe·ra·nō*	---	adv

πάντων πᾶς	all *__pan__·tōn*	GEN PL MASC	adj
τῶν ὁ	the ***tōn***	GEN PL MASC	article
οὐρανῶν οὐρανός	heavens *ou·ra·__nōn__*	GEN PL MASC	noun

10c **ἵνα πληρώσῃ τὰ πάντα.**

so that he might fill all things.

ἵνα ἵνα	so that *__hi__·na*	---	conj
πληρώσῃ πληρόω	he might fill *plē·__rō__·sē*	AOR ACT SUBJ 3RD SG	verb
τὰ ὁ	the ***ta***	ACC PL NEUT	article
πάντα πᾶς	all (things) *__pan__·ta*	ACC PL NEUT	adj

4:11–16

11a καὶ αὐτὸς ἔδωκεν

kai autos edōken

And he himself gave

11b τοὺς μὲν ἀποστόλους,

tous men apostolous,

some as apostles,

11c τοὺς δὲ προφήτας,

tous de prophētas,

some as prophets,

11d τοὺς δὲ εὐαγγελιστάς,

tous de euangelistas,

some as evangelists,

11e τοὺς δὲ ποιμένας καὶ διδασκάλους,

tous de poimenas kai didaskalous,

some as pastors and teachers

12a πρὸς τὸν καταρτισμὸν τῶν ἁγίων

pros ton katartismon tōn hagiōn

toward the equipping of the saints

12b εἰς ἔργον διακονίας,

eis ergon diakonias,

for the work of ministry,

12c εἰς οἰκοδομὴν τοῦ σώματος τοῦ χριστοῦ,

eis oikodomēn tou sōmatos tou christou,

for the edification of the body of Christ,

13a μέχρι καταντήσωμεν οἱ πάντες

**me**chri katan**tē**sōmen hoi **pan**tes

until we all should reach

13b εἰς τὴν ἑνότητα τῆς πίστεως

eis **tēn** he**no**tēta **tēs pis**teōs

καὶ τῆς ἐπιγνώσεως τοῦ υἱοῦ τοῦ θεοῦ,

**kai tēs** epi**gnō**seōs **tou** hui**ou tou** the**ou**,

the unity of faith and the knowledge of the Son of God,

13c εἰς ἄνδρα τέλειον,

eis **an**dra **te**leion,

the mature man,

13d εἰς μέτρον ἡλικίας τοῦ πληρώματος τοῦ χριστοῦ,

eis **me**tron hē**li**kias **tou** plē**rō**matos **tou** chri**stou**,

the measure of the full stature of the fullness of Christ,

14a ἵνα μηκέτι ὦμεν νήπιοι,

**hi**na mē**ke**ti **ō**men **nē**pioi,

so that we may no longer be children,

14b κλυδωνιζόμενοι καὶ περιφερόμενοι

klydōni**zo**menoi **kai** periphe**ro**menoi

παντὶ ἀνέμῳ τῆς διδασκαλίας

pan**ti** a**ne**mō **tēs** didaska**li**as

tossed back and forth by waves and being carried about by every wind of teaching

14c ἐν τῇ κυβίᾳ τῶν ἀνθρώπων

en **tē** ky**bi**a **tōn** an**thrō**pōn

in the trickery of men,

14d ἐν πανουργίᾳ πρὸς τὴν μεθοδίαν τῆς πλάνης,

en panour**gi**a **pros tēn** metho**di**an **tēs** pla**nēs**,

by craftiness, toward deceitful scheming.

15a ἀληθεύοντες δὲ ἐν ἀγάπῃ

*alē**theu**ontes **de** en a**gap**ē*

Rather, practicing the truth in love,

15b αὐξήσωμεν εἰς αὐτὸν τὰ πάντα,

*aux**ē**sōmen eis au**ton ta pan**ta,*

let us grow in respect to all things into him,

15c ὅς ἐστιν ἡ κεφαλή,

***hos** estin hē kepha**lē**,*

who is the head,

15d Χριστός,

*Chri**stos**,*

namely, Christ.

16a ἐξ οὗ πᾶν τὸ σῶμα

*ex **hou pan to sō**ma*

From whom the whole body,

16b συναρμολογούμενον καὶ συνβιβαζόμενον

*synarmolo**gou**menon **kai** synbiba**zo**menon*

joined and held together

16c διὰ πάσης ἁφῆς τῆς ἐπιχορηγίας

*di**a pa**sēs ha**phēs tēs** epichorē**gi**as*

through every supporting ligament,

16d κατ᾽ ἐνέργειαν ἐν μέτρῳ ἑνὸς ἑκάστου μέρους

*kat' ener**ge**ian en **met**rō he**nos** he**ka**stou **me**rous*

according to the working in the measure of each individual part,

16e τὴν αὔξησιν τοῦ σώματος ποιεῖται

***tēn au**xēsin **tou sō**matos poi**ei**tai*

promotes the growth of the body

16f εἰς οἰκοδομὴν ἑαυτοῦ

*eis oikodo**mēn** heau**tou***

for its own edification

16g ἐν ἀγάπῃ.

*en a**ga**pē.*

in love.

11a	**καὶ αὐτὸς ἔδωκεν**		
	And he himself gave		
καὶ καί	and ***kai***	---	conj
αὐτὸς αὐτός	he *au·**tos***	3RD NOM SG	personal pron
ἔδωκεν δίδωμι	(he) gave ***e**·dō·ken*	AOR ACT IND 3RD SG	verb

The emphasis on giving resumes the "gift" theme, now explaining what the gift is.

11b	**τοὺς μὲν ἀποστόλους,**		
	some as apostles,		
τοὺς ὁ	the ***tous***	ACC PL MASC	article
μὲν μέν	- ***men***	---	particle
ἀποστόλους ἀπόστολος	apostles *a·po·**sto**·lous*	ACC PL MASC	noun

Note the repetition of the definite article **τοὺς** in this verse. Articles can function in two ways. First, they could function straightforwardly as definite articles, in which case Paul is referring to "the apostles," "the prophets," etc., possibly as specific individuals in the church. Alternatively, the articles could be functioning here as indefinite pronouns—a common use of the article in Greek: he gave "some [to be] apostles," "some to be prophets," etc. This suggests an emphasis on the ministries rather than on specific individuals. Since these gifts are given for the ongoing nurturing of the body, it is likely that Paul has in mind the ministries themselves, which are to nurture continually the growth and maturity of the body.

11c **τοὺς δὲ προφήτας,**

some as prophets,

τοὺς ὁ	the ***tous***	ACC PL MASC	article
δὲ δέ	- ***de***	---	conj
προφήτας προφήτης	prophets *pro*·***phē***·*tas*	ACC PL MASC	noun

11d **τοὺς δὲ εὐαγγελιστάς,**

some as evangelists,

τοὺς ὁ	the ***tous***	ACC PL MASC	article
δὲ δέ	- ***de***	---	conj
εὐαγγελιστάς εὐαγγελιστής	evangelists *eu*·*an*·*ge*·*li*·***stas***	ACC PL MASC	noun

11e **τοὺς δὲ ποιμένας καὶ διδασκάλους,**

some as pastors and teachers

τοὺς ὁ	the ***tous***	ACC PL MASC	article
δὲ δέ	- ***de***	---	conj
ποιμένας ποιμήν	pastors *poi*·***me***·*nas*	ACC PL MASC	noun
καὶ καί	and ***kai***	---	conj

διδασκάλους διδάσκαλος	teachers *di·da·**ska**·lous*	ACC PL MASC	noun

Notice how **ποιμένας καὶ διδασκάλους** ("pastors and teachers") are put together with the coordinating conjunction **καὶ** ("and"). The coordination implies a closer link between the two ministries. It may indicate two facets of the same ministry, or more likely, that these two ministries should be exercised in tandem.

12a **πρὸς τὸν καταρτισμὸν τῶν ἁγίων**

toward the equipping of the saints

πρὸς πρός	toward ***pros***	---	prep
τὸν ὁ	the ***ton***	ACC SG MASC	article
καταρτισμὸν καταρτισμός	equipping *ka·tar·tis·**mon***	ACC SG MASC	noun
τῶν ὁ	of the ***tōn***	GEN PL MASC	article
ἁγίων ἅγιος	(of) saints *ha·**gi**·ōn*	GEN PL MASC	adj

Originally a medical term, the noun **καταρτισμὸν** ("equipping") denotes the "setting of a bone" and works well with Paul's metaphor of the body. More generally, it means "to furnish" or "to equip."

12b **εἰς ἔργον διακονίας,**

for the work of ministry,

εἰς εἰς	for *eis*	---	prep
ἔργον ἔργον	work ***er**·gon*	ACC SG NEUT	noun
διακονίας διακονία	of ministry *di·a·ko·**ni**·as*	GEN SG FEM	noun

Even though these gifts are given to certain individuals, they are meant to enable the broader church to minister.

12c	**εἰς οἰκοδομὴν τοῦ σώματος τοῦ χριστοῦ,**

for the edification of the body of Christ,

εἰς εἰς	for *eis*	---	prep
οἰκοδομὴν οἰκοδομή	edification *oi·ko·do·**mēn***	ACC SG FEM	noun
τοῦ ὁ	of the ***tou***	GEN SG NEUT	article
σώματος σῶμα	(of) body ***sō**·ma·tos*	GEN SG NEUT	noun
τοῦ ὁ	of the ***tou***	GEN SG MASC	article
χριστοῦ Χριστός	(of) Christ *chri·**stou***	GEN SG MASC	noun

The word **οἰκοδομὴν** ("edification") belongs with the architectural cluster of terms and alludes back to 2:20–21, where the apostles and prophets are the foundation of the building. Paul here applies it to the body metaphor. The edification of the body is a result of the work of service of the saints, which in turn is furnished by the ministries. The picture is of one well-arranged and integrated structure promoting its own edification.

13a	**μέχρι καταντήσωμεν οἱ πάντες**

until we all should reach

μέχρι μέχρι	until ***me**·chri*	---	adv
καταντήσωμεν καταντάω	we should reach *ka·tan·**tē**·sō·men*	AOR ACT SUBJ 1ST PL	verb
οἱ ὁ	the *hoi*	NOM PL MASC	article
πάντες πᾶς	all ***pan**·tes*	NOM PL MASC	adj

In the first section of Ephesians, Paul portrays the church as already sitting with Christ in the heavenly places (2:6) and refers to the unity of the body as something already accomplished in "one new person" (**ἕνα καινὸν ἄνθρωπον**, 2:15) in Christ. In this second section, Paul emphasizes the "not yet" part of the process with his use of the subjunctive **μέχρι καταντήσωμεν** ("until we should reach"). The church is growing into its identity and vocation.

13b **εἰς τὴν ἑνότητα τῆς πίστεως καὶ τῆς ἐπιγνώσεως τοῦ υἱοῦ τοῦ θεοῦ,**

the unity of faith and the knowledge of the Son of God,

εἰς εἰς	into *eis*	---	prep
τὴν ὁ	the ***tēn***	ACC SG FEM	article
ἑνότητα ἑνότης	unity *he*·***no***·*tē*·*ta*	ACC SG FEM	noun
τῆς ὁ	of the ***tēs***	GEN SG FEM	article
πίστεως πίστις	(of) faith ***pi***·*ste*·*ōs*	GEN SG FEM	noun
καὶ καί	and ***kai***	---	conj
τῆς ὁ	(of) the ***tēs***	GEN SG FEM	article
ἐπιγνώσεως ἐπίγνωσις	(of) knowledge *e*·*pi*·***gnō***·*se*·*ōs*	GEN SG FEM	noun
τοῦ ὁ	of the ***tou***	GEN SG MASC	article
υἱοῦ υἱός	(of) son *hui*·***ou***	GEN SG MASC	noun
τοῦ ὁ	of the ***tou***	GEN SG MASC	article
θεοῦ θεός	(of) God *the*·***ou***	GEN SG MASC	noun

13c **εἰς ἄνδρα τέλειον,**

the mature man,

εἰς εἰς	into *eis*	---	prep
ἄνδρα ἀνήρ	man ***an***·*dra*	ACC SG MASC	noun
τέλειον τέλειος	mature ***te***·*lei*·*on*	ACC SG MASC	adj

In talking about the maturity of the church, Paul uses the word **ἄνδρα** that identifies a male who has reached full maturity, which he will contrast with the **νήπιοι** ("children") in the next verse—an example of immaturity.

The emphasis of the metaphor is on maturity, not maleness. The image, as in 2:15, is a corporate one (cf. **οἱ πάντες**, "[we] all," in v. 13a).

13d	**εἰς μέτρον ἡλικίας τοῦ πληρώματος τοῦ χριστοῦ,**		
	the measure of the full stature of the fullness of Christ,		
εἰς εἰς	into *eis*	---	prep
μέτρον μέτρον	measure ***me**·tron*	ACC SG NEUT	noun
ἡλικίας ἡλικία	of full stature *hē·li·**ki**·as*	GEN SG FEM	noun
τοῦ ὁ	of the ***tou***	GEN SG NEUT	article
πληρώματος πλήρωμα	(of) fullness *plē·**rō**·ma·tos*	GEN SG NEUT	noun
τοῦ ὁ	of the ***tou***	GEN SG MASC	article
χριστοῦ Χριστός	(of) Christ *chri·**stou***	GEN SG MASC	noun

The noun **ἡλικία** ("full stature") can refer to time span, maturity, or stature. The association with **μέτρον** ("measure") seems to highlight quantity. Thus, stature is probably a better translation. This metaphorical "mature man" has "his" maturity measured according to Christ: the church grows into Christlikeness and has Christ as the standard of its maturity.

14a	**ἵνα μηκέτι ὦμεν νήπιοι,**		
	so that we may no longer be children,		
ἵνα ἵνα	so that ***hi**·na*	---	conj
μηκέτι μηκέτι	not longer *mē·**ke**·ti*	NEG	adv
ὦμεν εἰμί	we may be ***ō**·men*	PRES ACT SUBJ 1ST PL	verb
νήπιοι νήπιος	children ***nē**·pi·oi*	NOM PL MASC	adj

14b κλυδωνιζόμενοι καὶ περιφερόμενοι παντὶ ἀνέμῳ τῆς διδασκαλίας

tossed back and forth by waves and being carried about by every wind of teaching

κλυδωνιζόμενοι κλυδωνίζομαι	(we) (being) tossed back and forth by waves *kly·dō·ni·**zo**·me·noi*	PRES MID/PASS PTCP NOM PL MASC	verb
καὶ καί	and ***kai***	---	conj
περιφερόμενοι περιφέρω	(we) being carried about *pe·ri·phe·**ro**·me·noi*	PRES PASS PTCP NOM PL MASC	verb
παντὶ πᾶς	by every *pan·**ti***	DAT SG MASC	adj
ἀνέμῳ ἄνεμος	(by) wind *a·**ne**·mō*	DAT SG MASC	noun
τῆς ὁ	of the ***tēs***	GEN SG FEM	article
διδασκαλίας διδασκαλία	(of) teaching *di·da·ska·**li**·as*	GEN SG FEM	noun

14c ἐν τῇ κυβίᾳ τῶν ἀνθρώπων

in the trickery of men,

ἐν ἐν	in *en*	---	prep
τῇ ὁ	the ***tē***	DAT SG FEM	article
κυβίᾳ κυβεία	trickery *ky·**bi**·a*	DAT SG FEM	noun
τῶν ὁ	of the ***tōn***	GEN PL MASC	article
ἀνθρώπων ἄνθρωπος	(of) men *an·**thrō**·pōn*	GEN PL MASC	noun

14d ἐν πανουργίᾳ πρὸς τὴν μεθοδίαν τῆς πλάνης,

by craftiness, toward deceitful scheming.

ἐν ἐν	by *en*	---	prep

πανουργίᾳ πανουργία	craftiness *pan·our·**gi**·a*	DAT SG FEM	noun
πρὸς πρός	toward ***pros***	---	prep
τὴν ὁ	the ***tēn***	ACC SG FEM	article
μεθοδίαν μεθοδεία	scheming *me·tho·**di**·an*	ACC SG FEM	noun
τῆς ὁ	of the ***tēs***	GEN SG FEM	article
πλάνης πλάνη	(of) deceit/deceitful ***pla**·nēs*	GEN SG FEM	noun

15a **ἀληθεύοντες δὲ ἐν ἀγάπῃ**

Rather, practicing the truth in love,

ἀληθεύοντες ἀληθεύω	(we) practicing truth *a·lē·**theu**·on·tes*	PRES ACT PTCP NOM PL MASC	verb
δὲ δέ	rather ***de***	---	conj
ἐν ἐν	in *en*	---	prep
ἀγάπῃ ἀγάπη	love *a·**ga**·pē*	DAT SG FEM	noun

The verb **ἀληθεύοντες** ("practicing truth") relates to the noun **ἀλήθεια**, meaning truth. It denotes not only conveying the truth in speech but also practicing the truth in action and being truthful in character. It modifies the main verb **αὐξήσωμεν** ("grow" [v. 15b]) by indicating the manner by which we are to grow, and it is itself modified by **ἐν ἀγάπῃ** ("in love") also indicating manner. So we should grow in Christ by practicing truth, and we practice truth in love.

15b **αὐξήσωμεν εἰς αὐτὸν τὰ πάντα,**

let us grow in respect to all things into him,

αὐξήσωμεν αὐξάνω	let us grow *au·**xē**·sō·men*	AOR ACT SUBJ 1ST PL	verb
εἰς εἰς	into *eis*	---	prep

αὐτὸν αὐτός	him *au·**ton***	3RD ACC SG	personal pron
τὰ ὁ	the ***ta***	ACC PL NEUT	article
πάντα πᾶς	all (things) ***pan**·ta*	ACC PL NEUT	adj

Αὐξήσωμεν ("let us grow") is the main verb in this verse. Along with **συναρμολογούμενον** ("joined together") in v. 16b and **οἰκοδομὴν** ("edification") in vv. 12c and 16f, it recalls 2:21–22 and the image of the temple. Here, Paul uses the same three words but now in a more organic metaphor. The body and the building are Paul's most prominent church metaphors in the letter. The verb is a subjunctive but has the force of an imperative. The church is commanded to grow in maturity. In other words, growing in Christ is an expectation since he is the head (**κεφαλή**) of the body (cf. 1:22; 5:23) and since they have been given God's gift for this very purpose.

15c **ὅς ἐστιν ἡ κεφαλή,**

who is the head,

ὅς ὅς	who ***hos***	NOM SG MASC	relative pron
ἐστιν εἰμί	(he) is *e·stin*	PRES ACT IND 3RD SG	verb
ἡ ὁ	the *hē*	NOM SG FEM	article
κεφαλή κεφαλή	head *ke·pha·**lē***	NOM SG FEM	noun

In both Eph 1:22 and 5:23, **κεφαλή** ("head") indicates authority. Here Paul uses **κεφαλή** to indicate the source from whom the growth of the church flows.

15d **Χριστός,**

namely, Christ.

Χριστός Χριστός	Christ *Chri·**stos***	NOM SG MASC	noun

16a	**ἐξ οὗ πᾶν τὸ σῶμα**

From whom the whole body,

ἐξ ἐκ	from *ex*	---	prep
οὗ ὅς	whom ***hou***	GEN SG MASC	relative pron
πᾶν πᾶς	all ***pan***	NOM SG NEUT	adj
τὸ ὁ	the ***to***	NOM SG NEUT	article
σῶμα σῶμα	body ***sō***·*ma*	NOM SG NEUT	noun

Paul began with the focus on the individual parts of the body and now returns to the focus on the whole body (**πᾶν τὸ σῶμα**). The purpose of the individual ministries is the equipping of the saints for the work of ministry and the edification of the body (4:12). Accordingly, the body as a whole contributes to its own corporate growth. The image is one of organic and wholesome development.

16b	**συναρμολογούμενον καὶ συνβιβαζόμενον**

joined and held together

συναρμολογούμενον συναρμολογέω	(it) (being) joined together *syn·ar·mo·lo·***gou***·me·non*	PRES PASS PTCP NOM SG NEUT	verb
καὶ καί	and ***kai***	---	conj
συνβιβαζόμενον συμβιβάζω	(it) (being) held together *syn·bi·ba·***zo***·me·non*	PRES PASS PTCP NOM SG NEUT	verb

Another set of **συν-** verbs add to Paul's catalog of "together" words (cf. 2:5–6, 21–22; 4:16). The verb **συναρμολογέω** ("join together") is used in 2:21 in the metaphor of the building being joined together. The verb **συμβιβάζω** ("hold together") may mean "draw a conclusion together in the face of evidence" or "unite," as a synonym of **συναρμολογέω**, but with a less material connotation.

16c **διὰ πάσης ἁφῆς τῆς ἐπιχορηγίας**

through every supporting ligament,

διὰ διά	through *di·**a***	---	prep
πάσης πᾶς	every ***pa**·sēs*	GEN SG FEM	adj
ἁφῆς ἁφή	ligament *ha·**phēs***	GEN SG FEM	noun
τῆς ὁ	of the ***tēs***	GEN SG FEM	article
ἐπιχορηγίας ἐπιχορηγία	(of) support/supporting *e·pi·cho·rē·**gi**·as*	GEN SG FEM	noun

The word **ἁφῆς** can refer to ligaments in the body, but this is quite a technical and uncommon meaning. It can also refer simply to a "connection" in a more material or architectural sense. One might not need to adjudicate precisely between the two meanings since Paul has both the body and the building as his working metaphors.

16d **κατ᾽ ἐνέργειαν ἐν μέτρῳ ἑνὸς ἑκάστου μέρους**

according to the working in the measure
of each individual part,

κατ᾽ κατά	according to *kat᾽*	---	prep
ἐνέργειαν ἐνέργεια	working *en·**er**·gei·an*	ACC SG FEM	noun
ἐν ἐν	in *en*	---	prep
μέτρῳ μέτρον	measure ***me**·trō*	DAT SG NEUT	noun
ἑνὸς εἷς	of one *he·**nos***	GEN SG MASC	adj
ἑκάστου ἕκαστος	(of) each *he·**ka**·stou*	GEN SG MASC	adj
μέρους μέρος	(of) portion ***me**·rous*	GEN SG NEUT	noun

The phrase again highlights the contribution of each part to the whole.

16e	τὴν αὔξησιν τοῦ σώματος ποιεῖται		
	promotes the growth of the body		
τὴν ὁ	the ***tēn***	ACC SG FEM	article
αὔξησιν αὔξησις	growth ***au***·*xē*·*sin*	ACC SG FEM	noun
τοῦ ὁ	of the ***tou***	GEN SG NEUT	article
σώματος σῶμα	(of) body ***sō***·*ma*·*tos*	GEN SG NEUT	noun
ποιεῖται ποιέω	(it) makes *poi*·***ei***·*tai*	PRES MID IND 3RD SG	verb

The core sentence reads "the body promotes the growth of the body," with the "body" (**σῶμα**) being both the subject and the object of the action (note the objective genitive **τοῦ σώματος**). This indicates a self-generating growth—conveyed also in the reflexive **ἑαυτοῦ** (its own) at the end of the verse. But this self-generating growth is ultimately derived from its connection to the head (cf. **ἐξ οὗ**)—namely, Christ.

16f	εἰς οἰκοδομὴν ἑαυτοῦ		
	for its own edification		
εἰς εἰς	for *eis*	---	prep
οἰκοδομὴν οἰκοδομή	edification *oi*·*ko*·*do*·***mēn***	ACC SG FEM	noun
ἑαυτοῦ ἑαυτοῦ	of itself/its own *he*·*au*·***tou***	3RD GEN SG MASC	reflexive pron

16g	ἐν ἀγάπῃ.		
	in love.		
ἐν ἐν	in *en*	---	prep
ἀγάπῃ ἀγάπη	love *a*·***ga***·*pē*	DAT SG FEM	noun

 From Text to Sermon 

Main Exegetical Idea. God gives gifts to the church to promote both her growth and maturity.

Bridge to Theology. Paul continues with ecclesiology as his governing theological concept. Ecclesiology is couched in two larger theological ideas. The first is God's sovereignty and goodness. God orchestrates the edification of the church by giving her gifts, promoting her unity and maturity, and ultimately overseeing her growth. This aligns well with Paul's portrayal of God as the one who blesses his church and the one who carries out the administration of his plan for his household. Second, Paul grounds his ecclesiology in Christology, identifying Christ as the one who—through his death, resurrection, and exaltation—blesses his people just as YHWH himself does in Psalm 68. Christ is also the measure of the growth and maturity of the church. Thus, everything that happens in relation to the church is the result of God's agency and Christ's mediation.

On this foundation Paul builds his ecclesiology, portraying the five ministries as the very gifts Christ gives his church for her edification. The results of God's benevolent action are the church's unity, maturity, and growth. Paul highlights both individual and corporate aspects of this growth, painting a picture in which every member cooperates with the growth of the body as a whole, which derives its growth ultimately from Christ.

Possible Sermon Structure. This passage may be structured around three major themes:

1 The gifts of God
- 1.1 The gift of Christ (4:7–10)
- 1.2 The gift of ministries for the edification of the body (4:11–12)

2 The maturity of the church
- 2.1 Through the unity of faith (4:13a)
- 2.2 Toward Christlikeness (4:13b–14)

3 The growth of the church
- 3.1 Growing in truth and love (4:15a)
- 3.2 Growing into Christ (4:15b–16)
- 3.3 Growing together (4:16)

Points of Application. There are at least three aspects to be emphasized on Paul's teaching on maturity and growth in this passage. First, the maturity and growth of the church come from God and Christ. The church is sustained by God's grace and by its connection to the head—namely, Christ. In an age where human strategies for growth abound—both on a personal and institutional level—it is tempting for Christians to treat Christian life as a manageable sequence of logical steps toward self-improvement. It is equally tempting for leaders to think of church growth in terms of successful organizational strategies. Paul reminds us that the growth of the church is ultimately God's gift, not the result of human strategies.

Second, the apostle reminds us that even though growth and maturity are expected, these have to do with Christlikeness, not simply personal achievement or institutional success. Human strategies often focus on personal or institutional flourishing. Coaching techniques focus on strategies to achieve personal goals. Institutional planning, often applied to the church, emphasizes numeric growth and influence as ultimate goals. Self-improvement, growth, and success are not inherently bad, but they are not the goal of the Christian life, either individually or collectively, and can become a reductionistic pursuit if made an end in themselves. When it comes to the Christian life and the life of the church, the goal is maturity in Christ.

Finally, unity is the essential context for maturity and growth. We not only develop ourselves as individuals but also as members of the body of Christ. We grow together, contributing to the corporate growth and maturity of the body. As Paul emphasizes, the grace given to each one (4:7) is ultimately for the building up of the body (4:12). This is an excellent text to discuss ministry in the church. The five fundamental ministries and the image of the mutual building of the body should inspire Christians to see themselves as participants in the edification of the church. Here again, the preacher will do well to combat modern consumerist tendencies that lead people to see themselves as "clients" to be served or entertained and instead emphasize the critical need for the whole body to promote its own growth by serving one another.

Illustration Opportunities. Paul uses plenty of illustrations in this text. Images like the mature man contrasting with the child, the boat being tossed to and fro by the wind, and the connections in the body are very vivid analogies you can explore. You can also expand on illustrations of growth, such as that of a plant, a child, or the human body, as examples of healthy growth and maturity. For example, the image of a child trying to wear his/her parents' clothes or shoes (most parents would have funny

stories and pictures about that!) might help illustrate the need to grow in Christlikeness and the gradual nature of the process. If a child is well nourished, having everything he or she needs to mature, they may eventually grow up to be able to wear their parents' clothes (in most cases, at least). Similarly, Christians are expected to grow and mature as members of the body of Christ because God has given his gifts for their edification, and they are connected to the head, having everything they need to grow and attain the measure of the stature of the fullness of Christ. However, this implies collective growth as well as individual. Therefore, the image of the development of the human body, where organs and members grow proportionately to the growth of the whole body, will aid the illustration.

More concretely, you can use examples of how you have experienced growth in your own life because of the influence of other Christians, or how the congregation has shown signs of maturity as members of the body have learned to lean on one another. If you have particular situations where that growth has become evident, make sure you encourage the congregation.

LIVING ACCORDING TO THE NEW IDENTITY IN CHRIST

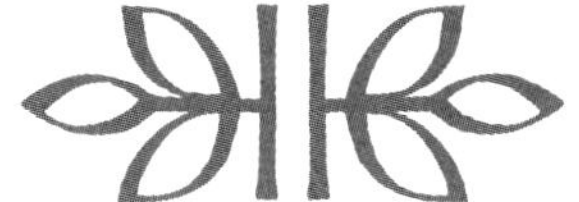

Having admonished the church concerning the unity of the body, Paul now moves on to an admonition concerning the conduct of believers. With rhetoric similar to the one he employs in 4:1–6, where the focus is on the internal relations of the members of the body, Paul now admonishes the church concerning their conduct, setting his admonition against the backdrop of unbelievers' practices. The contrast between the negative example of unbelievers and the expected Christlike conduct of believers remains in effect until 5:20. The Ephesians live among people who give themselves over to all sorts of wicked practices and do not even realize the perversion of their sinful practices. As those who are called by God, the believers cannot associate themselves with such practices.

4:17–19

17a Τοῦτο οὖν λέγω καὶ μαρτύρομαι ἐν κυρίῳ,

Touto oun legō kai martyromai en kyriō,

Therefore, I say this and testify in the Lord,

17b μηκέτι ὑμᾶς περιπατεῖν καθὼς καὶ τὰ ἔθνη περιπατεῖ

mēketi hymas peripatein kathōs kai ta ethnē peripatei

that you are no longer to walk as [also] the gentiles walk,

17c ἐν ματαιότητι τοῦ νοὸς αὐτῶν,

en mataiotēti tou noos autōn,

in the futility of their minds,

18a ἐσκοτωμένοι τῇ διανοίᾳ ὄντες,

eskotōmenoi tē dianoia ontes,

darkened in their understanding,

18b ἀπηλλοτριωμένοι τῆς ζωῆς τοῦ θεοῦ,

apēllotriōmenoi tēs zōēs tou theou,

alienated from the life of God,

18c διὰ τὴν ἄγνοιαν τὴν οὖσαν ἐν αὐτοῖς,

dia tēn agnoian tēn ousan en autois,

because of the ignorance that is in them,

18d διὰ τὴν πώρωσιν τῆς καρδίας αὐτῶν,

dia tēn pōrōsin tēs kardias autōn,

due to the hardness of their hearts,

19a οἵτινες ἀπηλγηκότες

hoitines apēlgēkotes

who, having become callous,

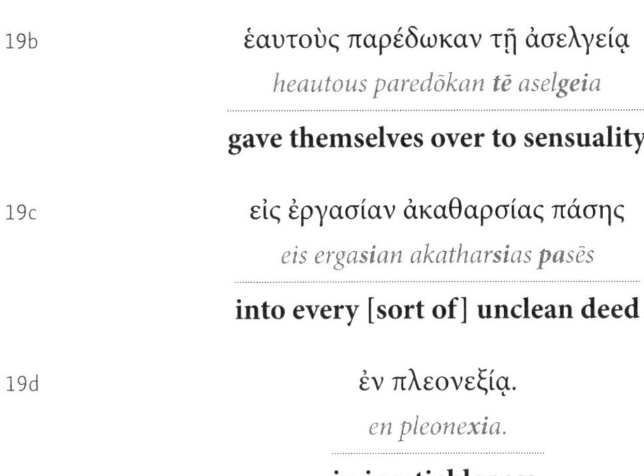

19b ἑαυτοὺς παρέδωκαν τῇ ἀσελγείᾳ

*heautous paredōkan **tē** asel**geia***

gave themselves over to sensuality

19c εἰς ἐργασίαν ἀκαθαρσίας πάσης

*eis erga**si**an akathar**si**as **pa**sēs*

into every [sort of] unclean deed

19d ἐν πλεονεξίᾳ.

*en pleone**xi**a.*

in insatiableness.

17a	**Τοῦτο οὖν λέγω καὶ μαρτύρομαι ἐν κυρίῳ,**		
	Therefore, I say this and testify in the Lord,		
Τοῦτο οὗτος	this ***Tou**·to*	ACC SG NEUT	demonstr pron
οὖν οὖν	therefore ***oun***	---	conj
λέγω λέγω	I say ***le**·gō*	PRES ACT IND 1ST SG	verb
καὶ καί	and ***kai***	---	conj
μαρτύρομαι μαρτύρομαι	(I) insist *mar·**ty**·ro·mai*	PRES MID/PASS IND 1ST SG	verb
ἐν ἐν	in *en*	---	prep
κυρίῳ κύριος	Lord *ky·**ri**·ō*	DAT SG MASC	noun

The verb **μαρτύρομαι** has a primary sense of "testifying" and indicates the gravity of Paul's appeal. Notice the similarity of this passage with 4:1, with the rhetoric of pleading (**παρακαλῶ** [4:1a]) and emphasis on conduct (**περιπατῆσαι** [4:1c]/**περιπατεῖν** [v. 17b]). The first appeal in 4:2 relates to ethical conduct among insiders regarding unity (**ἀνεχόμενοι ἀλλήλων** ["bearing with one another"]); the second relates to ethical conduct in relation to outsiders. These are two clear outcomes that the church, with a proper understanding of her new identity in Christ, could expect.

17b	**μηκέτι ὑμᾶς περιπατεῖν καθὼς καὶ τὰ ἔθνη περιπατεῖ**		
	that you are no longer to walk as [also] the gentiles walk,		
μηκέτι μηκέτι	no longer *mē·**ke**·ti*	NEG	adv
ὑμᾶς σύ	you (all) *hy·**mas***	2ND ACC PL	pron
περιπατεῖν περιπατέω	to walk *pe·ri·pa·**tein***	PRES ACT INF	verb
καθὼς καθώς	as *ka·**thōs***	---	adv
καὶ καί	also ***kai***	---	conj
τὰ ὁ	the ***ta***	NOM PL NEUT	article
ἔθνη ἔθνος	gentiles ***eth**·nē*	NOM PL NEUT	noun
περιπατεῖ περιπατέω	walk *pe·ri·pa·**tei***	PRES ACT IND 3RD SG	verb

The theme of "walking" (**περιπατέω**) recalls 2:2, when Paul refers to the Ephesians' former life; 2:10, with the reference to the good works prepared beforehand by God that the Ephesians should walk in them; and 4:1, with Paul's appeal for the Ephesians to walk in a manner worthy of their calling. The word will show up three more times (5:2, 8, 15), underscoring Paul's concern with the ethical living of the Ephesians. The powerful working of God in their lives should be evidenced by their holy conduct.

The gentiles (**τὰ ἔθνη**), as the subject of the comparative clause (cf. **καθὼς**), become the central focus of this section (they are mentioned again in v. 19a with the relative pronoun **οἵτινες** ["who"]). Paul's advice concerning conduct is expressed against the foil of the actions of this group. Since the Ephesian audience comprises mostly gentiles, Paul uses the term here to refer not exclusively to ethnicity but also to their state of alienation from God. In contrast to this group, the Ephesians have been made co-citizens with Israel (2:11–22) and have acquired a new covenantal identity. This understanding allows Paul to contrast these "gentiles-turned-Israel" with the gentile nonbelievers who are alienated from the life of God.

17c	**ἐν ματαιότητι τοῦ νοὸς αὐτῶν,**

in the futility of their minds,

ἐν ἐν	in *en*	---	prep
ματαιότητι ματαιότης	futility *ma·tai·**o**·tē·ti*	DAT SG FEM	noun
τοῦ ὁ	of the ***tou***	GEN SG MASC	article
νοὸς νοῦς	(of) mind *no·**os***	GEN SG MASC	noun
αὐτῶν αὐτός	of them/their *au·**tōn***	3RD GEN PL	personal pron

The noun **ματαιότητι** ("futility") is associated with idolatry elsewhere (Ps 31:6; Acts 14:15; Rom 1:21–23) and is likely what Paul has in mind. The New Testament condemns idolatry as worthless devotion. Idols are things that captivate our devotion but give us nothing in return. Perhaps a modern-day parallel to idolatry is any fruitless distraction that takes our attention captive and prevents us from looking to God.

18a	**ἐσκοτωμένοι τῇ διανοίᾳ ὄντες,**

darkened in their understanding,

ἐσκοτωμένοι σκοτόω	darkened *e·sko·tō·**me**·noi*	PERF PASS PTCP NOM PL MASC	verb
τῇ ὁ	in the ***tē***	DAT SG FEM	article
διανοίᾳ διάνοια	(in) understanding *di·a·**noi**·a*	DAT SG FEM	noun
ὄντες εἰμί	being ***on**·tes*	PRES ACT PTCP NOM PL MASC	verb

The darkness of the mind (**ἐσκοτωμένοι τῇ διανοίᾳ**) contrasts with the enlightenment of the eyes of the heart (1:18) and refers to one's state before conversion. The term **διάνοια** ("understanding") also shows up in 2:3 in reference to the passions of the mind that determine the conduct of those who are dead in their sins. The use of cognitive terminology continues an emphasis previously established in the letter (cf. 1:8–9, 17–18; 3:4, 10, 18–19; 4:13, 17–18, 23; 5:17; 6:19). The experience of conversion is characterized by the enlightenment of the mind, while unbelievers are darkened in their understanding. The mind is the starting point of conduct.

18b ἀπηλλοτριωμένοι τῆς ζωῆς τοῦ θεοῦ,

alienated from the life of God,

ἀπηλλοτριωμένοι ἀπαλλοτριόω	alienated *ap·ēl·lo·tri·ō·**me**·noi*	PERF PASS PTCP NOM PL MASC	verb
τῆς ὁ	from the ***tēs***	GEN SG FEM	article
ζωῆς ζωή	(from) life *zō·**ēs***	GEN SG FEM	noun
τοῦ ὁ	of the ***tou***	GEN SG MASC	article
θεοῦ θεός	(of) God *the·**ou***	GEN SG MASC	noun

The participle **ἀπηλλοτριωμένοι** ("alienated") recalls 2:12, when Paul talks about the Ephesians formerly being alienated from the citizenship of Israel, which is explained as being "without Christ" and "without God in the world." Similarly, gentile nonbelievers are alienated from the life of God.

18c διὰ τὴν ἄγνοιαν τὴν οὖσαν ἐν αὐτοῖς,

because of the ignorance that is in them,

διὰ διά	because of *di·**a***	---	prep
τὴν ὁ	the ***tēn***	ACC SG FEM	article
ἄγνοιαν ἄγνοια	ignorance ***ag**·noi·an*	ACC SG FEM	noun
τὴν ὁ	that ***tēn***	ACC SG FEM	article
οὖσαν εἰμί	it is ***ou**·san*	PRES ACT PTCP ACC SG FEM	verb
ἐν ἐν	in *en*	---	prep
αὐτοῖς αὐτός	them *au·**tois***	3RD DAT PL	personal pron

18d	**διὰ τὴν πώρωσιν τῆς καρδίας αὐτῶν,**		
	due to the hardness of their hearts,		
διὰ διά	due to *di·**a***	---	prep
τὴν ὁ	the ***tēn***	ACC SG FEM	article
πώρωσιν πώρωσις	hardness ***pō**·rō·sin*	ACC SG FEM	noun
τῆς ὁ	of the ***tēs***	GEN SG FEM	article
καρδίας καρδία	(of) heart *kar·**di**·as*	GEN SG FEM	noun
αὐτῶν αὐτός	of them/their *au·**tōn***	3RD GEN PL	personal pron

Hardness of heart (**πώρωσιν τῆς καρδίας**) is a weighty metaphor conveyed through various terms in the Old Testament that refer to the obduracy of both God's enemies and his people Israel (Exod 7:13; 8:15, 32; 1 Sam 6:6; Ps 95:8; Isa 63:17). In the New Testament, the metaphor is mostly used to refer to the rebelliousness of outsiders and Israel (Mark 3:5; John 12:40; Rom 11:7, 25; 2 Cor 3:14).

19a	**οἵτινες ἀπηλγηκότες**		
	who, having become callous,		
οἵτινες ὅστις	who ***hoi**·ti·nes*	NOM PL MASC	relative pron
ἀπηλγηκότες ἀπαλγέω	(they) having become callous *ap·ēl·gē·**ko**·tes*	PERF ACT PTCP NOM PL MASC	verb

The word **ἀπηλγηκότες** ("having become callous") evokes the idea of lack of sensitivity, either in a moral sense, as in someone incapable of sensing right or wrong, or in a sense of hopelessness, as in the inability to react and respond in life.

19b	**ἑαυτοὺς παρέδωκαν τῇ ἀσελγείᾳ**

gave themselves over to sensuality

ἑαυτοὺς ἑαυτοῦ	themselves *he·au·**tous***	3RD ACC PL MASC	reflexive pron
παρέδωκαν παραδίδωμι	(they) gave *pa·re·dō·kan*	AOR ACT IND 3RD PL	verb
τῇ ὁ	over to ***tē***	DAT SG FEM	article
ἀσελγείᾳ ἀσέλγεια	(over to) sensuality *a·sel·**gei**·a*	DAT SG FEM	noun

The phrase **ἑαυτοὺς παρέδωκαν** ("gave themselves") emphasizes culpability. Although their conduct is the result of the hardening of their hearts, they deliberately gave themselves over to all sorts of uncleanness.

19c	**εἰς ἐργασίαν ἀκαθαρσίας πάσης**

into every [sort of] unclean deed

εἰς εἰς	into *eis*	---	prep
ἐργασίαν ἐργασία	work/deed *er·ga·**si**·an*	ACC SG FEM	noun
ἀκαθαρσίας ἀκαθαρσία	unclean *a·ka·thar·**si**·as*	GEN SG FEM	noun
πάσης πᾶς	every ***pa**·sēs*	GEN SG FEM	adj

19d	**ἐν πλεονεξίᾳ.**

in insatiableness.

ἐν ἐν	in *en*	---	prep
πλεονεξίᾳ πλεονεξία	insatiableness *ple·o·ne·**xi**·a*	DAT SG FEM	noun

4:20–24

20 Ὑμεῖς δὲ οὐχ οὕτως ἐμάθετε τὸν χριστόν,

Hymeis de ouch houtōs emathete ton christon,

But you have not learned Christ in this way,

21a εἴ γε αὐτὸν ἠκούσατε

ei ge auton ēkousate

if indeed you heard him

21b καὶ ἐν αὐτῷ ἐδιδάχθητε,

kai en autō edidachthēte,

and were taught in him,

21c καθὼς ἔστιν ἀλήθεια ἐν τῷ Ἰησοῦ,

kathōs estin alētheia en tō Iēsou,

just as the truth is in Jesus,

22a ἀποθέσθαι ὑμᾶς κατὰ τὴν προτέραν ἀναστροφὴν

apothesthai hymas kata tēn proteran anastrophēn

τὸν παλαιὸν ἄνθρωπον

ton palaion anthrōpon

that you have put away, concerning the former way of life, the old self,

22b τὸν φθειρόμενον κατὰ τὰς ἐπιθυμίας τῆς ἀπάτης,

ton phtheiromenon kata tas epithymias tēs apatēs,

which is corrupted according to the lust of deceit,

23a ἀνανεοῦσθαι δὲ τῷ πνεύματι τοῦ νοὸς ὑμῶν,

ananeousthai de tō pneumati tou noos hymōn,

but are being renewed in the spirit of your mind

24a καὶ ἐνδύσασθαι τὸν καινὸν ἄνθρωπον

kai endysasthai ton kainon anthrōpon

and have put on the new self

24b τὸν κατὰ θεὸν κτισθέντα

ton kata theon ktisthenta

who has been created according to God

24c ἐν δικαιοσύνῃ καὶ ὁσιότητι τῆς ἀληθείας.

en dikaiosynē kai hosiotēti tēs alētheias.

in righteousness and holiness of truth.

20 **Ὑμεῖς δὲ οὐχ οὕτως ἐμάθετε τὸν χριστόν,**

But you have not learned Christ in this way,

Ὑμεῖς σύ	you (all) *Hy·meis*	2ND NOM PL	pron
δὲ δέ	but *de*	---	conj
οὐχ οὐ	not *ouch*	---	particle
οὕτως οὕτως	in this way *hou·tōs*	---	adv
ἐμάθετε μανθάνω	(you all) have learned *e·ma·the·te*	AOR ACT IND 2ND PL	verb
τὸν ὁ	the *ton*	ACC SG MASC	article
χριστόν Χριστός	Christ *chri·ston*	ACC SG MASC	noun

21a	**εἴ γε αὐτὸν ἠκούσατε**		
	if indeed you heard him		

εἴ εἰ	if ***ei***	---	cond
γε γέ	indeed *ge*	---	particle
αὐτὸν αὐτός	him *au*·***ton***	3RD ACC SG	personal pron
ἠκούσατε ἀκούω	you (all) heard *ē*·***kou***·*sa*·*te*	AOR ACT IND 2ND PL	verb

21b	**καὶ ἐν αὐτῷ ἐδιδάχθητε,**		
	and were taught in him,		

καὶ καί	and ***kai***	---	conj
ἐν ἐν	in *en*	---	prep
αὐτῷ αὐτός	him *au*·***tō***	3RD DAT SG	personal pron
ἐδιδάχθητε διδάσκω	(you all) were taught *e*·*di*·***dach***·*thē*·*te*	AOR PASS IND 2ND PL	verb

Three verbs—“learning” (**ἐμάθετε** [v. 20]) “hearing” (**ἠκούσατε** [v. 21a]), and “being taught” (**ἐδιδάχθητε** [v. 21b])—are used in reference to Christ. “Learning” and “hearing” have Christ as the direct object—an unusual construction, since they normally take impersonal objects. Christ himself is to be learned and heard, but since he is also the sphere of teaching, it is “in him” (**ἐν αὐτῷ**) that they are “being taught.” The three verbs combined give a sense of intense immersion in the knowledge of Christ.

21c	**καθὼς ἔστιν ἀλήθεια ἐν τῷ Ἰησοῦ,**		
	just as the truth is in Jesus,		

καθὼς καθώς	just as *ka*·***thōs***	---	adv
ἔστιν εἰμί	(it) is ***e***·*stin*	PRES ACT IND 3RD SG	verb
ἀλήθεια ἀλήθεια	truth *a*·***lē***·*thei*·*a*	NOM SG FEM	noun

ἐν ἐν	in *en*	---	prep
τῷ ὁ	the ***tō***	DAT SG MASC	article
Ἰησοῦ Ἰησοῦς	Jesus *I·ē·**sou***	DAT SG MASC	noun

22a **ἀποθέσθαι ὑμᾶς κατὰ τὴν προτέραν ἀναστροφὴν τὸν παλαιὸν ἄνθρωπον**

that you have put away, concerning the former way of life, the old self,

ἀποθέσθαι ἀποτίθημι	(you all) have put away *a·po·**thes**·thai*	AOR MID INF	verb
ὑμᾶς σύ	you (all) *hy·**mas***	2ND ACC PL	pron
κατὰ κατά	concerning *ka·**ta***	---	prep
τὴν ὁ	the ***tēn***	ACC SG FEM	article
προτέραν πρότερος	former *pro·**te**·ran*	ACC SG FEM	adj
ἀναστροφὴν ἀναστροφή	way of life *a·na·stro·**phēn***	ACC SG FEM	noun
τὸν ὁ	the ***ton***	ACC SG MASC	article
παλαιὸν παλαιός	old *pa·lai·**on***	ACC SG MASC	adj
ἄνθρωπον ἄνθρωπος	self ***an**·thrō·pon*	ACC SG MASC	noun

22b **τὸν φθειρόμενον κατὰ τὰς ἐπιθυμίας τῆς ἀπάτης,**

which is corrupted according to the lust of deceit,

τὸν ὁ	the one/which ***ton***	ACC SG MASC	article
φθειρόμενον φθείρω	(it) being/is corrupted *phthei·**ro**·me·non*	PRES PASS PTCP ACC SG MASC	verb
κατὰ κατά	according to *ka·**ta***	---	prep

τὰς ὁ	the ***tas***	ACC PL FEM	article
ἐπιθυμίας ἐπιθυμία	lust *e·pi·thy·**mi**·as*	ACC PL FEM	noun
τῆς ὁ	of the ***tēs***	GEN SG FEM	article
ἀπάτης ἀπάτη	(of) deceit *a·**pa**·tēs*	GEN SG FEM	noun

23a **ἀνανεοῦσθαι δὲ τῷ πνεύματι τοῦ νοὸς ὑμῶν,**

but are being renewed in the spirit of your mind

ἀνανεοῦσθαι ἀνανεόω	(you all) (are) being renewed *a·na·ne·**ous**·thai*	PRES PASS INF	verb
δὲ δέ	but ***de***	---	conj
τῷ ὁ	in the ***tō***	DAT SG NEUT	article
πνεύματι πνεῦμα	(in) spirit ***pneu**·ma·ti*	DAT SG NEUT	noun
τοῦ ὁ	of the ***tou***	GEN SG MASC	article
νοὸς νοῦς	(of) mind *no·**os***	GEN SG MASC	noun
ὑμῶν σύ	of you (all)/your *hy·**mōn***	2ND GEN PL	pron

24a **καὶ ἐνδύσασθαι τὸν καινὸν ἄνθρωπον**

and have put on the new self

καὶ καί	and ***kai***	---	conj
ἐνδύσασθαι ἐνδύω	(you all) have put on *en·**dy**·sas·thai*	AOR MID INF	verb
τὸν ὁ	the ***ton***	ACC SG MASC	article
καινὸν καινός	new *kai·**non***	ACC SG MASC	adj
ἄνθρωπον ἄνθρωπος	self ***an**·thrō·pon*	ACC SG MASC	noun

Three infinitives complete the thought begun in v. 21b with **ἐδιδάχθητε** ("being taught") and indicate three aspects of the new life that are to be taught in Christ: **ἀποθέσθαι** ("putting away the old self") in v. 22a, **ἀνανεοῦσθαι** ("being renewed in the mind") in v. 23a, and **ἐνδύσασθαι** ("putting on the new self") in v. 24a. They could be functioning as imperatives, but in context, the aorist tense of the first two infinitives—"putting away" and "putting on"—seems to suggest a reference to a previous experience of conversion. The metaphor is related to clothing. The church puts on its new "Christlike costume," as it were. "Being renewed" is a present passive infinitive and indicates an ongoing process.

Although **ἄνθρωπον** ("man") can be translated as "self" in context, it is important to recognize the thematic thread that the term continues. The language is of old and new creation.

24b **τὸν κατὰ θεὸν κτισθέντα**

who has been created according to God

τὸν ὁ	the (one)/who *ton*	ACC SG MASC	article
κατὰ κατά	according to *ka·ta*	---	prep
θεὸν θεός	God *the·on*	ACC SG MASC	noun
κτισθέντα κτίζω	(it) has been created *ktis·then·ta*	AOR PASS PTCP ACC SG MASC	verb

The image of a "new man" (**καινὸν ἄνθρωπον** [v. 24a]) being "created" (**κτισθέντα**) recalls both 2:15, where the corporate being created from Jews and gentiles is referred to as **ἕνα καινὸν ἄνθρωπον** ("one new man"), and 4:13, where **ἄνδρα τέλειον** ("perfect man") is used to express corporate maturity. Here the same language is employed but in a different way. Likely alluding to the creation of humanity in the image of God, Paul describes the new identity in a more individualized sense. Both the creation of the new collective man and the new self are the result of the recreative act of God in Christ.

24c **ἐν δικαιοσύνῃ καὶ ὁσιότητι τῆς ἀληθείας.**

in righteousness and holiness of truth.

ἐν ἐν	in *en*	---	prep
δικαιοσύνῃ δικαιοσύνη	righteousness *di·kai·o·**sy**·nē*	DAT SG FEM	noun
καὶ καί	and ***kai***	---	conj
ὁσιότητι ὁσιότης	holiness *ho·si·**o**·tē·ti*	DAT SG FEM	noun
τῆς ὁ	of the ***tēs***	GEN SG FEM	article
ἀληθείας ἀλήθεια	(of) truth *a·lē·**thei**·as*	GEN SG FEM	noun

From Text to Sermon

 ***Main Exegetical Idea.*** Believers should not walk as the gentiles do but should live according to their new identity in Christ.

Bridge to Theology. This passage marks the beginning of Paul's more practical discourse on conduct. His ethical exhortations, however, are firmly couched in a theological analysis of sin and conversion. Paul carefully evaluates the sinful conduct of gentile unbelievers, setting it up as a foil for his description of what happens in the lives of believers when they "learn Christ," a shorthand for conversion. This contrast is not merely informative but also meant to function as an admonition. Those who "learned Christ" are supposed to exhibit a radically different kind of attitude from that of unbelievers. It is significant that Paul talks about gentiles as distant outsiders, even though they are the majority of his audience. As pointed out previously, Paul argues for a new identity accomplished by the gracious work of God in Christ (cf. 2:1–22), to the extent that the believers are now distant from their compatriots when it comes to their identity and way of life.

Paul describes the process of corruption of the gentiles, from their compromised thought patterns to their hardness of hearts and their sinful conduct. The individual components of this corruption and the sequence in which they are presented are critical. It all starts with the futility of the mind and a darkened understanding, which then leads to a hardened heart and a callous attitude, which in turn is reflected in sensuality, greediness, and impure practices. Romans 1:18–32 serves as a good, expanded commentary on this passage. Sin emerges out of a corrupt mind and a stubborn and senseless heart alienated from God.

In contrast, believers are to live a transformed life. This transformation begins with conversion, when believers have "learned Christ" through hearing the gospel and being instructed in the ways of Christ. This "learning" then leads to a change in their very identity: they put off the old self, whose corruption used to follow the patterns of the gentiles, and put on the new self, created according to God. Theologically, Paul is alluding to the concept of the new creation, whereby the "new man" is "recreated" according to, or in the likeness of, God.

Notice that this transformation follows a reverse pattern to the sinful life. It involves the continual renewal of the mind (cf. Rom 12:1–2)—as opposed to a futile mind—and results in righteousness and holy conduct—as opposed to sinful practices.

Possible Sermon Structure. The passage can be divided into two major sections:

- 1 How not to live (4:17–19)
  - 1.1 Darkened mind
  - 1.2 Alienation from God
  - 1.3 Hardness of hearts
  - 1.4 Sinful lives
- 2 The new identity in Christ (4:20–24)
  - 2.1 Learning Christ
  - 2.2 Putting off the old self
  - 2.3 Renewing the mind
  - 2.4 Putting on the new self
  - 2.5 Living righteous and holy lives

Points of Application. The apostle dissects the sinful life, exposing the different aspects involved in that corruption. It is important to go through these different aspects with the congregation. What constitutes a darkened understanding? What does idolatrous futility look like in our day? How do thought patterns affect the way we react to God and ultimately the way we live our lives? Notice that Paul is admonishing his audience. To paraphrase the apostle, "If you indeed have learned Christ, your lives should be different! Your mindset and your conduct should be different!" Is it possible that, even though we have heard the gospel, we sometimes revert back to thought patterns that are typical of those who are alienated from God?

Finally, what does it mean to put off the old self and put on the new self? What does it mean to reject the old patterns and live into the new identity Christ has given to us? Although some clear examples may help, be careful not to restrict this application too much. The point is to encourage a personal reflection on what attitudes are perhaps part of old patterns of thought and action that should now be rejected in favor of a Christlike way of life.

Illustration Opportunities. The process of obduracy that Paul describes in vv. 17–19 draws on images of darkness, hardness of hearts, and callousness. All these have potential for illustrations. The experience of being in a dark room for too long or a disease that causes people to become insensitive to touch are just two examples. An example from the Bible could be Pharaoh's hardness of heart in Exod 4–14, which led to his inability to perceive God's action and respond to him even in the face of God's signs and wonders in Egypt. Another biblical example could come from the Gospels, where religious authorities—and sometimes even the disciples themselves—were unable to understand God's manifestation in Jesus (Mark 3:1–6; 6:45–52). Similarly, people living in alienation from God become unable to see and sense God and his actions in the world.

In addition, Paul's use of the words "putting off" and "putting on" provide great illustration opportunities, referring to clothing. There are certain clothes that reflect an identity, like the uniform of a soldier or the costume of an actor. According to certain studies, clothing may affect both the way the world perceives us and the way we perceive ourselves. In 2012, two psychologists, Hajo Adam and Adam Galinsky, came up with the concept of "enclothed cognition," which illustrates how clothing impacts human cognition. They ran a series of experiments. First they divided a group of undergraduates into two subgroups. To the first group they gave a doctor's lab coat to wear. The second group was told to wear their own clothes. The two groups were then given a test that required a lot of attention. The group wearing the doctor's lab coat made half as many errors than the group wearing their own clothes. Then they repeated the test with another group but now giving some participants a coat, telling them it was a doctor's coat, and to another group they gave a coat, telling them it was a painter's coat. Again, the group wearing the doctor's coat presented far superior results. Their conclusion was that both the physical experience of wearing certain clothes and the symbolic meaning of clothes affect people's self-perception and their performance.

While the effects of enclothed cognition may vary from people to people, the concept is a good illustration for this passage. If what we wear can shape our self-perception and the way the world perceives us, what happens if we are wearing our God-given Christlike "costume"? Taking off the old "costume" and putting on the new "Christlike costume" entails a new identity and conduct. In Paul's analogy it is a whole "self" that is to be abandoned and a whole new "self" that is to be put on— a new self that is "according to God" and designed in the mold of Christ.

EPHESIANS 4:25–32

LIVING AS MEMBERS OF ONE ANOTHER

The contrast established between the conduct of believers and non-believers gives way to a focus on internal relationships. Those who have put on the new self according to God are now told how that reality should be expressed in their relationships with their neighbors. The emphasis falls heavily on truthful and edifying speech and avoidance of anger.

4:25–32

25a Διὸ ἀποθέμενοι τὸ ψεῦδος

*Dio apo**the**menoi **to pseu**dos*

Therefore, having put aside falsehood,

25b λαλεῖτε ἀλήθειαν ἕκαστος μετὰ τοῦ πλησίον αὐτοῦ,

*la**lei**te a**lē**theian **he**kastos me**ta tou** plē**si**on au**tou**,*

each [of you] are to speak the truth with his neighbor,

25c ὅτι ἐσμὲν ἀλλήλων μέλη.

***ho**ti es**men** al**lē**lōn **me**lē.*

because we are members of one another.

26a ὀργίζεσθε

*or**gi**zesthe*

Be angry

26b καὶ μὴ ἁμαρτάνετε·

***kai mē** hamar**ta**nete;*

and do not sin.

26c ὁ ἥλιος μὴ ἐπιδυέτω ἐπὶ παροργισμῷ ὑμῶν,

*ho **hē**lios **mē** epidy**e**tō e**pi** parorgis**mō** hy**mōn**,*

Let not the sun go down upon that which angers you.

27 μηδὲ δίδοτε τόπον τῷ διαβόλῳ.

*mē**de di**dote **to**pon **tō** dia**bo**lō.*

Neither give place to the devil.

28a ὁ κλέπτων μηκέτι κλεπτέτω,

*ho **klēp**tōn mē**ke**ti klep**te**tō,*

Let those who steal no longer steal,

28b μᾶλλον δὲ κοπιάτω ἐργαζόμενος ταῖς χερσὶν τὸ ἀγαθόν,

mallon de kopiatō ergazomenos tais chersin to agathon,

rather let them labor by doing good with [their] hands,

28c ἵνα ἔχῃ μεταδιδόναι τῷ χρείαν ἔχοντι.

hina echē metadidonai tō chreian echonti.

that they might share with those in need.

29a πᾶς λόγος σαπρὸς ἐκ τοῦ στόματος ὑμῶν μὴ ἐκπορευέσθω,

pas logos sapros ek tou stomatos hymōn mē ekporeuesthō,

Do not let any corrupt speech come out from your mouth,

29b ἀλλὰ εἴ τις ἀγαθὸς πρὸς οἰκοδομὴν τῆς χρείας,

alla ei tis agathos pros oikodomēn tēs chreias,

but only [a speech that is] good toward building up [where there is] need,

29c ἵνα δῷ χάριν τοῖς ἀκούουσιν.

hina dō charin tois akouousin

so that [it] should give grace to those who hear [it].

30a καὶ μὴ λυπεῖτε τὸ πνεῦμα τὸ ἅγιον τοῦ θεοῦ,

kai mē lypeite to pneuma to hagion tou theou,

And do not grieve the Holy Spirit of God,

30b ἐν ᾧ ἐσφραγίσθητε

en hō esphragisthēte

by whom you have been sealed

30c εἰς ἡμέραν ἀπολυτρώσεως.

eis hēmeran apolytrōseōs.

for the day of redemption.

31a πᾶσα πικρία καὶ θυμὸς καὶ ὀργὴ

pasa pikria kai thymos kai orgē

καὶ κραυγὴ καὶ βλασφημία ἀρθήτω ἀφ’ ὑμῶν

kai kraugē kai blasphēmia arthētō aph’ hymōn

Let every bitterness and wrath and anger and clamor and blasphemy be taken away from you

31b σὺν πάσῃ κακίᾳ.

syn pasē kakia.

along with all malice

32a γίνεσθε δὲ εἰς ἀλλήλους χρηστοί, εὔσπλαγχνοι,

ginesthe de eis allēlous chrēstoi, eusplanchnoi,

But be kind to one another, tenderhearted,

32b χαριζόμενοι ἑαυτοῖς

charizomenoi heautois

showing grace to one another

32c καθὼς καὶ ὁ θεὸς ἐν Χριστῷ ἐχαρίσατο ὑμῖν.

kathōs kai ho theos en Christō echarisato hymin.

just as God has also shown grace to you in Christ.

25a **Διὸ ἀποθέμενοι τὸ ψεῦδος**

Therefore, having put aside falsehood,

Διὸ διό	therefore *Di·o*	---	conj
ἀποθέμενοι ἀποτίθημι	(you all) having put aside *a·po·the·me·noi*	AOR MID PTCP NOM PL MASC	verb
τὸ ὁ	the *to*	ACC SG NEUT	article
ψεῦδος ψεῦδος	falsehood *pseu·dos*	ACC SG NEUT	noun

25b λαλεῖτε ἀλήθειαν ἕκαστος μετὰ τοῦ πλησίον αὐτοῦ,

each [of you] are to speak the truth with his neighbor,

λαλεῖτε λαλέω	you (all) are to speak *la·**lei**·te*	PRES ACT IMPV 2ND PL	verb
ἀλήθειαν ἀλήθεια	truth *a·**lē**·thei·an*	ACC SG FEM	noun
ἕκαστος ἕκαστος	each ***he**·ka·stos*	NOM SG MASC	adj
μετὰ μετά	with *me·**ta***	---	prep
τοῦ ὁ	the ***tou***	GEN SG MASC	article
πλησίον πλησίον	neighbor *plē·**si**·on*	---	adv
αὐτοῦ αὐτός	of him/his *au·**tou***	3RD GEN SG	personal pron

This phrase appears almost verbatim in the Septuagint in Zech 8:16. The Zechariah passage envisions a new era to be inaugurated by the return of YHWH to Zion—an era characterized by truth, peace, and reconciliation. In this context, the people of God are required to speak the truth to one another. In Ephesians, Paul describes a reality in which Jews and gentiles form a "new corporate person" in Christ, which he likely sees as the fulfillment of the eschatological promise. In this new reality, the same ethics are required.

25c ὅτι ἐσμὲν ἀλλήλων μέλη.

because we are members of one another.

ὅτι ὅτι	because ***ho**·ti*	---	conj
ἐσμὲν εἰμί	we are *es·**men***	PRES ACT IND 1ST PL	verb
ἀλλήλων ἀλλήλων	of one another *al·**lē**·lōn*	GEN PL MASC	reciprocal pron
μέλη μέλος	members ***me**·lē*	NOM PL NEUT	noun

26a	**ὀργίζεσθε**		
	Be angry		
ὀργίζεσθε ὀργίζω	(you all) be angry *or·**gi**·zes·the*	PRES PASS IMPV 2ND PL	verb

26b	**καὶ μὴ ἁμαρτάνετε·**		
	and do not sin.		
καὶ καί	and ***kai***	---	conj
μὴ μή	not ***mē***	---	particle
ἁμαρτάνετε ἁμαρτάνω	(you all) sin *ha·mar·**ta**·ne·te*	PRES ACT IMPV 2ND PL	verb

Verses 26a and 26b constitute another verbatim quotation, this time from Ps 4:4. The two imperatives are coordinated, which entails a connection between them. The first verb, **ὀργίζεσθε**, relates to the noun **ὀργή** ("anger") and was often used to refer to violent expressions of anger. In Paul's understanding, anger carries the potential for sinning (hence the next prohibition in 26b). The admonition, therefore, is a prohibition against sinning when one is angry rather than a provision for justified anger.

26c	**ὁ ἥλιος μὴ ἐπιδυέτω ἐπὶ παροργισμῷ ὑμῶν,**		
	Let not the sun go down upon that which angers you.		
ὁ ὁ	the *ho*	NOM SG MASC	article
ἥλιος ἥλιος	sun ***hē**·li·os*	NOM SG MASC	noun
μὴ μή	not ***mē***	---	particle
ἐπιδυέτω ἐπιδύω	(you all) let (it) go down *e·pi·dy·**e**·tō*	PRES ACT IMPV 3RD SG	verb
ἐπὶ ἐπί	upon *e·**pi***	---	prep
παροργισμῷ παροργισμός	that which angers *par·or·gis·**mō***	DAT SG MASC	noun
ὑμῶν σύ	you (all) *hy·**mōn***	2ND GEN PL	pron

The noun **παροργισμῷ** relates to the verb **παροργίζω**, meaning to provoke to anger. With the genitive **ὑμῶν** likely functioning as an objective genitive, the sense of the phrase is "that which angers you," which means that Paul is concerned with not only internally appeasing one's angry feelings but also actively dealing with the cause of the anger.

27	**μηδὲ δίδοτε τόπον τῷ διαβόλῳ.**		
	Neither give place to the devil.		
μηδὲ μηδέ	neither *mē·**de***	NEGATIVE	conj
δίδοτε δίδωμι	give ***di**·do·te*	PRES ACT IMPV 2ND PL	verb
τόπον τόπος	place ***to**·pon*	ACC SG MASC	noun
τῷ ὁ	to the ***tō***	DAT SG MASC	article
διαβόλῳ διάβολος	(to) devil *di·a·**bo**·lō*	DAT SG MASC	adj

The term **διαβόλῳ** is an adjective that literally means "slanderous," but in early Christianity it almost always refers to the devil (including in Eph 6:11). The connotation of slander, however, contrasts with the emphasis on "speaking truth," and Paul may have used this term intentionally to make that connection. The devil is known as the father of lies (John 8:44).

28a	**ὁ κλέπτων μηκέτι κλεπτέτω,**		
	Let those who steal no longer steal,		
ὁ ὁ	the *ho*	NOM SG MASC	article
κλέπτων κλέπτω	one who steals ***klēp**·tōn*	PRES ACT PTCP NOM SG MASC	verb
μηκέτι μηκέτι	no longer *mē·**ke**·ti*	NEG	adv
κλεπτέτω κλέπτω	(you all) let him/her steal *klep·**te**·tō*	PRES ACT IMPV 3RD SG	verb

28b μᾶλλον δὲ κοπιάτω ἐργαζόμενος ταῖς χερσὶν τὸ ἀγαθόν,

rather let them labor by doing good with [their] hands,

μᾶλλον μᾶλλον	rather ***mal***·*lon*	---	adv
δὲ δέ	but ***de***	---	conj
κοπιάτω κοπιάω	(you all) let (him/her) labor *ko*·*pi*·***a***·*tō*	PRES ACT IMPV 3RD SG	verb
ἐργαζόμενος ἐργάζομαι	by doing *er*·*ga*·***zo***·*me*·*nos*	PRES MID/PASS PTCP NOM SG MASC	verb
ταῖς ὁ	with the ***tais***	DAT PL FEM	article
χερσὶν χείρ	hands *cher*·***sin***	DAT PL FEM	noun
τὸ ὁ	the ***to***	ACC SG NEUT	article
ἀγαθόν ἀγαθός	good *a*·*ga*·***thon***	ACC SG NEUT	adj

28c ἵνα ἔχῃ μεταδιδόναι τῷ χρείαν ἔχοντι.

that they might share with those in need.

ἵνα ἵνα	that ***hi***·*na*	---	conj
ἔχῃ ἔχω	(he/she) might ***e***·*chē*	PRES ACT SUBJ 3RD SG	verb
μεταδιδόναι μεταδίδωμι	share *me*·*ta*·*di*·***do***·*nai*	PRES ACT INF	verb
τῷ ὁ	with the (one)/those ***tō***	DAT SG MASC	article
χρείαν χρεία	need ***chrei***·*an*	ACC SG FEM	noun
ἔχοντι ἔχω	(he/she) having ***e***·*chon*·*ti*	PRES ACT PTCP DAT SG MASC	verb

29a πᾶς λόγος σαπρὸς ἐκ τοῦ στόματος ὑμῶν μὴ ἐκπορευέσθω,

Do not let any corrupt speech come out from your mouth,

πᾶς πᾶς	any ***pas***	NOM SG MASC	adj

λόγος λόγος	word ***lo***·*gos*	NOM SG MASC	noun
σαπρὸς σαπρός	corrupt *sa*·***pros***	NOM SG MASC	adj
ἐκ ἐκ	from *ek*	---	prep
τοῦ ὁ	the ***tou***	GEN SG NEUT	article
στόματος στόμα	mouth ***sto***·*ma*·*tos*	GEN SG NEUT	noun
ὑμῶν σύ	of you (all)/your *hy*·***mōn***	2ND GEN PL	pron
μὴ μή	not ***mē***	---	particle
ἐκπορευέσθω ἐκπορεύομαι	(you all) let it come out *ek*·*po*·*reu*·***es***·*thō*	PRES MID/PASS IMPV 3RD SG	verb

The word **σαπρὸς** ("corrupt") is used in literature contemporary to Ephesians to refer to things that are rotten or putrid. More generally, it refers to something corrupt, worthless, or unwholesome.

29b **ἀλλὰ εἴ τις ἀγαθὸς πρὸς οἰκοδομὴν τῆς χρείας,**

but only [a speech that is] good toward
building up [where there is] need,

ἀλλὰ ἀλλά	but *al*·***la***	---	conj
εἴ εἰ	if ***ei***	---	cond
τις τίς~1	something *tis*	NOM SG MASC	indef pron
ἀγαθὸς ἀγαθός	good *a*·*ga*·***thos***	NOM SG MASC	adj
πρὸς πρός	toward ***pros***	---	prep
οἰκοδομὴν οἰκοδομή	building up *oi*·*ko*·*do*·***mēn***	ACC SG FEM	noun
τῆς ὁ	of the ***tēs***	GEN SG FEM	article
χρείας χρεία	need ***chrei***·*as*	GEN SG FEM	noun

Notice how Paul again uses the word **οἰκοδομὴν** ("building up"), recalling the reference to the edification of the body (4:12, 16).

29c	**ἵνα δῷ χάριν τοῖς ἀκούουσιν.**		
	so that [it] should give grace to those who hear [it].		
ἵνα ἵνα	so that ***hi***·*na*	---	conj
δῷ δίδωμι	it should give ***dō***	AOR ACT SUBJ 3RD SG	verb
χάριν χάρις	grace ***cha***·*rin*	ACC SG FEM	noun
τοῖς ὁ	to the ***tois***	DAT PL MASC	article
ἀκούουσιν ἀκούω	(to) those who hear *a*·***kou***·*ou*·*sin*	PRES ACT PTCP DAT PL MASC	verb

30a	**καὶ μὴ λυπεῖτε τὸ πνεῦμα τὸ ἅγιον τοῦ θεοῦ,**		
	And do not grieve the Holy Spirit of God,		
καὶ καί	and ***kai***	---	conj
μὴ μή	not ***mē***	---	particle
λυπεῖτε λυπέω	(you all) grieve *ly*·***pei***·*te*	PRES ACT IMPV 2ND PL	verb
τὸ ὁ	the ***to***	ACC SG NEUT	article
πνεῦμα πνεῦμα	Spirit ***pneu***·*ma*	ACC SG NEUT	noun
τὸ ὁ	the ***to***	ACC SG NEUT	article
ἅγιον ἅγιος	Holy ***ha***·*gi*·*on*	ACC SG NEUT	adj
τοῦ ὁ	of the ***tou***	GEN SG MASC	article
θεοῦ θεός	(of) God *the*·***ou***	GEN SG MASC	noun

30b	**ἐν ᾧ ἐσφραγίσθητε**		
	by whom you have been sealed		
ἐν ἐν	by *en*	---	prep
ᾧ ὅς	whom ***hō***	DAT SG NEUT	relative pron
ἐσφραγίσθητε σφραγίζω	you (all) have been sealed *es·phra·**gis**·thē·te*	AOR PASS IND 2ND PL	verb

30c	**εἰς ἡμέραν ἀπολυτρώσεως.**		
	for the day of redemption.		
εἰς εἰς	for *eis*	---	prep
ἡμέραν ἡμέρα	day *hē·**me**·ran*	ACC SG FEM	noun
ἀπολυτρώσεως ἀπολύτρωσις	of redemption *a·po·ly·**trō**·se·ōs*	GEN SG FEM	noun

Notice how vv. 30b and 30c—**ἐν ᾧ ἐσφραγίσθητε εἰς ἡμέραν ἀπολυτρώσεως** ("by whom you have been sealed for the day of redemption")—echo Paul's words from ch. 1 where we read that the believers "were sealed with the promised Holy Spirit, who is the down payment of our inheritance until the redemption of [God's] possession" (Eph 1:13–14).

31a	**πᾶσα πικρία καὶ θυμὸς καὶ ὀργὴ καὶ κραυγὴ καὶ βλασφημία ἀρθήτω ἀφ' ὑμῶν**		
	Let every bitterness and wrath and anger and clamor and blasphemy be taken away from you		
πᾶσα πᾶς	every ***pa**·sa*	NOM SG FEM	adj
πικρία πικρία	bittnerness *pi·**kri**·a*	NOM SG FEM	noun
καὶ καί	and ***kai***	---	conj
θυμὸς θυμός	wrath *thy·**mos***	NOM SG MASC	noun

καὶ καί	and ***kai***	---	conj
ὀργὴ ὀργή	anger *or·**gē***	NOM SG FEM	noun
καὶ καί	and ***kai***	---	conj
κραυγὴ κραυγή	clamor *krau·**gē***	NOM SG FEM	noun
καὶ καί	and ***kai***	---	conj
βλασφημία βλασφημία	blasphemy *blas·phē·**mi**·a*	NOM SG FEM	noun
ἀρθήτω αἴρω	(you all) let it be taken away *ar·**thē**·tō*	AOR PASS IMPV 3RD SG	verb
ἀφ᾽ ἀπό	from *aph᾽*	---	prep
ὑμῶν σύ	you (all) *hy·**mōn***	2ND GEN PL	pron

31b σὺν πάσῃ κακίᾳ.

along with all malice

σὺν σύν	with ***syn***	---	prep
πάσῃ πᾶς	all *__pa__·sē*	DAT SG FEM	adj
κακίᾳ κακία	malice *ka·**ki**·a*	DAT SG FEM	noun

32a γίνεσθε δὲ εἰς ἀλλήλους χρηστοί, εὔσπλαγχνοι,

But be kind to one another, tenderhearted,

γίνεσθε γίνομαι	(you all) be *__gi__·nes·the*	PRES MID/PASS IMPV 2ND PL	verb
δὲ δέ	but ***de***	---	conj
εἰς εἰς	to *eis*	---	prep
ἀλλήλους ἀλλήλων	one another *al·**lē**·lous*	ACC PL MASC	reciprocal pron

χρηστοί χρηστός	kind *chrē·**stoi***	NOM PL MASC	adj
εὔσπλαγχνοι εὔσπλαγχνος	tenderhearted ***eu**·splanch·noi*	NOM PL MASC	adj

32b **χαριζόμενοι ἑαυτοῖς**

showing grace to one another

χαριζόμενοι χαρίζομαι	showing grace *cha·ri·**zo**·me·noi*	PRES MID/PASS PTCP NOM PL MASC	verb
ἑαυτοῖς ἑαυτοῦ	to one another *he·au·**tois***	2ND DAT PL MASC	reflexive pron

32c **καθὼς καὶ ὁ θεὸς ἐν Χριστῷ ἐχαρίσατο ὑμῖν.**

just as God has also shown grace to you in Christ.

καθὼς καθώς	just as *ka·**thōs***	---	adv
καὶ καί	also ***kai***	---	conj
ὁ ὁ	the *ho*	NOM SG MASC	article
θεὸς θεός	God *the·**os***	NOM SG MASC	noun
ἐν ἐν	in *en*	---	prep
Χριστῷ Χριστός	Christ *Chri·**stō***	DAT SG MASC	noun
ἐχαρίσατο χαρίζομαι	(he) has shown grace *e·cha·**ri**·sa·to*	AOR MID IND 3RD SG	verb
ὑμῖν σύ	to you (all) *hy·**min***	2ND DAT PL	pron

The verbs **χαριζόμενοι** in v. 32b and **ἐχαρίσατο** in v. 32c are related to the noun **χάρις**, meaning "grace" or "gift," which is employed throughout the letter in relation to the grace God shows to his people (Eph 1:6–7; 2:5, 7–8; 4:7, 29). The verbs can have the connotation of showing grace by means of forgiveness. Believers are told to extend grace in forgiveness as a result of having been forgiven by God through Christ.

From Text to Sermon

Main Exegetical Idea. As those who have put on the new identity in Christ, believers should live lives characterized by truth, peace, generosity, kindness, and graciousness.

Bridge to Theology. This passage is a practical admonition, heavily dependent on the previous one (4:17–24). In that passage, Paul contrasted the conduct of believers with the conduct of unbelievers and admonished believers to live a transformed life, having put off the old self and having put on the new self created according to God. The apostle now gives five practical areas in which that change should manifest itself, all of them focused on interpersonal relations in the church. The number of imperatives indicates the authoritative nature of Paul's admonitions. He clearly prescribes the things to avoid and the things to do. It is tempting to see these admonitions as a mere ethical code—a list of dos and don'ts. However, the admonitions are situated in the larger theological picture Paul has been painting. Just like in Zech 8:16, which the apostle cites, where ethical commands are part of an eschatological reality inaugurated by the return of YHWH to Zion, so too in Ephesians are the ethics of the people of God shaped by God's work of election, redemption, and formation of his people, reflecting the outworking of the gospel. Because they learned Christ and were recreated in God's image, they are to live in a new manner. Therefore, the ethical living is itself part of the new reality God has accomplished for his people.

Possible Sermon Structure. The passage contains a series of ethical admonitions, highlighting things to put away and things to do:

1 Put off falsehood and speak the truth to one another (4:25)
2 Put off anger and don't sin (4:26–27)
3 Put off stealing and work to share with those in need (4:28)
4 Put off corrupt talk and build up those in need (4:29–30)
5 Put off bitterness and show kindness to one another (4:31–32)

Notice that the admonitions concerning anger (4:26–27) and corrupt talk (4:29–30) come with additional admonitions: "do not give place to the devil" and "do not grieve the Holy Spirit." The preacher should make sure to highlight those important emphases.

 ***Points of Application.*** The fact that Paul focuses on interpersonal relationships as areas in which the new identity in Christ should be manifested is significant. A transformed life is reflected in how we treat one another. It is also clear that these interpersonal relationships primarily envision the relationships among believers (cf. 4:25). The church is, therefore, the primary context where the work of God in Christ in the lives of the believers is supposed to be evidenced. The preacher, particularly the pastor of a congregation, should take this opportunity to expose the danger of a divided church, where members of the same body attack and defraud one another through gossip and bitterness.

The areas addressed are part of a broad range. It is somewhat surprising that the apostle would have to condemn overtly bad behavior like stealing or corrupt talk in a public letter to Christians. More internalized sins, such as anger and bitterness, are perhaps things that are more commonly perceived in interpersonal relationships. The difference, of course, is that internalized sins are more difficult to confront in someone's life. Yet, it is clear that both the blatant sins and the more internalized ones are observed even in the best of Christian communities. Whether they are explicit or hidden, they are all part of that which Christians must put off as they take on their new self in Christ. This is, perhaps, a good point for application. Are there things that we promptly condemn for their evident nature while indulging other, less explicit, sins, such as anger, bitterness, and falsehood?

What about the positive aspects mentioned? The apostle not only condemns bad behavior but prescribes good conduct. It is not enough not to lie; we have to speak the truth to one another. It is not enough not to steal; we have to be generous toward one another. It is not enough not to curse; we have to build up one another with good words. It is not enough not to be bitter; we have to show kindness to one another. And those positive attitudes have as their very point of reference the grace shown to us by God in Christ (Eph 4:32). Therefore, we have to resist a "low bar" Christianity defined simply by avoiding bad behavior. We have been created in Christ for good works (Eph 2:10), which are to be manifested directly in our relationships with brothers and sisters in Christ. That is an essential part of what it means to be the people of God.

Finally, it is significant that the apostle situates interpersonal sins in relation to the devil on the one hand and the Holy Spirit on the other. "Giving place to the devil" and "grieving the Holy Spirit" sound like very "spiritual" problems, but they are clearly linked to how we treat one another. What we do toward our neighbors has clear consequences and can leave us exposed to the devil and grieving the Spirit of God.

 ***Illustration Opportunities.*** The best illustrations for this text are those unfortunate real-life situations involving disunity in which some churches and families find themselves. Unfortunately, many preachers know too many of these stories. These cautionary tales should stand as warnings for any congregation. Things like gossip, lies, rudeness, and lack of grace are very common expressions of our sinful nature, and they open space for the devil, grieve the Spirit of God, and divide the body of Christ. Use these illustrations carefully, preserving anonymity, so that they serve not as a means of exposing people but of emphasizing how vulnerable we can be to our sinful tendencies and how destructive those sins can be to the body of Christ.

EPHESIANS 5:1–20

LIVING AS CHILDREN OF LIGHT

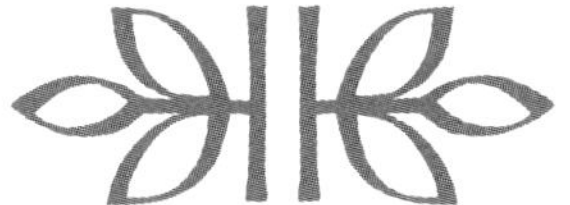

Since Paul is contrasting the conduct of the saints with that of non-believers, it is fitting to offer a positive paradigm. For Paul, that positive paradigm is God himself—who is to be imitated—and Christ—whose sacrificial love establishes the pattern upon which believers should live. This positive paradigm then leads to Paul's continued admonition on conduct, still with the contrast with the pagans as a foil. A more comprehensive list of vices is provided, with emphasis on immorality, greed, and vulgar speech. Closing his contrastive admonition, Paul frames his discourse in terms of a dichotomy between light and darkness. Believers are to expose the works of darkness with their good, righteous, and truthful living and to pursue wisdom, discernment, and a Spirit-filled life.

 5:1–2 

1a γίνεσθε οὖν μιμηταὶ τοῦ θεοῦ,

*ginesthe **oun** mimē**tai tou** the**ou**,*

Therefore, be imitators of God,

1b ὡς τέκνα ἀγαπητά,

*hōs **tek**na agapē**ta**,*

as beloved children,

2a καὶ περιπατεῖτε ἐν ἀγάπῃ,

***kai** peripa**tei**te en **aga**pē,*

And walk in love,

2b καθὼς καὶ ὁ χριστὸς ἠγάπησεν ἡμᾶς

*ka**thōs kai** ho chri**stos** ē**ga**pēsen hē**mas***

just as Christ also loved us

2c καὶ παρέδωκεν ἑαυτὸν ὑπὲρ ἡμῶν

kai** pare**dō**ken heau**ton** hy**per** hē**mōn

προσφορὰν καὶ θυσίαν τῷ θεῷ

*prospho**ran kai** thy**si**an **tō** theō*

and gave himself for us
as an offering and a sacrifice to God,

2d εἰς ὀσμὴν εὐωδίας.

*eis os**mēn** euō**di**as.*

as a fragrant smell.

1a	**γίνεσθε οὖν μιμηταὶ τοῦ θεοῦ,**

Therefore, be imitators of God,

γίνεσθε γίνομαι	(you all) be ***gi***·*nes*·*the*	PRES MID/PASS IMPV 2ND PL	verb
οὖν οὖν	therefore ***oun***	---	conj
μιμηταὶ μιμητής	imitators *mi*·*mē*·***tai***	NOM PL MASC	noun
τοῦ ὁ	of the ***tou***	GEN SG MASC	article
θεοῦ θεός	(of) God *the*·***ou***	GEN SG MASC	noun

The concept of imitation was prevalent in the ancient world. Ancient children would learn how to read and write by copying the great Greek poets, especially Homer. Imitation is also the paradigm for discipleship and learning. Paul's appeal for the Ephesians to imitate God is somewhat uncommon, since the term **μιμηταὶ** ("imitators") is mostly used to refer to the imitation of people, including Paul himself (1 Cor 4:16; 11:1; 1 Thess 1:6; 2:14; Heb 6:12).

1b	**ὡς τέκνα ἀγαπητά,**

as beloved children,

ὡς ὡς	as *hōs*	---	adv
τέκνα τέκνον	children ***tek***·*na*	NOM PL NEUT	noun
ἀγαπητά ἀγαπητός	beloved *a*·*ga*·*pē*·***ta***	NOM PL NEUT	adj

2a	**καὶ περιπατεῖτε ἐν ἀγάπῃ,**

And walk in love,

καὶ καί	and ***kai***	---	conj
περιπατεῖτε περιπατέω	(you all) walk *pe*·*ri*·*pa*·***tei***·*te*	PRES ACT IMPV 2ND PL	verb
ἐν ἐν	in *en*	---	prep

ἀγάπῃ ἀγάπη	love *a·**ga**·pē*	DAT SG FEM	noun

The two imperatives—be imitators (**γίνεσθε μιμηταὶ**) in v. 1a and walk in love (**περιπατεῖτε ἐν ἀγάπῃ**) here—are coordinated with a **καὶ**, and each is followed by comparative clause with a reference to love—"as beloved children" (**ὡς τέκνα ἀγαπητά** [v. 1b]) and "just as Christ also loved you" (**καθὼς καὶ ὁ χριστὸς ἠγάπησεν ὑμᾶς** [v. 2b]), respectively. Rhetorically, the two imperative clauses might be seen either as two separate commands in a series or, more likely, as relating to one another in an explanatory manner. In this case, "being imitators of God" is explained in terms of "walking in love."

2b **καθὼς καὶ ὁ χριστὸς ἠγάπησεν ἡμᾶς**

just as Christ also loved us

καθὼς καθώς	just as *ka·**thōs***	---	adv
καὶ καί	also ***kai***	---	conj
ὁ ὁ	the *ho*	NOM SG MASC	article
χριστὸς Χριστός	Christ *chri·**stos***	NOM SG MASC	noun
ἠγάπησεν ἀγαπάω	(he) loved *ē·**ga**·pē·sen*	AOR ACT IND 3RD SG	verb
ἡμᾶς ἐγώ	us *hē·**mas***	1ST ACC PL	pron

2c **καὶ παρέδωκεν ἑαυτὸν ὑπὲρ ἡμῶν**
προσφορὰν καὶ θυσίαν τῷ θεῷ

and gave himself for us
as an offering and a sacrifice to God,

καὶ καί	and ***kai***	---	conj
παρέδωκεν παραδίδωμι	(he) gave *par·**e**·dō·ken*	AOR ACT IND 3RD SG	verb
ἑαυτὸν ἑαυτοῦ	himself *he·au·**ton***	3RD ACC SG MASC	reflexive pron

ὑπὲρ ὑπέρ	for *hy·**per***	---	prep
ἡμῶν ἐγώ	us *hē·**mōn***	1ST GEN PL	pron
προσφορὰν προσφορά	offering *pros·pho·**ran***	ACC SG FEM	noun
καὶ καί	and ***kai***	---	conj
θυσίαν θυσία	sacrifice *thy·**si**·an*	ACC SG FEM	noun
τῷ ὁ	to the ***tō***	DAT SG MASC	article
θεῷ θεός	(to) God *the·**ō***	DAT SG MASC	noun

Imitating God is concretely expressed in reference to Christ and his sacrificial love. The adverb of comparison in 2b, **καθὼς** ("just as"), sets up the love of Christ as the pattern upon which the believers are to model their walking in love: **καὶ ὁ χριστὸς ἠγάπησεν ἡμᾶς** ("Christ also loved us"). Similarly, Christ's sacrificial "giving of himself" (**παρέδωκεν ἑαυτὸν**) specifies the way in which his love is expressed.

2d **εἰς ὀσμὴν εὐωδίας.**

as a fragrant smell.

εἰς εἰς	as *eis*	---	prep
ὀσμὴν ὀσμή	smell *os·**mēn***	ACC SG FEM	noun
εὐωδίας εὐωδία	fragrent *eu·ō·**di**·as*	GEN SG FEM	noun

5:3–5

3a Πορνεία δὲ καὶ ἀκαθαρσία πᾶσα ἢ πλεονεξία

Porneia de kai akatharsia pasa ē pleonexia

μηδὲ ὀνομαζέσθω ἐν ὑμῖν,

mēde onomazesthō en hymin,

But sexual immorality and all uncleanness or greediness must not be even mentioned among you,

3b καθὼς πρέπει ἁγίοις,

kathōs prepei hagiois,

just as it is fitting to saints

4a καὶ αἰσχρότης καὶ μωρολογία ἢ εὐτραπελία,

kai aischrotēs kai mōrologia ē eutrapelia,

and shamefulness and foolish talk or vulgar joking,

4b ἃ οὐκ ἀνῆκεν,

ha ouk anēken,

which is improper,

4c ἀλλὰ μᾶλλον εὐχαριστία.

alla mallon eucharistia.

but instead, thanksgiving.

5a τοῦτο γὰρ ἴστε γινώσκοντες

touto gar iste ginōskontes

For you may be sure of this,

5b ὅτι πᾶς πόρνος ἢ ἀκάθαρτος ἢ πλεονέκτης,

hoti pas pornos ē akathartos ē pleonektēs,

that every sexually immoral person or unclean, or greedy,

5c ὅ ἐστιν εἰδωλολάτρης,

ho estin eidōlolatrēs,

(that is, an idolater),

5d οὐκ ἔχει κληρονομίαν ἐν τῇ βασιλείᾳ τοῦ χριστοῦ καὶ θεοῦ.

ouk echei klēronomian en tē basileia tou christou kai theou.

does not have an inheritance in the kingdom of Christ and God.

3a **Πορνεία δὲ καὶ ἀκαθαρσία πᾶσα ἢ πλεονεξία μηδὲ ὀνομαζέσθω ἐν ὑμῖν,**

But sexual immorality and all uncleanness or greediness must not be even mentioned among you,

Πορνεία πορνεία	sexual immorality *Por·nei·a*	NOM SG FEM	noun
δὲ δέ	but *de*	---	conj
καὶ καί	and *kai*	---	conj
ἀκαθαρσία ἀκαθαρσία	uncleaness *a·ka·thar·si·a*	NOM SG FEM	noun
πᾶσα πᾶς	all *pa·sa*	NOM SG FEM	adj
ἢ ἤ	or *ē*	---	particle
πλεονεξία πλεονεξία	greediness *ple·o·ne·xi·a*	NOM SG FEM	noun
μηδὲ μηδέ	not even *mē·de*	NEGATIVE	conj
ὀνομαζέσθω ὀνομάζω	(it) must be mentioned *o·no·ma·zes·thō*	PRES PASS IMPV 3RD SG	verb
ἐν ἐν	among *en*	---	prep
ὑμῖν σύ	you (all) *hy·min*	2ND DAT PL	pron

3b	**καθὼς πρέπει ἁγίοις,**		
	just as it is fitting to saints		
καθὼς καθώς	just as *ka·**thōs***	---	adv
πρέπει πρέπω	it is fitting ***pre**·pei*	PRES ACT IND 3RD SG	verb
ἁγίοις ἅγιος	to saints *ha·**gi**·ois*	DAT PL MASC	adj

4a	**καὶ αἰσχρότης καὶ μωρολογία ἢ εὐτραπελία,**		
	and shamefulness and foolish talk or vulgar joking,		
καὶ καί	and ***kai***	---	conj
αἰσχρότης αἰσχρότης	shamefulness *ais·**chro**·tēs*	NOM SG FEM	noun
καὶ καί	and ***kai***	---	conj
μωρολογία μωρολογία	foolish talk *mō·ro·lo·**gi**·a*	NOM SG FEM	noun
ἢ ἤ	or *ē*	---	particle
εὐτραπελία εὐτραπελία	vulgar joking *eu·tra·pe·**li**·a*	NOM SG FEM	noun

The list of vices—**πορνεία** ("sexual immorality"), **ἀκαθαρσία** ("uncleanness"), **πλεονεξία** ("greediness"), **αἰσχρότης** ("shamefulness"), **μωρολογία** ("foolish talk"), and **εὐτραπελία** ("vulgar joking")—encompasses the categories of sexual sin, greed, and filthy speech. The association of terms could be related to the practice of orgies in the Greco-Roman world, where one would find sumptuous banquets marked by prostitution and all sorts of filthy talk.

4b	**ἃ οὐκ ἀνῆκεν,**		
	which is improper,		
ἃ ὅς	which ***ha***	NOM PL NEUT	relative pron
οὐκ οὐ	not *ouk*	---	particle

ἀνῆκεν ἀνήκω	(it) is proper *a·**nē**·ken*	IMPF ACT IND 3RD SG	verb

4c ἀλλὰ μᾶλλον εὐχαριστία.

but instead, thanksgiving.

ἀλλὰ ἀλλά	but *al·**la***	---	conj
μᾶλλον μᾶλλον	instead ***mal**·lon*	---	adv
εὐχαριστία εὐχαριστία	thanksgiving *eu·cha·ri·**sti**·a*	NOM SG FEM	noun

If the contrast with the Greco-Roman banquets is intended, then the word "thanksgiving" (**εὐχαριστία**) would certainly evoke the Lord's Supper (cf. 1 Cor 10:16)—a banquet characterized by thanksgiving—which fits well with the reference to Christ's sacrifice in the previous verse.

5a τοῦτο γὰρ ἴστε γινώσκοντες

For you may be sure of this,

τοῦτο οὗτος	this ***tou**·to*	ACC SG NEUT	demonstr pron
γὰρ γάρ	for ***gar***	---	conj
ἴστε εἰδῶ	you (all) know ***i**·ste*	PERF ACT IMPV 2ND PL	verb
γινώσκοντες γινώσκω	knowing *gi·**nō**·skon·tes*	PRES ACT PTCP NOM PL MASC	verb

5b ὅτι πᾶς πόρνος ἢ ἀκάθαρτος ἢ πλεονέκτης,

that every sexually immoral person or unclean, or greedy,

ὅτι ὅτι	that ***ho**·ti*	---	conj
πᾶς πᾶς	every ***pas***	NOM SG MASC	adj
πόρνος πόρνος	sexually immoral person ***por**·nos*	NOM SG MASC	noun

ἢ ἤ	or *ē*	---	particle
ἀκάθαρτος ἀκάθαρτος	unclean *a·**ka**·thar·tos*	NOM SG MASC	adj
ἢ ἤ	or *ē*	---	particle
πλεονέκτης πλεονέκτης	greedy *ple·o·**nek**·tēs*	NOM SG MASC	noun

5c **ὅ ἐστιν εἰδωλολάτρης,**

(that is, an idolater),

ὅ ὅς	that ***ho***	NOM SG NEUT	relative pron
ἐστιν εἰμί	is *e·stin*	PRES ACT IND 3RD SG	verb
εἰδωλολάτρης εἰδωλολάτρης	idolater *ei·dō·lo·**la**·trēs*	NOM SG MASC	noun

The association of greed (**πλεονέκτης**) and idolatry (**εἰδωλολάτρης**) is present elsewhere in Paul (1 Cor 5:10–11; 6:9; Col 3:5). This is an evaluation of greed as a matter of divided allegiance—the worship of possessions. It is fitting, therefore, that those who are devoted to wealth in this way are deprived of the true inheritance of the kingdom of God (below, v. 5d).

5d **οὐκ ἔχει κληρονομίαν ἐν τῇ βασιλείᾳ τοῦ χριστοῦ καὶ θεοῦ.**

does not have an inheritance
in the kingdom of Christ and God.

οὐκ οὐ	not *ouk*	---	particle
ἔχει ἔχω	(he/she) has ***e**·chei*	PRES ACT IND 3RD SG	verb
κληρονομίαν κληρονομία	inheritance *klē·ro·no·**mi**·an*	ACC SG FEM	noun
ἐν ἐν	in *en*	---	prep
τῇ ὁ	the ***tē***	DAT SG FEM	article
βασιλείᾳ βασιλεία	kingdom *ba·si·**lei**·a*	DAT SG FEM	noun

τοῦ ὁ	of the ***tou***	GEN SG MASC	article
χριστοῦ Χριστός	(of) Christ *chri*·***stou***	GEN SG MASC	noun
καὶ καί	and ***kai***	---	conj
θεοῦ θεός	(of) God *the*·***ou***	GEN SG MASC	noun

Verse 5d contains the last of three references to **κληρονομίαν** ("inheritance") in the letter (1:14, 18), now in a context of warning rather than hope.

6a Μηδεὶς ὑμᾶς ἀπατάτω κενοῖς λόγοις,

Mēdeis hymas apatatō kenois logois

Let no one deceive you with empty words,

6b διὰ ταῦτα γὰρ ἔρχεται ἡ ὀργὴ τοῦ θεοῦ

dia tauta gar erchetai hē orgē tou theou

ἐπὶ τοὺς υἱοὺς τῆς ἀπειθίας.

epi tous huious tēs apeithias.

for because of them the wrath of God comes upon the sons of disobedience.

7 μὴ οὖν γίνεσθε συνμέτοχοι αὐτῶν·

mē oun ginesthe synmetochoi autōn;

Therefore do not be partakers of them,

8a ἦτε γάρ ποτε σκότος,

ēte gar pote skotos,

for you were once darkness,

8b νῦν δὲ φῶς ἐν κυρίῳ·

nyn de phōs en kyriō;

but now [you are] light in the Lord.

8c ὡς τέκνα φωτὸς περιπατεῖτε,

hōs tekna phōtos peripateite

Walk as children of light—

9 ὁ γὰρ καρπὸς τοῦ φωτὸς ἐν πάσῃ ἀγαθωσύνῃ

ho gar karpos tou phōtos en pasē agathōsynē

καὶ δικαιοσύνῃ καὶ ἀληθείᾳ,

kai dikaiosynē kai alētheia,

for the fruit of light [consists in] all goodness and righteousness and truth—

10 δοκιμάζοντες τί ἐστιν εὐάρεστον τῷ κυρίῳ·

dokimazontes ti estin euareston tō kyriō;

discerning what is pleasing to the Lord.

11a καὶ μὴ συνκοινωνεῖτε τοῖς ἔργοις τοῖς ἀκάρποις τοῦ σκότους,

kai mē synkoinōneite tois ergois tois akarpois tou skotous,

And do not participate in the unfruitful works of darkness,

11b μᾶλλον δὲ καὶ ἐλέγχετε,

mallon de kai elenchete,

but rather [you should] even expose them.

12 τὰ γὰρ κρυφῇ γινόμενα ὑπ᾽ αὐτῶν αἰσχρόν ἐστιν καὶ λέγειν·

ta gar krypsē ginomena hyp' autōn aischron estin kai legein;

For it is shameful even to speak of the things they do secretly.

13 τὰ δὲ πάντα ἐλεγχόμενα ὑπὸ τοῦ φωτὸς φανεροῦται,

ta de panta elenchomena hypo tou phōtos phaneroutai,

But all things being exposed by the light are revealed,

14a πᾶν γὰρ τὸ φανερούμενον φῶς ἐστίν.

pan gar to phaneroumenon phōs estin.

for all that is being revealed is light.

14b διὸ λέγει

dio legei

Therefore it says,

14c Ἔγειρε, ὁ καθεύδων,

Egeire, ho katheudōn,

Awake, sleeper,

14d καὶ ἀνάστα ἐκ τῶν νεκρῶν,

kai anasta ek tōn nekrōn,

and arise from the dead,

14e καὶ ἐπιφαύσει σοι ὁ χριστός.

***kai** epiphau**sei soi ho chris**tos.*

and Christ will shine on you.

6a **Μηδεὶς ὑμᾶς ἀπατάτω κενοῖς λόγοις,**

Let no one deceive you with empty words,

Μηδεὶς μηδείς	no one *Mē·**deis***	NOM SG MASC	adj
ὑμᾶς σύ	you (all) *hy·**mas***	2ND ACC PL	pron
ἀπατάτω ἀπατάω	(you all) let (him/her) deceive *a·pa·**ta**·tō*	PRES ACT IMPV 3RD SG	verb
κενοῖς κενός	(with) empty *ke·**nois***	DAT PL MASC	adj
λόγοις λόγος	with words ***lo**·gois*	DAT PL MASC	noun

6b **διὰ ταῦτα γὰρ ἔρχεται ἡ ὀργὴ τοῦ θεοῦ ἐπὶ τοὺς υἱοὺς τῆς ἀπειθίας.**

for because of them the wrath of God comes upon the sons of disobedience.

διὰ διά	because of *di·**a***	---	prep
ταῦτα οὗτος	them ***tau**·ta*	ACC PL NEUT	demonstr pron
γὰρ γάρ	for ***gar***	---	conj
ἔρχεται ἔρχομαι	(it) comes ***er**·che·tai*	PRES MID/PASS IND 3RD SG	verb
ἡ ὁ	the *hē*	NOM SG FEM	article
ὀργὴ ὀργή	wrath *or·**gē***	NOM SG FEM	noun

τοῦ ὁ	of the ***tou***	GEN SG MASC	article
θεοῦ θεός	(of) God *the*·***ou***	GEN SG MASC	noun
ἐπὶ ἐπί	upon *e*·***pi***	---	prep
τοὺς ὁ	the ***tous***	ACC PL MASC	article
υἱοὺς υἱός	sons *hui*·***ous***	ACC PL MASC	noun
τῆς ὁ	of the ***tēs***	GEN SG FEM	article
ἀπειθίας ἀπείθεια	(of) disobedience *a*·*pei*·***thi***·*as*	GEN SG FEM	noun

The phrase **ἡ ὀργὴ τοῦ θεοῦ ἐπὶ τοὺς υἱοὺς τῆς ἀπειθίας** ("the wrath of God comes upon the sons of disobedience") recalls 2:1–3, where Paul describes the believers' former status as children of wrath, living among the sons of disobedience. Paul uses similar language now to admonish the believers not to revert back to old sinful patterns. It is noticeable that throughout the letter, Paul goes back and forth in his emphasis on the believers' new identity and their former identity to admonish them.

7 **μὴ οὖν γίνεσθε συνμέτοχοι αὐτῶν·**

Therefore do not be partakers of them,

μὴ μή	not ***mē***	---	particle
οὖν οὖν	therefore ***oun***	---	conj
γίνεσθε γίνομαι	(you all) be ***gi***·*nes*·*the*	PRES MID/PASS IMPV 2ND PL	verb
συνμέτοχοι συμμέτοχος	partakers *syn*·***me***·*to*·*choi*	NOM PL MASC	adj
αὐτῶν αὐτός	of them *au*·***tōn***	3RD GEN PL	personal pron

The same word **συνμέτοχοι** ("partakers") is used in 3:6 to talk about gentiles being partakers of the promises given to Israel. If believers are "partakers" with the covenant people, they cannot be "partakers" with nonbelievers.

8a	**ἦτε γάρ ποτε σκότος,**		
	for you were once darkness,		
ἦτε εἰμί	you (all) were *ē · te*	IMPF ACT IND 2ND PL	verb
γάρ γάρ	for ***gar***	---	conj
ποτε ποτέ	once *po · te*	---	particle
σκότος σκότος	darkness ***sko** · tos*	NOM SG NEUT	noun

8b	**νῦν δὲ φῶς ἐν κυρίῳ·**		
	but now [you are] light in the Lord.		
νῦν νῦν	now ***nyn***	---	adv
δὲ δέ	but ***de***	---	conj
φῶς φῶς	light ***phōs***	NOM SG NEUT	noun
ἐν ἐν	in *en*	---	prep
κυρίῳ κύριος	Lord *ky · **ri** · ō*	DAT SG MASC	noun

The darkness (**σκότος**) and light (**φῶς**) contrast, which recalls 1:18, emphasizes the radical nature of the transformation that is expected to come as a result of one's conversion.

8c	**ὡς τέκνα φωτὸς περιπατεῖτε,**		
	Walk as children of light—		
ὡς ὡς	as *hōs*	---	adv
τέκνα τέκνον	children ***tek** · na*	NOM PL NEUT	noun
φωτὸς φῶς	of light *phō · **tos***	GEN SG NEUT	noun
περιπατεῖτε περιπατέω	(you all) walk *pe · ri · pa · **tei** · te*	PRES ACT IMPV 2ND PL	verb

9 **ὁ γὰρ καρπὸς τοῦ φωτὸς ἐν πάσῃ ἀγαθωσύνῃ καὶ δικαιοσύνῃ καὶ ἀληθείᾳ,**

for the fruit of light [consists in] all goodness and righteousness and truth—

ὁ ὁ	the *ho*	NOM SG MASC	article
γὰρ γάρ	for ***gar***	---	conj
καρπὸς καρπός~1	fruit *kar*·***pos***	NOM SG MASC	noun
τοῦ ὁ	of the ***tou***	GEN SG NEUT	article
φωτὸς φῶς	(of) light *phō*·***tos***	GEN SG NEUT	noun
ἐν ἐν	[consists] in *en*	---	prep
πάσῃ πᾶς	all ***pa***·*sē*	DAT SG FEM	adj
ἀγαθωσύνῃ ἀγαθωσύνη	goodness *a*·*ga*·*thō*·***sy***·*nē*	DAT SG FEM	noun
καὶ καί	and ***kai***	---	conj
δικαιοσύνῃ δικαιοσύνη	righteousness *di*·*kai*·*o*·***sy***·*nē*	DAT SG FEM	noun
καὶ καί	and ***kai***	---	conj
ἀληθείᾳ ἀλήθεια	truth *a*·*lē*·***thei***·*a*	DAT SG FEM	noun

The reference to fruit (**καρπὸς**) is reminiscent of the list of the fruit of the Spirit in Gal 5:22, although only "goodness" shows up in both. As in Galatians, the "fruit" is singular but encompasses multiple virtues: here it includes goodness, righteousness, and truth. The language of fruit denotes a sense of result but also refers to the capacity to produce, which comes forward in the contrast with the unfruitfulness of darkness in the next verse. In other words, these virtues are the expected fruit that results from the believer's walking in the light.

10	**δοκιμάζοντες τί ἐστιν εὐάρεστον τῷ κυρίῳ·**
	discerning what is pleasing to the Lord.

δοκιμάζοντες δοκιμάζω	(you all) discerning *do·ki·**ma**·zon·tes*	PRES ACT PTCP NOM PL MASC	verb
τί τίς~2	what ***ti***	NOM SG NEUT	interr pron
ἐστιν εἰμί	is *e·stin*	PRES ACT IND 3RD SG	verb
εὐάρεστον εὐάρεστος	pleasimg *eu·**a**·re·ston*	NOM SG NEUT	adj
τῷ ὁ	to the ***tō***	DAT SG MASC	article
κυρίῳ κύριος	(to) Lord *ky·**ri**·ō*	DAT SG MASC	noun

The verb **δοκιμάζοντες** has the sense of testing and approving something. Goodness, righteousness, and truth are the criteria for discernment.

11a	**καὶ μὴ συνκοινωνεῖτε τοῖς ἔργοις τοῖς ἀκάρποις τοῦ σκότους,**
	And do not participate in the unfruitful works of darkness,

καὶ καί	and ***kai***	---	conj
μὴ μή	not ***mē***	---	particle
συνκοινωνεῖτε συγκοινωνέω	(you all) participate *syn·koi·nō·**nei**·te*	PRES ACT IMPV 2ND PL	verb
τοῖς ὁ	in the ***tois***	DAT PL NEUT	article
ἔργοις ἔργον	(in) works ***er**·gois*	DAT PL NEUT	noun
τοῖς ὁ	(in) the ***tois***	DAT PL NEUT	article
ἀκάρποις ἄκαρπος	(in) unfruitful *a·**kar**·pois*	DAT PL NEUT	adj
τοῦ ὁ	of the ***tou***	GEN SG NEUT	article
σκότους σκότος	(of) darkness ***sko**·tous*	GEN SG NEUT	noun

The verb **συνκοινωνεῖτε** is related to the word **κοινωνία**, meaning “fellowship” or “participation,” with the added prefix **συν** (“with”). What is envisioned is not simply practicing the acts but participating in the acts with nonbelievers. The admonition seems to imply there are members of the Christian community secretly engaging in such activities. Paul, therefore, calls for exposing such acts with their righteous living.

The dichotomy between light (**φωτὸς** [9]) and darkness (**σκότους**) sets a clear contrast between the two groups. There is no middle space between them.

11b	**μᾶλλον δὲ καὶ ἐλέγχετε,**
	but rather [you should] even expose them.

μᾶλλον μᾶλλον	rather *mal·lon*	---	adv
δὲ δέ	but *de*	---	conj
καὶ καί	even *kai*	---	conj
ἐλέγχετε ἐλέγχω	(you all) expose *e·len·che·te*	PRES ACT IMPV 2ND PL	verb

The verb **ἐλέγχω** means "to expose" or "to reproach." It may carry the intent of correction (Matt 18:15; 1 Tim 5:20; 2 Tim 4:2; Titus 1:9, 13; 2:15) or judgment (John 3:20; 16:8; Jas 2:9; Jude 15). Here, used with the metaphor of light and darkness, the idea is one of "exposing" in the sense of bringing the hidden deeds into the light so they would be seen for what they are.

12	**τὰ γὰρ κρυφῇ γινόμενα ὑπ' αὐτῶν αἰσχρόν ἐστιν καὶ λέγειν·**
	For it is shameful even to speak of the things they do secretly.

τὰ ὁ	the things *ta*	NOM PL NEUT	article
γὰρ γάρ	for *gar*	---	conj
κρυφῇ κρυφῇ	secretly *kry·phē*	---	adv
γινόμενα γίνομαι	(those) coming *gi·no·me·na*	PRES MID/PASS PTCP ACC PL NEUT	verb
ὑπ' ὑπό	by *hyp'*	---	prep
αὐτῶν αὐτός	(of) them *au·tōn*	3RD GEN PL	personal pron

αἰσχρόν αἰσχρός	shameful *ais·**chron***	NOM SG NEUT	adj
ἐστιν εἰμί	it is *e·stin*	PRES ACT IND 3RD SG	verb
καὶ καί	even ***kai***	---	conj
λέγειν λέγω	to speak ***le**·gein*	PRES ACT INF	verb

The phrase **τὰ γὰρ κρυφῇ γινόμενα ὑπ' αὐτῶν** literally means the "things done secretly by them." The pronoun **αὐτῶν** may refer to nonbelievers or to believers who are engaged secretly in shameful acts. Since Paul is very descriptive of the sins committed by gentiles (cf. 5:3–4), these secret practices seem to constitute a different, more serious level of condemnable actions, which go beyond what the apostle has already mentioned.

13 **τὰ δὲ πάντα ἐλεγχόμενα ὑπὸ τοῦ φωτὸς φανεροῦται,**

But all things being exposed by the light are revealed,

τὰ ὁ	the ***ta***	NOM PL NEUT	article
δὲ δέ	but ***de***	---	conj
πάντα πᾶς	all (things) ***pan**·ta*	NOM PL NEUT	adj
ἐλεγχόμενα ἐλέγχω	(they) being exposed *e·len·**cho**·me·na*	PRES PASS PTCP NOM PL NEUT	verb
ὑπὸ ὑπό	by *hy·**po***	---	prep
τοῦ ὁ	the ***tou***	GEN SG NEUT	article
φωτὸς φῶς	light *phō·**tos***	GEN SG NEUT	noun
φανεροῦται φανερόω	(they) are revealed *pha·ne·**rou**·tai*	PRES PASS IND 3RD SG	verb

14a **πᾶν γὰρ τὸ φανερούμενον φῶς ἐστίν.**

for all that is being revealed is light.

πᾶν πᾶς	all ***pan***	NOM SG NEUT	adj

γὰρ γάρ	for *gar*	---	conj
τὸ ὁ	that *to*	NOM SG NEUT	article
φανερούμενον φανερόω	(it) is being revealed *pha·ne·rou·me·non*	PRES PASS PTCP NOM SG NEUT	verb
φῶς φῶς	light *phōs*	NOM SG NEUT	noun
ἐστίν εἰμί	(it) is *e·stin*	PRES ACT IND 3RD SG	verb

It is difficult to understand precisely what the phrase in v. 13b means. How do the things manifested by light become light? One should refrain from seeing this in terms of transformation—as if the works of darkness themselves become essentially light through exposure. Paul is simply saying that the hidden things exposed by light are no longer hidden in darkness. But the overall idea seems to be that, when these actions are exposed, those who practice them finally see them for what they truly are. It is this that leads to the enlightenment of others. The goal of the exposure, in this case, is restorative, which is confirmed by the following verse.

14b **διὸ λέγει**

Therefore it says,

διὸ διό	therefore *di·o*	---	conj
λέγει λέγω	it says *le·gei*	PRES ACT IND 3RD SG	verb

Paul is citing a text, but if it comes from Scripture, it is unclear to which text specifically he refers. The closest possibility is a paraphrase of Isa 60:1. The citation compares the state of being in darkness with sleep and death, and Christ's shining upon people as that which brings them back from this state of alienation.

14c **Ἔγειρε, ὁ καθεύδων,**

Awake, sleeper,

Ἔγειρε ἐγείρω	(you) awake *E·gei·re*	PRES ACT IMPV 2ND SG	verb

ὁ ὁ	the *ho*	NOM SG MASC	article
καθεύδων καθεύδω	sleeper *ka·**theu**·dōn*	PRES ACT PTCP NOM SG MASC	verb

14d καὶ ἀνάστα ἐκ τῶν νεκρῶν,

and arise from the dead,

καὶ καί	and ***kai***	---	conj
ἀνάστα ἀνίστημι	(you) arise *a·**na**·sta*	AOR ACT IMPV 2ND SG	verb
ἐκ ἐκ	from *ek*	---	prep
τῶν ὁ	the ***tōn***	GEN PL MASC	article
νεκρῶν νεκρός	dead *ne·**krōn***	GEN PL MASC	adj

14e καὶ ἐπιφαύσει σοι ὁ χριστός.

and Christ will shine on you.

καὶ καί	and ***kai***	---	conj
ἐπιφαύσει ἐπιφαύσκω	(he) will shine *e·pi·**phau**·sei*	FUT ACT IND 3RD SG	verb
σοι σύ	on you *soi*	2ND DAT SG	pron
ὁ ὁ	the *ho*	NOM SG MASC	article
χριστός Χριστός	Christ *chri·**stos***	NOM SG MASC	noun

5:15–20

15a Βλέπετε οὖν ἀκριβῶς πῶς περιπατεῖτε,

Blepete oun akribōs pōs peripateite,

Therefore look carefully how you are walking,

15b μὴ ὡς ἄσοφοι

mē hōs asophoi

not as unwise

15c ἀλλ᾽ ὡς σοφοί,

all' hōs sophoi,

but as wise,

16a ἐξαγοραζόμενοι τὸν καιρόν,

exagorazomenoi ton kairon,

Making the most of the time,

16b ὅτι αἱ ἡμέραι πονηραί εἰσιν.

hoti hai hēmerai ponērai eisin.

because the days are evil.

17a διὰ τοῦτο μὴ γίνεσθε ἄφρονες,

dia touto mē ginesthe aphrones,

For this reason do not be foolish,

17b ἀλλὰ συνίετε τί τὸ θέλημα τοῦ κυρίου·

alla syniete ti to thelēma tou kyriou;

but understand what the will of the Lord is.

18a καὶ μὴ μεθύσκεσθε οἴνῳ,

kai mē methyskesthe oinō,

And do not get drunk with wine,

18b ἐν ᾧ ἐστὶν ἀσωτία,

*en **hō estin** asōtia,*

in which there is debauchery,

18c ἀλλὰ πληροῦσθε ἐν πνεύματι,

*al**la** plē**rous**the en **pneu**mati,*

but be filled by the Spirit.

19a λαλοῦντες ἑαυτοῖς ψαλμοῖς

*la**loun**tes heau**tois** psal**mois***

καὶ ὕμνοις καὶ ᾠδαῖς πνευματικαῖς,

***kai hym**nois **kai** ō**dais** pneumati**kais**,*

**Speaking to one another with psalms
and hymns and spiritual songs,**

19b ᾄδοντες καὶ ψάλλοντες τῇ καρδίᾳ ὑμῶν τῷ κυρίῳ,

***a**dontes **kai psal**lontes **tē** kar**di**a hy**mōn tō** ky**ri**ō,*

singing and making melody to the Lord with your heart,

20a εὐχαριστοῦντες πάντοτε

*euchari**stoun**tes **pan**tote*

always giving thanks

20b ὑπὲρ πάντων

*hy**per pan**tōn*

for everything

20c ἐν ὀνόματι τοῦ κυρίου ἡμῶν Ἰησοῦ Χριστοῦ

*en o**no**mati **tou** ky**ri**ou hē**mōn** Iēsou Chri**stou***

in the name of our Lord Jesus Christ

20d τῷ θεῷ καὶ πατρί,

***tō** theō **kai** pa**tri**,*

to [our] God and Father

15a	**Βλέπετε οὖν ἀκριβῶς πῶς περιπατεῖτε,**
	Therefore look carefully how you are walking,

Βλέπετε βλέπω	(you all) look ***Ble***·*pe*·*te*	PRES ACT IMPV 2ND PL	verb
οὖν οὖν	therefore ***oun***	---	conj
ἀκριβῶς ἀκριβῶς	carefully *a*·*kri*·***bōs***	---	adv
πῶς πῶς~2	how ***pōs***	---	adv
περιπατεῖτε περιπατέω	you (all) are walking *pe*·*ri*·*pa*·***tei***·*te*	PRES ACT IND 2ND PL	verb

15b	**μὴ ὡς ἄσοφοι**
	not as unwise

μὴ μή	not ***mē***	---	particle
ὡς ὡς	as *hōs*	---	adv
ἄσοφοι ἄσοφος	unwise ***a***·*so*·*phoi*	NOM PL MASC	adj

15c	**ἀλλ᾽ ὡς σοφοί,**
	but as wise,

ἀλλ᾽ ἀλλά	but *all'*	---	conj
ὡς ὡς	as *hōs*	---	adv
σοφοί σοφός	wise *so*·***phoi***	NOM PL MASC	adj

16a	**ἐξαγοραζόμενοι τὸν καιρόν,**

Making the most of the time,

ἐξαγοραζόμενοι ἐξαγοράζω	(you all) redeeming/ buying out *e·xa·go·ra·**zo**·me·noi*	PRES MID PTCP NOM PL MASC	verb
τὸν ὁ	the ***ton***	ACC SG MASC	article
καιρόν καιρός	time *kai·**ron***	ACC SG MASC	noun

The verb **ἐξαγοραζόμενοι** means literally "redeeming" or "buying out/ from" (cf. Gal 3:13; 4:5). Its use with **τὸν καιρόν** ("the time") makes it more likely that Paul is using this word metaphorically. Given the clause in 16b—**ὅτι αἱ ἡμέραι πονηραί εἰσιν** ("because the days are evil")—"making the most of the time" is not simply about taking advantage of opportunities but about living life in a discerning way, not wasting time but seeking to understand the will of God at every moment and with every opportunity.

16b	**ὅτι αἱ ἡμέραι πονηραί εἰσιν.**

because the days are evil.

ὅτι ὅτι	because ***ho**·ti*	---	conj
αἱ ὁ	the *hai*	NOM PL FEM	article
ἡμέραι ἡμέρα	days *hē·**me**·rai*	NOM PL FEM	noun
πονηραί πονηρός	evil *po·nē·**rai***	NOM PL FEM	adj
εἰσιν εἰμί	(they) are *ei·sin*	PRES ACT IND 3RD PL	verb

17a	**διὰ τοῦτο μὴ γίνεσθε ἄφρονες,**

For this reason do not be foolish,

διὰ διά	for *di·**a***	---	prep
τοῦτο οὗτος	this (reason) ***tou**·to*	ACC SG NEUT	demonstr pron

μὴ μή	not ***mē***	---	particle
γίνεσθε γίνομαι	(you all) be ***gi*** *· nes · the*	PRES MID/PASS IMPV 2ND PL	verb
ἄφρονες ἄφρων	foolish ***a*** *· phro · nes*	NOM PL MASC	adj

17b	**ἀλλὰ συνίετε τί τὸ θέλημα τοῦ κυρίου·**
	but understand what the will of the Lord is.

ἀλλὰ ἀλλά	but *al ·* ***la***	---	conj
συνίετε συνίημι	(you all) understand *sy ·* ***ni*** *· e · te*	PRES ACT IMPV 2ND PL	verb
τί τίς~2	what ***ti***	NOM SG NEUT	interr pron
τὸ ὁ	the ***to***	NOM SG NEUT	article
θέλημα θέλημα	will ***the*** *· lē · ma*	NOM SG NEUT	noun
τοῦ ὁ	of the ***tou***	GEN SG MASC	article
κυρίου κύριος	(of) Lord *ky ·* ***ri*** *· ou*	GEN SG MASC	noun

Note Paul's use of wisdom language in vv. 15–17: "not as unwise (**ἄσοφοι**) but as wise (**σοφοί**)"; "do not be foolish (**ἄφρονες**) but understand (**συνίετε**)." He has highlighted the darkening of the mind as the reason for the gentiles' shameful behavior (cf. 4:17–19). Now, he uses wisdom language again to affirm the need for discernment.

18a	**καὶ μὴ μεθύσκεσθε οἴνῳ,**
	And do not get drunk with wine,

καὶ καί	and ***kai***	---	conj
μὴ μή	not ***mē***	---	particle
μεθύσκεσθε μεθύσκω	(you all) get drunk *me ·* ***thy*** *· skes · the*	PRES PASS IMPV 2ND PL	verb

οἴνῳ οἶνος	with wine ***oi***·*nō*	DAT SG MASC	noun

Drunkenness is associated with confusion and lack of discernment in the Old Testament (cf. Isa 28:7; 29:9–10). Therefore, this admonition assumes that drunkenness is a concrete way in which the foolishness and lack of wisdom of the previous verses are expressed. The image of intoxication, which matches well the social background of pagan parties, also evokes the idea of lack of control.

18b **ἐν ᾧ ἐστὶν ἀσωτία,**

in which there is debauchery,

ἐν ἐν	in *en*	---	prep
ᾧ ὅς	which ***hō***	DAT SG MASC	relative pron
ἐστὶν εἰμί	(it) is *e*·***stin***	PRES ACT IND 3RD SG	verb
ἀσωτία ἀσωτία	debauchery *a*·*sō*·***ti***·*a*	NOM SG FEM	noun

The term **ἀσωτία** ("debauchery") denotes wastefulness and recklessness. Therefore, it contrasts with the wise and purposeful "redeeming of time."

18c **ἀλλὰ πληροῦσθε ἐν πνεύματι,**

but be filled by the Spirit.

ἀλλὰ ἀλλά	but *al*·***la***	---	conj
πληροῦσθε πληρόω	(you all) be filled *plē*·***rous***·*the*	PRES PASS IMPV 2ND PL	verb
ἐν ἐν	by *en*	---	prep
πνεύματι πνεῦμα	Spirit ***pneu***·*ma*·*ti*	DAT SG NEUT	noun

In light of the contrast with wastefulness, **πληροῦσθε ἐν πνεύματι** ("being filled by the Spirit") indicates surrendering control to the purposeful agency of the Holy Spirit.

19a	**λαλοῦντες ἑαυτοῖς ψαλμοῖς καὶ ὕμνοις καὶ ᾠδαῖς πνευματικαῖς,**

Speaking to one another with psalms
and hymns and spiritual songs,

λαλοῦντες λαλέω	(you all) speaking *la·**loun**·tes*	PRES ACT PTCP NOM PL MASC	verb
ἑαυτοῖς ἑαυτοῦ	to one another *he·au·**tois***	2ND DAT PL MASC	reflexive pron
ψαλμοῖς ψαλμός	with psalms *psal·**mois***	DAT PL MASC	noun
καὶ καί	and ***kai***	---	conj
ὕμνοις ὕμνος	(with) hymns ***hym**·nois*	DAT PL MASC	noun
καὶ καί	and ***kai***	---	conj
ᾠδαῖς ᾠδή	(with) songs *ō·**dais***	DAT PL FEM	noun
πνευματικαῖς πνευματικός	(with) spiritual *pneu·ma·ti·**kais***	DAT PL FEM	adj

In keeping with 1:3, the adjective **πνευματικαῖς** ("spiritual") that modifies **ᾠδαῖς** ("songs") refers to that which comes from the Holy Spirit rather than to a specific genre of songs.

19b	**ᾄδοντες καὶ ψάλλοντες τῇ καρδίᾳ ὑμῶν τῷ κυρίῳ,**

singing and making melody to the Lord with your heart,

ᾄδοντες ᾄδω	singing ***a**·don·tes*	PRES ACT PTCP NOM PL MASC	verb
καὶ καί	and ***kai***	---	conj
ψάλλοντες ψάλλω	(you all) making melody ***psal**·lon·tes*	PRES ACT PTCP NOM PL MASC	verb
τῇ ὁ	with the ***tē***	DAT SG FEM	article
καρδίᾳ καρδία	(with) heart *kar·**di**·a*	DAT SG FEM	noun
ὑμῶν σύ	of you (all)/your *hy·**mōn***	2ND GEN PL	pron
τῷ ὁ	to the ***tō***	DAT SG MASC	article

κυρίῳ κύριος	(to) Lord *ky·**ri**·ō*	DAT SG MASC	noun

20a **εὐχαριστοῦντες πάντοτε**

always giving thanks

εὐχαριστοῦντες εὐχαριστέω	(you all) giving thanks *eu·cha·ri·**stoun**·tes*	PRES ACT PTCP NOM PL MASC	verb
πάντοτε πάντοτε	always ***pan**·to·te*	---	adv

Four participles in vv. 19–20, all of which relate to worship in community, modify the main verb in v. 18c, **πληροῦσθε** ("be filled"): **λαλοῦντες** ("speaking [to one another]"), **ᾄδοντες** ("singing"), **ψάλλοντες** ("making melody"), and **εὐχαριστοῦντες** ("giving thanks"). They are best seen as participles of result, indicating the consequences of being filled with the Spirit.

20b **ὑπὲρ πάντων**

for everything

ὑπὲρ ὑπέρ	for *hy·**per***	---	prep
πάντων πᾶς	everything ***pan**·tōn*	GEN PL NEUT	adj

20c **ἐν ὀνόματι τοῦ κυρίου ἡμῶν Ἰησοῦ Χριστοῦ**

in the name of our Lord Jesus Christ

ἐν ἐν	in *en*	---	prep
ὀνόματι ὄνομα	name *o·**no**·ma·ti*	DAT SG NEUT	noun
τοῦ ὁ	of the ***tou***	GEN SG MASC	article
κυρίου κύριος	(of) Lord *ky·**ri**·ou*	GEN SG MASC	noun
ἡμῶν ἐγώ	of us/our *hē·**mōn***	1ST GEN PL	pron

Ἰησοῦ Ἰησοῦς	Jesus *I·ē·**sou***	GEN SG MASC	noun
Χριστοῦ Χριστός	Christ *Chri·**stou***	GEN SG MASC	noun

20d **τῷ θεῷ καὶ πατρί,**

to [our] God and Father

τῷ ὁ	to the ***tō***	DAT SG MASC	article
θεῷ θεός	(to) God *the·**ō***	DAT SG MASC	noun
καὶ καί	and ***kai***	---	conj
πατρί πατήρ	father *pa·**tri***	DAT SG MASC	noun

From Text to Sermon

Main Exegetical Ideas. Believers should imitate God, according to the self-giving example of Christ. They should also distance themselves from all sinful practices and environments, exposing such practices as works of darkness, and live with discernment, being filled with the Spirit.

Bridge to Theology. More generally, the passage continues the contrast between the life of those who walk with God and the life of those who live in sin. Paul uses the outstanding concept of the imitation of God to refer to the way believers are expected to conduct themselves. Paul often mentions imitation in his letters referring to himself or Christ as the models to be imitated (1 Cor 4:16; 11:1; Phil 3:17; 1 Thess 1:6; 2:14), but this is the only place Paul mentions the imitation of God. More immediately, the concept of imitation draws from common practices of learning in the ancient world, where pupils would imitate their masters and apprentices would imitate artisans. Theologically, imitating God is connected to the idea of being made in God's image—which Paul alluded to in Eph 4:13—and also finds a point of reference in the appeal for Israel to imitate YHWH (Lev 11:44–45; Deut 15:12–15). However, Paul offers a more direct point of reference to the idea of imitation of God: Christ is the model by which the imitation of God is patterned, more specifically his sacrifice on our behalf. Christ's loving sacrifice is the ultimate example of God's love, the incarnate model by which God's children can imitate him.

This incredible appeal, however, is not abstract but is expressed in very clear ethical terms. Those who have their new creation identity must not live in sin. More importantly, because they are children of light, their holy living should expose the hidden works of darkness and bring Christ's light wherever they go. The contrast between light and darkness is a creation motif (cf. Gen 1:3–4; John 1:1–13). Light always exposes and defeats darkness, and the children of God are to walk with such an understanding. Therefore, as children of light, believers are to live a discerning life, not being numbed by the appetites of the flesh but filled with the Spirit.

The filling with the Spirit is framed in two ways. First, it contrasts with "getting drunk with wine," which both condemns the debauchery seen in the Greco-Roman parties and warns against the numbness to and lack of awareness of God's will (5:15–17). Second, and more positively, being filled with the Spirit is expressed in the communal practice of singing and ministering to one another in the context of the gathering of the people of

God. Paul contrasts the wastefulness of the parties of the unbelievers with the joyful, purposeful gathering of the people of God. In other words, the filling with the Spirit is experienced in the thanksgiving-filled gathering of the church.

Possible Sermon Structure. This passage can be broken down into four sections:

1. Being imitators of God (5:1–2)
2. Avoiding sin (5:3–5)
3. Walking as children of light and exposing darkness (5:6–14)
4. Living with discernment and being filled with the Spirit (5:15–21)

Because the four sections form one coherent argument, it is possible to preach one sermon highlighting these four points. Alternatively, one can approach the passage in a two-part sermon:

1. Being imitators of God in a sinful world (5:1–6)
2. Walking as children of light in a world of darkness (5:7–14)

Points of Application. The detailed descriptions of the sins to be avoided and the appeal to live according to God's standards foster straightforward points of application. Perhaps one aspect that can sometimes go unnoticed is the discerning life. Discussions on the prohibition of wine often miss Paul's more important point. In a context where people would give themselves to wasteful entertainment—characterized by sexual immorality, drunkenness, and foolish talk (see commentary)—Paul urges his audience to remain attentive by discerning the time in order to make the most of it, being filled with the Spirit, and ministering spiritually to one another. The point is hardly about the permissibility of alcohol consumption—although the abusive consumption of alcohol certainly aligns with the larger problem Paul is addressing—but rather the danger of living according to the sinful wastefulness and numbness of this world. We can certainly relate to Paul's exposure to the environment of wasteful entertainment in modern culture. What does it mean to live with discernment in the midst of the intoxicating distractions of our days?

Illustration Opportunities. Examples of imitation, such as children imitating their parents, or pupils imitating their teacher, will help illustrate Paul's appeal to imitate God. Furthermore, Paul's use of the images of light and darkness lends itself immediately to illustrations. Any examples of how light exposes what is hidden would serve as a good way to introduce the idea.

Finally, the ever-increasing alcohol, drug, and opioid abuse in society is clear evidence of the numbness that characterizes our times. Sometimes overwhelmed by oppressing realities, sometimes unable to resist the appetites of the flesh, people give in to coping mechanisms to desensitize and detach themselves from the problems around them. Even things like food and entertainment can become ways to escape the harsh realities of life. That is a good frame of reference to apply what Paul is saying to a contemporary context. The apostle urges us to avoid such wastefulness and live with awareness and discernment, being filled with the Spirit and reminding one another of God's will.

EPHESIANS 5:21–6:9

LIVING IN THE HOUSEHOLD OF GOD

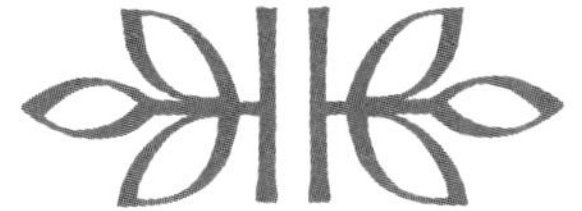

After discussing the conduct of believers in contrast with that of non-believers, Paul directs his focus to a more particular context—that of the household. His admonitions still focus on unity and conduct, but now with household relationships in view. The household was the most basic social unit in the Greco-Roman world, providing the model for fundamental hierarchical relationships in society and the empire at large. Paul's understanding of the household, however, does not have the state or a general social context as its primary framework; rather he is focused on the reality of the church as the household of God (recall the many words we have seen containing the οἰκ- root throughout the letter). Therefore, the principles that guide the relationships in the Christian household derive their thrust from the more fundamental understanding of Christ's headship over the church as emphasized by Paul in his argument thus far. This difference notwithstanding, Paul addresses the conventional hierarchical pairings found in ethical discussions of his day: wives/husbands, children/parents, and slaves/masters.

5:21

21a ὑποτασσόμενοι ἀλλήλοις

hypotassomenoi allēlois

Submitting to one another

21b ἐν φόβῳ Χριστοῦ.

en phobō Christou.

out of reverence of Christ

21a ὑποτασσόμενοι ἀλλήλοις

Submitting to one another

ὑποτασσόμενοι ὑποτάσσω	(you all) submitting *hy·po·tas·so·me·noi*	PRES PASS PTCP NOM PL MASC	verb
ἀλλήλοις ἀλλήλων	to one another *al·lē·lois*	DAT PL MASC	reciprocal pron

The verb **ὑποτάσσω** implies submission, typically within a hierarchical relationship. Here it is used in participial form—the last in a chain of participles that begins in 5:19–20—and is syntactically related to the main verb in 5:18: "*be filled (***πληροῦσθε***)* by the Spirit." Therefore, the submission to one another is still a result of believers' Spirit-filled lives. Rhetorically, this begins a new section, with the subject matter moving from worship in the community to relations in the household. Participles can sometimes function as imperatives, which is reflected in many translations of this passage. However, in light of Paul's purposeful use of imperatives, including in this passage (cf. 5:25, 33; 6:1–2, 4–5, 9), it is significant that the apostle chooses a participle to convey the idea of submission, subordinating it to the work of the Spirit and portraying it as a result thereof. Effectively, though, the participle carries a sense of command, but one that is derived from the command to be filled by the Spirit.

The idea of submitting to one another (**ἀλλήλοις**) would likely have seemed strange to an audience who understood household relations in hierarchical terms. How can two people in unequal positions submit to one another? How can someone in authority submit themselves to someone under their authority? There are two elements that explain such a counterintuitive command. The first is the absolute lordship of Christ. Since all are in submission to Christ as members of the body, they are all in equal footing in this respect, and that makes mutual submission possible even in socially uneven relationships. The second, as Paul will make clear, is that those in positions of authority in the household—whether husbands, parents, or masters—are not to abuse their position but rather adopt a loving, self-sacrificial posture, which effectively makes them subject to those they are called to love and nurture.

21b	**ἐν φόβῳ Χριστοῦ.**		
	out of reverence of Christ		
ἐν ἐν	out of *en*	---	prep
φόβῳ φόβος	reverence ***pho***·*bō*	DAT SG MASC	noun
Χριστοῦ Χριστός	of Christ *Chri*·***stou***	GEN SG MASC	noun

The noun **φόβῳ** literally means "fear" but is here used to denote reverence rather than terror.

5:22–24

22a Αἱ γυναῖκες τοῖς ἰδίοις ἀνδράσιν

*Hai gy**nai**kes **tois** i**di**ois an**dra**sin*

Wives [submit] to [your] husbands

22b ὡς τῷ κυρίῳ,

*hōs **tō** ky**ri**ō,*

as to the Lord,

23a ὅτι ἀνήρ ἐστιν κεφαλὴ τῆς γυναικὸς

ho**ti a**nēr** estin kepha**lē** **tēs** gynai**kos

because the husband is the head of the wife

23b ὡς καὶ ὁ χριστὸς κεφαλὴ τῆς ἐκκλησίας,

*hōs **kai** ho chri**stos** kepha**lē** **tēs** ekklē**si**as,*

as also Christ is the head of the church—

23c αὐτὸς σωτὴρ τοῦ σώματος.

*au**tos** sō**tēr** **tou** **sō**matos.*

himself [being] the savior of the body.

24a ἀλλὰ ὡς ἡ ἐκκλησία ὑποτάσσεται τῷ χριστῷ,

*al**la** hōs hē ekklē**si**a hypo**tas**setai **tō** chri**stō**,*

But as the church submits to Christ,

24b οὕτως καὶ αἱ γυναῖκες τοῖς ἀνδράσιν ἐν παντί.

***hou**tōs **kai** hai gy**nai**kes **tois** an**dra**sin en pan**ti**.*

thus also the wives [should submit]
to [their] husbands in everything.

22a	Αἱ γυναῖκες τοῖς ἰδίοις ἀνδράσιν		
	Wives [submit] to [your] husbands		
Αἱ ὁ	the *Hai*	NOM PL FEM	article
γυναῖκες γυνή	wives *gy·**nai**·kes*	NOM PL FEM	noun
τοῖς ὁ	to the ***tois***	DAT PL MASC	article
ἰδίοις ἴδιος	(to) their *i·**di**·ois*	DAT PL MASC	adj
ἀνδράσιν ἀνήρ	(to) husbands *an·**dra**·sin*	DAT PL MASC	noun

The verb "submit" is not in the Greek text but is implied from the previous verse.

22b	ὡς τῷ κυρίῳ,		
	as to the Lord,		
ὡς ὡς	as *hōs*	---	adv
τῷ ὁ	to the ***tō***	DAT SG MASC	article
κυρίῳ κύριος	(to) Lord *ky·**ri**·ō*	DAT SG MASC	noun

The household codes are punctuated with comparative phrases—note the conjunctions **ὡς** ("as") in 5:22–24, 28, 33; 6:5–7 and **καθὼς** ("just as") in 5:25, 29, as well as the adverb **οὕτως** ("in this way") in 5:24, 28, 33—which Paul uses to ground the admonitions for interactions among family members in Christ's relationship with the church. Here, the comparative clause **ὡς τῷ κυρίῳ** ("as to the Lord") indicates that the posture of the wives' submission to Christ should inform their submission to their husbands, since Christ is the one to whom they are ultimately subject. The same principle is reflected in the admonition to slaves to render service to their masters "as to the Lord and not to men" (6:7).

23a **ὅτι ἀνήρ ἐστιν κεφαλὴ τῆς γυναικὸς**

because the husband is the head of the wife

ὅτι ὅτι	because ***ho*** *·ti*	---	conj
ἀνήρ ἀνήρ	husband *a·* ***nēr***	NOM SG MASC	noun
ἐστιν εἰμί	(he) is *e·stin*	PRES ACT IND 3RD SG	verb
κεφαλὴ κεφαλή	head *ke·pha·* ***lē***	NOM SG FEM	noun
τῆς ὁ	of the ***tēs***	GEN SG FEM	article
γυναικὸς γυνή	(of) wife *gy·nai·* ***kos***	GEN SG FEM	noun

Paul explains the husband's role as the "head" (**κεφαλὴ**) of the wife in relation to Christ's headship over the church, which he discusses in 1:22 and 4:15 in reference to Christ's supremacy over all things and his role as the source of the growth of the body. Although much discussion has ensued concerning the exact sense of the "head" metaphor in 5:23, the context of submission suggests that "authority" is the most immediate meaning in view (cf. 1 Cor 11:3–10). This is also how an audience familiar with the hierarchical structure of the household would have understood the metaphor. Paul's understanding of this authority, however, has as a paradigm Christ's sacrificial love for the church, which inevitably informs the notion of authority in the passage. Rather than in power, authority is expressed in love.

23b **ὡς καὶ ὁ χριστὸς κεφαλὴ τῆς ἐκκλησίας,**

as also Christ is the head of the church—

ὡς ὡς	as *hōs*	---	adv
καὶ καί	also ***kai***	---	conj
ὁ ὁ	the *ho*	NOM SG MASC	article
χριστὸς Χριστός	Christ *chri·* ***stos***	NOM SG MASC	noun
κεφαλὴ κεφαλή	head *ke·pha·* ***lē***	NOM SG FEM	noun

τῆς ὁ	of the *tēs*	GEN SG FEM	article
ἐκκλησίας ἐκκλησία	(of) church *ek·klē·**si**·as*	GEN SG FEM	noun

23c **αὐτὸς σωτὴρ τοῦ σώματος.**

himself [being] the savior of the body.

αὐτὸς αὐτός	himself *au·**tos***	3RD NOM SG	personal pron
σωτὴρ σωτήρ	savior *sō·**tēr***	NOM SG MASC	noun
τοῦ ὁ	of the ***tou***	GEN SG NEUT	article
σώματος σῶμα	(of) body ***sō**·ma·tos*	GEN SG NEUT	noun

The phrase **αὐτὸς σωτὴρ τοῦ σώματος** ("himself [being] the savior of the body") explains the way in which Christ is understood as head of the church, i.e., by his act of saving her. Paul's use of the contrastive conjunction **ἀλλὰ** (but) in the next verse, although difficult, may suggest that there is some disjunction in the metaphor as it relates to Christ and to husbands—husbands are not saviors of their wives. However, the principle that Christ's authority over the church is ultimately predicated on his self-sacrificial act of salvation will inform Paul's command for husbands to love their wives. The self-giving impetus of Christ's authority over the church should guide the husbands in their position of authority. The issue is not authority for the sake of authority but authority exercised for the sake of the other. Most importantly, the paradigm of Christ's self-giving authority should inform the wives' understanding of their submission to their husbands. The command is not simply for them to submit to authority in an unqualified manner but to submit to authority that is expressed in love.

24a **ἀλλὰ ὡς ἡ ἐκκλησία ὑποτάσσεται τῷ χριστῷ,**

But as the church submits to Christ,

ἀλλὰ ἀλλά	but *al·**la***	---	conj

ὡς ὡς	as *hōs*	---	adv
ἡ ὁ	the *hē*	NOM SG FEM	article
ἐκκλησία ἐκκλησία	church *ek·klē·**si**·a*	NOM SG FEM	noun
ὑποτάσσεται ὑποτάσσω	(it) submits *hy·po·**tas**·se·tai*	PRES PASS IND 3RD SG	verb
τῷ ὁ	to the ***tō***	DAT SG MASC	article
χριστῷ Χριστός	(to) Christ *chri·**stō***	DAT SG MASC	noun

24b **οὕτως καὶ αἱ γυναῖκες τοῖς ἀνδράσιν ἐν παντί.**

thus also the wives [should submit] to [their] husbands in everything.

οὕτως οὕτως	thus ***hou**·tōs*	---	adv
καὶ καί	also ***kai***	---	conj
αἱ ὁ	the *hai*	NOM PL FEM	article
γυναῖκες γυνή	wives *gy·**nai**·kes*	NOM PL FEM	noun
τοῖς ὁ	to the ***tois***	DAT PL MASC	article
ἀνδράσιν ἀνήρ	(to) husbands *an·**dra**·sin*	DAT PL MASC	noun
ἐν ἐν	in *en*	---	prep
παντί πᾶς	everything *pan·**ti***	DAT SG NEUT	adj

The unqualified **ἐν παντί** ("everything") has caused discomfort in many interpreters. However, this is likely another instance of hyperbolic language so common in Ephesians (Eph 1:8, 23; 4:6; 5:9, 24; 6:18), here encouraging an unreserved relationship. More importantly, the notion of sacrificial love that shapes the entire discourse also plays an important part here. The wives' submission "in everything" to their husbands is "as the church submits to Christ." Therefore, the paradigm of Christ's loving headship over the church determines the scope of "everything." In other words, this unreserved submission is only possible in the context of the love that finds its ultimate meaning in Christ. Any attempt to justify unqualified subjugation, particularly abusive actions, on the basis of this text is a profound violation of its meaning.

5:25–33

25a Οἱ ἄνδρες, ἀγαπᾶτε τὰς γυναῖκας,

Hoi andres, agapate tas gynaikas,

Husbands, love [your] wives,

25b καθὼς καὶ ὁ χριστὸς ἠγάπησεν τὴν ἐκκλησίαν

kathōs kai ho christos ēgapēsen tēn ekklēsian

just as also Christ loved the church

25c καὶ ἑαυτὸν παρέδωκεν ὑπὲρ αὐτῆς,

kai heauton paredōken hyper autēs,

and gave himself for her,

26 ἵνα αὐτὴν ἁγιάσῃ καθαρίσας

hina autēn hagiasē katharisas

τῷ λουτρῷ τοῦ ὕδατος ἐν ῥήματι,

tō loutrō tou hydatos en rhēmati,

so that he should sanctify her, having cleansed [her]
by the washing of water with the word,

27a ἵνα παραστήσῃ αὐτὸς ἑαυτῷ ἔνδοξον τὴν ἐκκλησίαν,

hina parastēsē autos heautō endoxon tēn ekklēsian,

So that he should present the church to himself as glorious,

27b μὴ ἔχουσαν σπίλον ἢ ῥυτίδα ἤ τι τῶν τοιούτων,

mē echousan spilon ē rhytida ē ti tōn toioutōn,

not having a stain or a wrinkle or anything of such kind,

27c ἀλλ᾽ ἵνα ᾖ ἁγία καὶ ἄμωμος.

all' hina ē hagia kai amōmos.

but that she should be holy and blameless.

28a οὕτως ὀφείλουσιν [καὶ] οἱ ἄνδρες

houtōs opheilousin kai hoi andres

ἀγαπᾶν τὰς ἑαυτῶν γυναῖκας

agapan tas heautōn gynaikas

In the same way, husbands also ought to love their own wives

28b ὡς τὰ ἑαυτῶν σώματα·

hōs ta heautōn sōmata;

as their own bodies.

28c ὁ ἀγαπῶν τὴν ἑαυτοῦ γυναῖκα ἑαυτὸν ἀγαπᾷ,

ho agapōn tēn heautou gynaika heauton agapa

He who loves his own wife loves himself,

29a οὐδεὶς γάρ ποτε τὴν ἑαυτοῦ σάρκα ἐμίσησεν,

oudeis gar pote tēn heautou sarka emisēsen,

For no one ever hated his own flesh,

29b ἀλλὰ ἐκτρέφει καὶ θάλπει αὐτήν,

alla ektrephei kai thalpei autēn,

but nourishes and cares for it,

29c καθὼς καὶ ὁ χριστὸς τὴν ἐκκλησίαν,

kathōs kai ho christos tēn ekklēsian,

just as also Christ [does] the church,

30 ὅτι μέλη ἐσμὲν τοῦ σώματος αὐτοῦ.

hoti melē esmen tou sōmatos autou.

because we are members of his body.

31a ἀντὶ τούτου καταλείψει ἄνθρωπος

anti toutou kataleipsei anthrōpos

τὸν πατέρα καὶ τὴν μητέρα

ton patera kai tēn mētera

For this reason a man will leave
[his] father and mother

31b καὶ προσκολληθήσεται πρὸς τὴν γυναῖκα αὐτοῦ,

kai proskollēthēsetai pros tēn gynaika autou,

and will be joined to his wife,

31c καὶ ἔσονται οἱ δύο εἰς σάρκα μίαν.

kai esontai hoi dyo eis sarka mian.

and the two will be one flesh.

32a τὸ μυστήριον τοῦτο μέγα ἐστίν,

to mystērion touto mega estin,

This mystery is great,

32b ἐγὼ δὲ λέγω εἰς Χριστὸν καὶ εἰς τὴν ἐκκλησίαν.

egō de legō eis Christon kai eis tēn ekklēsian.

but I myself am speaking about Christ and the church.

33a πλὴν καὶ ὑμεῖς

plēn kai hymeis

Nevertheless, you—

33b οἱ καθ᾽ ἕνα ἕκαστος

hoi kath' hena hekastos

each one of you—

33c τὴν ἑαυτοῦ γυναῖκα οὕτως ἀγαπάτω ὡς ἑαυτόν,

tēn heautou gynaika houtōs agapatō hōs heauton,

should also love his own wife as himself in this way,

33d ἡ δὲ γυνὴ ἵνα φοβῆται τὸν ἄνδρα.

hē dē gynē hina phobētai ton andra.

and the wife should respect the husband.

25a	**Οἱ ἄνδρες, ἀγαπᾶτε τὰς γυναῖκας,**
	Husbands, love [your] wives,

Οἱ ὁ	the *Hoi*	NOM PL MASC	article
ἄνδρες ἀνήρ	husbands *an·dres*	NOM PL MASC	noun
ἀγαπᾶτε ἀγαπάω	(you all) love *a·ga·pa·te*	PRES ACT IMPV 2ND PL	verb
τὰς ὁ	the *tas*	ACC PL FEM	article
γυναῖκας γυνή	wives *gy·nai·kas*	ACC PL FEM	noun

Although the imperative for husbands to love their wives (**ἀγαπᾶτε**) can be found in other ancient texts, Paul brings it to another level by stating that marital love is patterned upon Christ's self-sacrificial giving for the church. The command also recalls Eph 5:2 ("walk in love"), which comes with a similar comparison to Christ's sacrifice for the church. For Paul, Christ's love is the fundamental paradigm that informs love in human relationships.

25b	**καθὼς καὶ ὁ χριστὸς ἠγάπησεν τὴν ἐκκλησίαν**
	just as also Christ loved the church

καθὼς καθώς	just as *ka·thōs*	---	adv
καὶ καί	also *kai*	---	conj
ὁ ὁ	the *ho*	NOM SG MASC	article

χριστὸς Χριστός	Christ *chri·**stos***	NOM SG MASC	noun
ἠγάπησεν ἀγαπάω	(he) loved *ē·**ga**·pē·sen*	AOR ACT IND 3RD SG	verb
τὴν ὁ	the ***tēn***	ACC SG FEM	article
ἐκκλησίαν ἐκκλησία	church *ek·klē·**si**·an*	ACC SG FEM	noun

25c **καὶ ἑαυτὸν παρέδωκεν ὑπὲρ αὐτῆς,**

and gave himself for her,

καὶ καί	and ***kai***	---	conj
ἑαυτὸν ἑαυτοῦ	himself *he·au·**ton***	3RD ACC SG MASC	reflexive pron
παρέδωκεν παραδίδωμι	(he) gave *par·**e**·dō·ken*	AOR ACT IND 3RD SG	verb
ὑπὲρ ὑπέρ	for *hy·**per***	---	prep
αὐτῆς αὐτός	her *au·**tēs***	3RD GEN SG	personal pron

26 **ἵνα αὐτὴν ἁγιάσῃ καθαρίσας**
τῷ λουτρῷ τοῦ ὕδατος ἐν ῥήματι,

so that he should sanctify her, having cleansed [her]
by the washing of water with the word,

ἵνα ἵνα	so that ***hi**·na*	---	conj
αὐτὴν αὐτός	her *au·**tēn***	3RD ACC SG	personal pron
ἁγιάσῃ ἁγιάζω	he should sanctify *ha·gi·**a**·sē*	AOR ACT SUBJ 3RD SG	verb
καθαρίσας καθαρίζω	(he) having cleansed *ka·tha·**ri**·sas*	AOR ACT PTCP NOM SG MASC	verb
τῷ ὁ	her ***tō***	DAT SG NEUT	article
λουτρῷ λουτρόν	by washing *lou·**trō***	DAT SG NEUT	noun

τοῦ ὁ	of the ***tou***	GEN SG NEUT	article
ὕδατος ὕδωρ	(of) water ***hy***·*da*·*tos*	GEN SG NEUT	noun
ἐν ἐν	with *en*	---	prep
ῥήματι ῥῆμα	word ***rhē***·*ma*·*ti*	DAT SG NEUT	noun

The aorist participle **καθαρίσας** ("having cleansed") denotes a perfective aspect that conveys an action holistically: the cleansing of the church is envisioned as an accomplished reality—the result of Christ's self-giving. This is in line with Paul's view of the exalted church in 2:5–6—a "snapshot" of a spiritual reality that is still unfolding in an "already/not yet" continuum and that will climax with the presentation of the church as holy and blameless to Christ (cf. Rev 19:7). In other words, Christ has already done what is necessary to present the church blameless to himself, but that cleansing is still unfolding in history until its final consummation.

The word **ῥήματι** ("word") is likely a reference to the preached gospel (cf. Rom 10:8). The image of washing with water and the presentation of the church as radiant, without a stain or wrinkle, may have as a background the ancient baths that were given to brides in preparation for the wedding ceremony. Echoes of Ezek 16:8–14, which draws from the same image, may also be in play here.

27a **ἵνα παραστήσῃ αὐτὸς ἑαυτῷ ἔνδοξον τὴν ἐκκλησίαν,**

So that he should present the church to himself as glorious,

ἵνα ἵνα	so that ***hi***·*na*	---	conj
παραστήσῃ παρίστημι	he should present *pa*·*ra*·***stē***·*sē*	AOR ACT SUBJ 3RD SG	verb
αὐτὸς αὐτός	he *au*·***tos***	3RD NOM SG	personal pron
ἑαυτῷ ἑαυτοῦ	to himself *he*·*au*·***tō***	3RD DAT SG MASC	reflexive pron
ἔνδοξον ἔνδοξος	glorious ***en***·*do*·*xon*	ACC SG FEM	adj
τὴν ὁ	the ***tēn***	ACC SG FEM	article
ἐκκλησίαν ἐκκλησία	church *ek*·*klē*·***si***·*an*	ACC SG FEM	noun

Paul uses reflexive language throughout the discourse to speak of both Christ and the husbands. Christ gave himself (**ἑαυτὸν**) for the church (5:25) and presents the church to himself (**ἑαυτῷ**, 5:27). The husbands should love their own (**ἑαυτῶν**) wives as their own (**ἑαυτῶν**) bodies (5:28). The one loving his own (**ἑαυτοῦ**) wife loves himself (**ἑαυτὸν**, 5:28). No one hates his own (**ἑαυτοῦ**) flesh (5:29). The husband should love his own (**ἑαυτοῦ**) wife as himself (**ἑαυτόν**, 5:33). The repetition of the reflexive language creates a sense of profound connection between the husband and the wife, which is predicated on the fact that they are one flesh (5:31), a connection that Paul also understands as a mysterious union between Christ and the church (5:32).

27b **μὴ ἔχουσαν σπίλον ἢ ῥυτίδα ἤ τι τῶν τοιούτων,**

not having a stain or a wrinkle or anything of such kind,

μὴ μή	not *mē*	---	particle
ἔχουσαν ἔχω	(it) having *e·chou·san*	PRES ACT PTCP ACC SG FEM	verb
σπίλον σπίλος	stain *spi·lon*	ACC SG MASC	noun
ἢ ἤ	or *ē*	---	particle
ῥυτίδα ῥυτίς	wrinkle *rhy·ti·da*	ACC SG FEM	noun
ἤ ἤ	or *ē*	---	particle
τι τίς~1	anything *ti*	ACC SG NEUT	indef pron
τῶν ὁ	of the *tōn*	GEN PL NEUT	article
τοιούτων τοιοῦτος	(of) such kind *toi·ou·tōn*	GEN PL NEUT	demonstr pron

27c **ἀλλ' ἵνα ᾖ ἁγία καὶ ἄμωμος.**

but that she should be holy and blameless.

ἀλλ' ἀλλά	but *all'*	---	conj
ἵνα ἵνα	that *hi·na*	---	conj

ἦ εἰμί	she *ē*	PRES ACT SUBJ 3RD SG	verb
ἁγία ἅγιος	holy *ha·**gi**·a*	NOM SG FEM	adj
καὶ καί	and ***kai***	---	conj
ἄμωμος ἄμωμος	blameless ***a**·mō·mos*	NOM SG FEM	adj

28a **οὕτως ὀφείλουσιν [καὶ] οἱ ἄνδρες ἀγαπᾶν τὰς ἑαυτῶν γυναῖκας**

In the same way, husbands also ought to love their own wives

οὕτως οὕτως	in the same way ***hou**·tōs*	---	adv
ὀφείλουσιν ὀφείλω	(they) ought *o·**phei**·lou·sin*	PRES ACT IND 3RD PL	verb
καὶ καί	also ***kai***	---	conj
οἱ ὁ	the *hoi*	NOM PL MASC	article
ἄνδρες ἀνήρ	husbands ***an**·dres*	NOM PL MASC	noun
ἀγαπᾶν ἀγαπάω	to love *a·ga·**pan***	PRES ACT INF	verb
τὰς ὁ	the/their ***tas***	ACC PL FEM	article
ἑαυτῶν ἑαυτοῦ	own *he·au·**tōn***	3RD GEN PL MASC	reflexive pron
γυναῖκας γυνή	wives *gy·**nai**·kas*	ACC PL FEM	noun

The verb **ὀφείλουσιν** ("ought"), often used with reference to a debt, carries a sense of obligation. Along with the imperative "love" in 5:25, this puts the husband in a situation of dependence on his wife. This is a clear way in which the mutual submission of 5:21 works out in the discourse. Furthermore, the sense of obligation implies that, for Paul, love involves intentionality. Different from modern perceptions of love as a feeling, which is regarded almost as an agent with its own will that comes and goes impulsively, Paul portrays love between a husband and his wife as a commitment and a command.

28b **ὡς τὰ ἑαυτῶν σώματα·**

as their own bodies.

ὡς ὡς	as ***hōs***	---	adv
τὰ ὁ	the/their ***ta***	ACC PL NEUT	article
ἑαυτῶν ἑαυτοῦ	own *he·au·**tōn***	3RD GEN PL MASC	reflexive pron
σώματα σῶμα	bodies ***sō**·ma·ta*	ACC PL NEUT	noun

28c **ὁ ἀγαπῶν τὴν ἑαυτοῦ γυναῖκα ἑαυτὸν ἀγαπᾷ,**

He who loves his own wife loves himself,

ὁ ὁ	the one/he *ho*	NOM SG MASC	article
ἀγαπῶν ἀγαπάω	who loves *a·ga·**pōn***	PRES ACT PTCP NOM SG MASC	verb
τὴν ὁ	the ***tēn***	ACC SG FEM	article
ἑαυτοῦ ἑαυτοῦ	of his/his own *he·au·**tou***	3RD GEN SG MASC	reflexive pron
γυναῖκα γυνή	wife *gy·**nai**·ka*	ACC SG FEM	noun
ἑαυτὸν ἑαυτοῦ	himself *he·au·**ton***	3RD ACC SG MASC	reflexive pron
ἀγαπᾷ ἀγαπάω	(he) loves *a·ga·**pa***	PRES ACT IND 3RD SG	verb

29a **οὐδεὶς γάρ ποτε τὴν ἑαυτοῦ σάρκα ἐμίσησεν,**

For no one ever hated his own flesh,

οὐδεὶς οὐδείς	no one *ou·**deis***	NOM SG MASC	adj
γάρ γάρ	for ***gar***	---	conj
ποτε ποτέ	ever *po·te*	---	particle
τὴν ὁ	the ***tēn***	ACC SG FEM	article

ἑαυτοῦ ἑαυτοῦ	of himself/his own *he·au·**tou***	3RD GEN SG MASC	reflexive pron
σάρκα σάρξ	flesh ***sar**·ka*	ACC SG FEM	noun
ἐμίσησεν μισέω	(he) hated *e·**mi**·sē·sen*	AOR ACT IND 3RD SG	verb

29b **ἀλλὰ ἐκτρέφει καὶ θάλπει αὐτήν,**

but nourishes and cares for it,

ἀλλὰ ἀλλά	but *al·**la***	---	conj
ἐκτρέφει ἐκτρέφω	(he) nourishes *ek·**tre**·phei*	PRES ACT IND 3RD SG	verb
καὶ καί	and ***kai***	---	conj
θάλπει θάλπω	(he) cares for ***thal**·pei*	PRES ACT IND 3RD SG	verb
αὐτήν αὐτός	it *au·**tēn***	3RD ACC SG	personal pron

29c **καθὼς καὶ ὁ χριστὸς τὴν ἐκκλησίαν,**

just as also Christ [does] the church,

καθὼς καθώς	just as *ka·**thōs***	---	adv
καὶ καί	also ***kai***	---	conj
ὁ ὁ	the *ho*	NOM SG MASC	article
χριστὸς Χριστός	Christ *chri·**stos***	NOM SG MASC	noun
τὴν ὁ	the ***tēn***	ACC SG FEM	article
ἐκκλησίαν ἐκκλησία	church *ek·klē·**si**·an*	ACC SG FEM	noun

30 ὅτι μέλη ἐσμὲν τοῦ σώματος αὐτοῦ.

because we are members of his body.

ὅτι ὅτι	because *ho·ti*	---	conj
μέλη μέλος	members *me·lē*	NOM PL NEUT	noun
ἐσμὲν εἰμί	we are *es·men*	PRES ACT IND 1ST PL	verb
τοῦ ὁ	of the *tou*	GEN SG NEUT	article
σώματος σῶμα	(of) body *sō·ma·tos*	GEN SG NEUT	noun
αὐτοῦ αὐτός	of him/his *au·tou*	3RD GEN SG	personal pron

Paul portrays husband and wife in a physical union through the use of the words "bodies" (**σώματα** [28b]) and "flesh" (**σάρκα** [29a]). This is predicated on the mystical union between husband and wife (5:33), which makes loving the wife an act of self-love, and conversely, hating the wife an act of self-hatred. At the same time, Paul grounds the husband's care for his wife in Christ's care for the members "of his body" (**τοῦ σώματος αὐτοῦ**), i.e., the church, of which both husbands and wives are members. The reference to the body of Christ is not incidental, as if Paul were simply digressing. Rather, given Paul's purposeful use of the analogy of the body to refer to the church throughout the letter (Eph 1:23; 2:16; 4:4, 12, 16; 5:23), the apostle wants to tie the husbands' mandate to love their wives with one of the most important theological realities explored in the letter thus far. In this way, Paul at the same time situates the husbands' mandate to love their wives in relation to their most intimate understanding of themselves—their body—and in relation to their understanding that they and their wives are members of Christ's body.

31a ἀντὶ τούτου καταλείψει ἄνθρωπος τὸν πατέρα καὶ τὴν μητέρα

For this reason a man will leave [his] father and mother

ἀντὶ ἀντί	for *anti*	---	prep
τούτου οὗτος	this reason *tou·tou*	GEN SG NEUT	demonstr pron

καταλείψει καταλείπω	(he) will leave *ka·ta·**lei**·psei*	FUT ACT IND 3RD SG	verb
ἄνθρωπος ἄνθρωπος	man ***an**·thrō·pos*	NOM SG MASC	noun
τὸν ὁ	the ***ton***	ACC SG MASC	article
πατέρα πατήρ	father *pa·**te**·ra*	ACC SG MASC	noun
καὶ καί	and ***kai***	---	conj
τὴν ὁ	the ***tēn***	ACC SG FEM	article
μητέρα μήτηρ	mother *mē·**te**·ra*	ACC SG FEM	noun

Paul offers a quotation from Gen 2:24 as the basis of what he has just said concerning the union between husband and wife on the one hand and Christ and the church on the other. The quotation would explain more directly the former, since that is the meaning in its original context, but Paul applies it explicitly, and perhaps counterintuitively, to the union of Christ with his church. In this way, Paul establishes marriage as a prefiguration of the union between Christ and the church, which is, by Paul's own admission, a great mystery (v. 32a).

31b **καὶ προσκολληθήσεται πρὸς τὴν γυναῖκα αὐτοῦ,**

and will be joined to his wife,

καὶ καί	and ***kai***	---	conj
προσκολληθήσεται προσκολλάω	(he) will be joined *pros·kol·lē·**thē**·se·tai*	FUT PASS IND 3RD SG	verb
πρὸς πρός	to ***pros***	---	prep
τὴν ὁ	the ***tēn***	ACC SG FEM	article
γυναῖκα γυνή	wife *gy·**nai**·ka*	ACC SG FEM	noun
αὐτοῦ αὐτός	of him/his *au·**tou***	3RD GEN SG	personal pron

31c	**καὶ ἔσονται οἱ δύο εἰς σάρκα μίαν.**

and the two will be one flesh.

καὶ καί	and ***kai***	---	conj
ἔσονται εἰμί	(they) will be *e·son·tai*	FUT MID IND 3RD PL	verb
οἱ ὁ	the *hoi*	NOM PL MASC	article
δύο δύο	two ***dy**·o*	---	number
εἰς εἰς	into *eis*	---	prep
σάρκα σάρξ	flesh ***sar**·ka*	ACC SG FEM	noun
μίαν εἷς	one ***mi**·an*	ACC SG FEM	adj

32a	**τὸ μυστήριον τοῦτο μέγα ἐστίν,**

This mystery is great,

τὸ ὁ	the ***to***	NOM SG NEUT	article
μυστήριον μυστήριον	mystery *my·**stē**·ri·on*	NOM SG NEUT	noun
τοῦτο οὗτος	this ***tou**·to*	NOM SG NEUT	demonstr pron
μέγα μέγας	great ***me**·ga*	NOM SG NEUT	adj
ἐστίν εἰμί	(it) is *e·**stin***	PRES ACT IND 3RD SG	verb

The phrase **ἔσονται οἱ δύο εἰς σάρκα μίαν** ("the two will be one flesh"), although part of the citation from Gen 2:24, recalls Eph 2:15 and the creation of one new person in Christ out of two groups, Jews and gentiles, with new creation overtones (**τοὺς δύο κτίσῃ ἐν αὐτῷ εἰς ἕνα καινὸν ἄνθρωπον**). Interestingly, Paul also considers the union of Jews and gentiles into one body in Christ a "mystery" (**μυστήριον**) (cf. Eph 3:3–6). This is perhaps part of Paul's understanding of how marriage reflects the reality of the church. The mysterious union between husband and wife in one flesh is, like the mysterious oneness of the body of the church, a union of two into one (husband and wife; Jew and gentile) and a union with Christ (**ἐν αὐτῷ**).

32b	**ἐγὼ δὲ λέγω εἰς Χριστὸν καὶ εἰς τὴν ἐκκλησίαν.**		
	but I myself am speaking about Christ and the church.		
ἐγὼ ἐγώ	I *e·**gō***	1ST NOM SG	pron
δὲ δέ	but ***de***	---	conj
λέγω λέγω	(I) am speaking ***le**·gō*	PRES ACT IND 1ST SG	verb
εἰς εἰς	about *eis*	---	prep
Χριστὸν Χριστός	Christ *Chri·**ston***	ACC SG MASC	noun
καὶ καί	and ***kai***	---	conj
εἰς εἰς	about *eis*	---	prep
τὴν ὁ	the ***tēn***	ACC SG FEM	article
ἐκκλησίαν ἐκκλησία	church *ek·klē·**si**·an*	ACC SG FEM	noun

33a	**πλὴν καὶ ὑμεῖς**		
	Nevertheless, you—		
πλὴν πλήν	nevertheless ***plēn***	---	adv
καὶ καί	also ***kai***	---	conj
ὑμεῖς σύ	you (all) *hy·**meis***	2ND NOM PL	pron

33b οἱ καθ᾽ ἕνα ἕκαστος

each one of you—

οἱ ὁ	the (ones) *hoi*	NOM PL MASC	article
καθ᾽ κατά	according to *kath'*	---	prep
ἕνα εἷς	one ***he***·*na*	ACC SG MASC	adj
ἕκαστος ἕκαστος	each ***he***·*ka*·*stos*	NOM SG MASC	adj

33c τὴν ἑαυτοῦ γυναῖκα οὕτως ἀγαπάτω ὡς ἑαυτόν,

should also love his own wife as himself in this way,

τὴν ὁ	the ***tēn***	ACC SG FEM	article
ἑαυτοῦ ἑαυτοῦ	of himself/his own *he*·*au*·***tou***	3RD GEN SG MASC	reflexive pron
γυναῖκα γυνή	wife *gy*·***nai***·*ka*	ACC SG FEM	noun
οὕτως οὕτως	in this way ***hou***·*tōs*	---	adv
ἀγαπάτω ἀγαπάω	(he) should love *a*·*ga*·***pa***·*tō*	PRES ACT IMPV 3RD SG	verb
ὡς ὡς	as *hōs*	---	adv
ἑαυτόν ἑαυτοῦ	himself *he*·*au*·***ton***	3RD ACC SG MASC	reflexive pron

33d ἡ δὲ γυνὴ ἵνα φοβῆται τὸν ἄνδρα.

and the wife should respect the husband.

ἡ ὁ	the *hē*	NOM SG FEM	article
δὲ δέ	and ***dē***	---	conj
γυνὴ γυνή	wife *gy*·***nē***	NOM SG FEM	noun
ἵνα ἵνα	in order that ***hi***·*na*	---	conj

φοβῆται φοβέω	(she) should respect *pho*·***bē***·*tai*	PRES MID/PASS SUBJ 3RD SG	verb
τὸν ὁ	the ***ton***	ACC SG MASC	article
ἄνδρα ἀνήρ	husband ***an***·*dra*	ACC SG MASC	noun

6:1–3

1a Τὰ τέκνα, ὑπακούετε τοῖς γονεῦσιν ὑμῶν ἐν κυρίῳ,

Ta tekna, hypakouete tois goneusin hymōn en kyriō,

Children, obey your parents in the Lord,

1b τοῦτο γάρ ἐστιν δίκαιον·

touto gar estin dikaion;

for this is right.

2a τίμα τὸν πατέρα σου καὶ τὴν μητέρα,

tima ton patera sou kai tēn mētera,

Honor your father and mother,

2b ἥτις ἐστὶν ἐντολὴ πρώτη ἐν ἐπαγγελίᾳ,

hētis estin entolē prōtē en epangelia,

which is the first commandment with a promise,

3a ἵνα εὖ σοι γένηται

hina eu soi genētai

so that it should be well with you

3b καὶ ἔσῃ μακροχρόνιος ἐπὶ τῆς γῆς.

kai esē makrochronios epi tēs gēs.

and you will live long on the earth.

1a **Τὰ τέκνα, ὑπακούετε τοῖς γονεῦσιν ὑμῶν ἐν κυρίῳ,**

Children, obey your parents in the Lord,

Τὰ ὁ	the *Ta*	NOM PL NEUT	article

τέκνα τέκνον	children ***tek***·*na*	NOM PL NEUT	noun
ὑπακούετε ὑπακούω	(you all) obey *hy*·*pa*·***kou***·*e*·*te*	PRES ACT IMPV 2ND PL	verb
τοῖς ὁ	the ***tois***	DAT PL MASC	article
γονεῦσιν γονεύς	parents *go*·***neu***·*sin*	DAT PL MASC	noun
ὑμῶν σύ	of you (all)/your *hy*·***mōn***	2ND GEN PL	pron
ἐν ἐν	in *en*	---	prep
κυρίῳ κύριος	Lord *ky*·***ri***·*ō*	DAT SG MASC	noun

1b **τοῦτο γάρ ἐστιν δίκαιον·**

for this is right.

τοῦτο οὗτος	this ***tou***·*to*	NOM SG NEUT	demonstr pron
γάρ γάρ	for ***gar***	---	conj
ἐστιν εἰμί	(it) is *e*·*stin*	PRES ACT IND 3RD SG	verb
δίκαιον δίκαιος	right ***di***·*kai*·*on*	NOM SG NEUT	adj

2a **τίμα τὸν πατέρα σου καὶ τὴν μητέρα,**

Honor your father and mother,

τίμα τιμάω	(you) honor ***ti***·*ma*	PRES ACT IMPV 2ND SG	verb
τὸν ὁ	the ***ton***	ACC SG MASC	article
πατέρα πατήρ	father *pa*·***te***·*ra*	ACC SG MASC	noun
σου σύ	of you/your *sou*	2ND GEN SG	pron
καὶ καί	and ***kai***	---	conj

τὴν ὁ	the ***tēn***	ACC SG FEM	article
μητέρα μήτηρ	mother *mē*·***te***·*ra*	ACC SG FEM	noun

2b **ἥτις ἐστὶν ἐντολὴ πρώτη ἐν ἐπαγγελίᾳ,**

which is the first commandment with a promise,

ἥτις ὅστις	which ***hē***·*tis*	NOM SG FEM	relative pron
ἐστὶν εἰμί	(it) is *e*·***stin***	PRES ACT IND 3RD SG	verb
ἐντολὴ ἐντολή	commandment *en*·*to*·***lē***	NOM SG FEM	noun
πρώτη πρῶτος	first ***prō***·*tē*	NOM SG FEM	adj
ἐν ἐν	with *en*	---	prep
ἐπαγγελίᾳ ἐπαγγελία	promise *e*·*pan*·*ge*·***li***·*a*	DAT SG FEM	noun

3a **ἵνα εὖ σοι γένηται**

so that it should be well with you

ἵνα ἵνα	so that ***hi***·*na*	---	conj
εὖ εὖ	well ***eu***	---	adv
σοι σύ	with you *soi*	2ND DAT SG	pron
γένηται γίνομαι	it should be ***ge***·*nē*·*tai*	AOR MID SUBJ 3RD SG	verb

3b **καὶ ἔσῃ μακροχρόνιος ἐπὶ τῆς γῆς.**

and you will live long on the earth.

καὶ καί	and ***kai***	---	conj

ἔσῃ εἰμί	you (all) will be ***e***·*sē*	FUT MID IND 2ND SG	verb
μακροχρόνιος μακροχρόνιος	long-lived *ma*·*kro*·***chro***·*ni*·*os*	NOM SG MASC	adj
ἐπὶ ἐπί	on *e*·***pi***	---	prep
τῆς ὁ	the ***tēs***	GEN SG FEM	article
γῆς γῆ	earth ***gēs***	GEN SG FEM	noun

4a Καὶ οἱ πατέρες, μὴ παροργίζετε τὰ τέκνα ὑμῶν,

__kai__ hoi pa__te__res, __mē__ paror__gi__zete __ta tek__na hy__mōn__,

And Fathers, do not provoke your children to anger,

4b ἀλλὰ ἐκτρέφετε αὐτὰ

al__la__ ek__tre__phete au__ta__

but nurture them

4c ἐν παιδείᾳ καὶ νουθεσίᾳ Κυρίου.

en paidei__a kai__ nouthe__si__a Ky__ri__ou.

in the instruction and admonition of the Lord.

4a **Καὶ οἱ πατέρες, μὴ παροργίζετε τὰ τέκνα ὑμῶν,**

And Fathers, do not provoke your children to anger,

Καὶ καί	and ***kai***	---	conj
οἱ ὁ	the *hoi*	NOM PL MASC	article
πατέρες πατήρ	fathers *pa·__te__·res*	NOM PL MASC	noun
μὴ μή	not ***mē***	---	particle
παροργίζετε παροργίζω	(you all) provoke to anger *par·or·__gi__·ze·te*	PRES ACT IMPV 2ND PL	verb
τὰ ὁ	the ***ta***	ACC PL NEUT	article
τέκνα τέκνον	children *__tek__·na*	ACC PL NEUT	noun
ὑμῶν σύ	of you (all)/your *hy·__mōn__*	2ND GEN PL	pron

The verb **παροργίζω**, meaning "to provoke to anger," is related to the noun **παροργισμῷ** used in 4:26 in the admonition against anger. Since Paul seems very concerned with anger in the community, the admonition "not to anger" children is important.

4b	**ἀλλὰ ἐκτρέφετε αὐτὰ**		
	but nurture them		
ἀλλὰ ἀλλά	but *al·**la***	---	conj
ἐκτρέφετε ἐκτρέφω	(you all) nurture *ek·**tre**·phe·te*	PRES ACT IMPV 2ND PL	verb
αὐτὰ αὐτός	them *au·**ta***	3RD ACC PL	personal pron

The word **ἐκτρέφετε** ("nurture") is also used in 5:29 referring to Christ's care for the church. This is a subtle but important way by which Paul connects the relationship between parents and children with the relationship between Christ and the church. After all, this is ultimately the household of God.

4c	**ἐν παιδείᾳ καὶ νουθεσίᾳ Κυρίου.**		
	in the instruction and admonition of the Lord.		
ἐν ἐν	in *en*	---	prep
παιδείᾳ παιδεία	instruction *pai·dei·**a***	DAT SG FEM	noun
καὶ καί	and ***kai***	---	conj
νουθεσίᾳ νουθεσία	admonition *nou·the·**si**·a*	DAT SG FEM	noun
Κυρίου κύριος	of Lord *Ky·**ri**·ou*	GEN SG MASC	noun

6:5–8

5a Οἱ δοῦλοι, ὑπακούετε τοῖς κατὰ σάρκα κυρίοις

*Hoi **dou**loi, hypa**kou**ete **tois** ka**ta** **sar**ka ky**ri**ois*

Slaves, obey [your] masters according to the flesh

5b μετὰ φόβου καὶ τρόμου

*me**ta** **pho**bou **kai** **tro**mou*

with fear and trembling

5c ἐν ἁπλότητι τῆς καρδίας ὑμῶν

*en ha**plo**tēti **tēs** kar**di**as hy**mōn***

with the sincerity of your heart,

5d ὡς τῷ χριστῷ,

*hōs **tō** chri**stō**,*

as [you obey] Christ

6a μὴ κατ᾽ ὀφθαλμοδουλίαν ὡς ἀνθρωπάρεσκοι

***mē** kat' ophthalmodou**li**an hōs anthrō**pa**reskoi*

not as those who serve only to impress, as people-pleasers,

6b ἀλλ᾽ ὡς δοῦλοι Χριστοῦ

*all' hōs **dou**loi Chri**stou***

but as slaves of Christ,

6c ποιοῦντες τὸ θέλημα τοῦ θεοῦ,

*poi**oun**tes **to** **the**lēma **tou** the**ou**,*

doing the will of God,

6d ἐκ ψυχῆς,

***ek** psy**chēs**,*

from the heart,

7a μετ᾽ εὐνοίας δουλεύοντες,

*met' eu**noi**as dou**leu**ontes,*

rendering service with good will,

7b ὡς τῷ κυρίῳ καὶ οὐκ ἀνθρώποις,

*hōs **tō** ky**ri**ō **kai** ouk an**thrō**pois,*

as to the Lord and not to men,

8a εἰδότες ὅτι ἕκαστος,

*ei**do**tes **ho**ti **he**kastos,*

knowing that each one,

8b ἐάν τι ποιήσῃ ἀγαθόν,

*e**an** ti poi**ē**sē aga**thon**,*

if he does something good,

8c τοῦτο κομίσεται παρὰ κυρίου,

***tou**to ko**mi**setai pa**ra** ky**ri**ou,*

he will receive this back from the Lord,

8d εἴτε δοῦλος εἴτε ἐλεύθερος.

***ei**tē **dou**los **ei**tē e**leu**theros.*

whether slave or free.

5a **Οἱ δοῦλοι, ὑπακούετε τοῖς κατὰ σάρκα κυρίοις**

Slaves, obey [your] masters according to the flesh

Οἱ ὁ	the *Hoi*	NOM PL MASC	article
δοῦλοι δοῦλος	slaves ***dou**·loi*	NOM PL MASC	noun
ὑπακούετε ὑπακούω	(you all) obey *hy·pa·**kou**·e·te*	PRES ACT IMPV 2ND PL	verb

τοῖς ὁ	the ***tois***	DAT PL MASC	article
κατὰ κατά	according to *ka*·***ta***	---	prep
σάρκα σάρξ	flesh ***sar***·*ka*	ACC SG FEM	noun
κυρίοις κύριος	masters *ky*·***ri***·*ois*	DAT PL MASC	noun

The term **δοῦλοι** refers to someone who belongs to another person. Slavery was a common social practice in the Greco-Roman world. Seeing this sort of admonition in Scripture can be unsettling in light of the oppressive reality of slavery in recent history in America and other parts of the world. Although different from slavery in modern history, especially when it comes to its racial components, slavery in the ancient world is still an oppressive system, often characterized by physical and sexual abuse. The fact that Paul operates with the assumption of slavery relates to its ubiquitous nature as an integral part of the household in his context, something over which the early church has no control. In fact, subverting the institution of slavery would be understood as an attempt to destabilize the empire. However, by emphasizing the slaves' ultimate allegiance to Christ, and situating both slaves and masters as "slaves of Christ" (6:9), Paul creates a dynamic radically different from the normal standards of the time—a dynamic that effectively protected both the slaves' dignity as members of the body of Christ and their lives.

5b **μετὰ φόβου καὶ τρόμου**

with fear and trembling

μετὰ μετά	with *me*·***ta***	---	prep
φόβου φόβος	fear ***pho***·*bou*	GEN SG MASC	noun
καὶ καί	and ***kai***	---	conj
τρόμου τρόμος	trembling ***tro***·*mou*	GEN SG MASC	noun

5c	ἐν ἁπλότητι τῆς καρδίας ὑμῶν		
	with the sincerity of your heart,		
ἐν ἐν	with *en*	---	prep
ἁπλότητι ἁπλότης	sincerity *ha·**plo**·tē·ti*	DAT SG FEM	noun
τῆς ὁ	of the ***tēs***	GEN SG FEM	article
καρδίας καρδία	heart *kar·**di**·as*	GEN SG FEM	noun
ὑμῶν σύ	of you (all)/your *hy·**mōn***	2ND GEN PL	pron

5d	ὡς τῷ χριστῷ,		
	as [you obey] Christ		
ὡς ὡς	as *hōs*	---	adv
τῷ ὁ	the ***tō***	DAT SG MASC	article
χριστῷ Χριστός	Christ *chri·**stō***	DAT SG MASC	noun

We saw this same phrase in 5:22–24. The slaves' ultimate allegiance is to Christ, and their submission to Christ as their Master should inform their obedience to their earthly masters.

6a	μὴ κατ᾽ ὀφθαλμοδουλίαν ὡς ἀνθρωπάρεσκοι		
	not as those who serve only to impress, as people-pleasers,		
μὴ μή	not ***mē***	---	particle
κατ᾽ κατά	as *kat'*	---	prep
ὀφθαλμοδουλίαν ὀφθαλμοδουλία	eye-service *oph·thal·mo·dou·**li**·an*	ACC SG FEM	noun
ὡς ὡς	as *hōs*	---	adv
ἀνθρωπάρεσκοι ἀνθρωπάρεσκος	people-pleasers *an·thrō·**pa**·re·skoi*	NOM PL MASC	adj

6b ἀλλ᾽ ὡς δοῦλοι Χριστοῦ

but as slaves of Christ,

ἀλλ᾽ ἀλλά	but *all'*	---	conj
ὡς ὡς	as *hōs*	---	adv
δοῦλοι δοῦλος	slaves ***dou***·*loi*	NOM PL MASC	noun
Χριστοῦ Χριστός	of Christ *Chri*·***stou***	GEN SG MASC	noun

6c ποιοῦντες τὸ θέλημα τοῦ θεοῦ,

doing the will of God,

ποιοῦντες ποιέω	(you all) doing *poi*·***oun***·*tes*	PRES ACT PTCP NOM PL MASC	verb
τὸ ὁ	the ***to***	ACC SG NEUT	article
θέλημα θέλημα	will ***the***·*lē*·*ma*	ACC SG NEUT	noun
τοῦ ὁ	of the ***tou***	GEN SG MASC	article
θεοῦ θεός	(of) God *the*·***ou***	GEN SG MASC	noun

6d ἐκ ψυχῆς,

from the heart,

ἐκ ἐκ	from ***ek***	---	prep
ψυχῆς ψυχή	soul *psy*·***chēs***	GEN SG FEM	noun

In this admonition to slaves, Paul offers an ethic of work that is applicable to other modern situations, such as paid employment. The standards for a Christian's work ethic are found here—**ποιοῦντες τὸ θέλημα τοῦ θεοῦ, ἐκ ψυχῆς**, "doing the will of God from the heart"—and in v. 7 below—**μετ᾽ εὐνοίας δουλεύοντες, ὡς τῷ κυρίῳ καὶ οὐκ ἀνθρώποις**, "rendering service with good will as to the Lord and not to men."

7a	**μετ᾽ εὐνοίας δουλεύοντες,**		
	rendering service with good will,		

μετ᾽ μετά	with *met᾽*	---	prep
εὐνοίας εὔνοια	good will *eu·**noi**·as*	GEN SG FEM	noun
δουλεύοντες δουλεύω	(you all) rendering service *dou·**leu**·on·tes*	PRES ACT PTCP NOM PL MASC	verb

7b	**ὡς τῷ κυρίῳ καὶ οὐκ ἀνθρώποις,**		
	as to the Lord and not to men,		

ὡς ὡς	as *hōs*	---	adv
τῷ ὁ	to the ***tō***	DAT SG MASC	article
κυρίῳ κύριος	Lord *ky·**ri**·ō*	DAT SG MASC	noun
καὶ καί	and ***kai***	---	conj
οὐκ οὐ	not *ouk*	---	particle
ἀνθρώποις ἄνθρωπος	to men *an·**thrō**·pois*	DAT PL MASC	noun

8a	**εἰδότες ὅτι ἕκαστος,**		
	knowing that each one,		

εἰδότες εἰδώ	(you all) knowing *ei·**do**·tes*	PERF ACT PTCP NOM PL MASC	verb
ὅτι ὅτι	that ***ho**·ti*	---	conj
ἕκαστος ἕκαστος	each (one) ***he**·ka·stos*	NOM SG MASC	adj

8b	**ἐάν τι ποιήσῃ ἀγαθόν,**		
	if he does something good,		
ἐάν ἐάν	if *e·**an***	---	cond
τι τίς~1	something *ti*	ACC SG NEUT	indef pron
ποιήσῃ ποιέω	he does *poi·ē·sē*	AOR ACT SUBJ 3RD SG	verb
ἀγαθόν ἀγαθός	good *a·ga·**thon***	ACC SG NEUT	adj

8c	**τοῦτο κομίσεται παρὰ κυρίου,**		
	he will receive this back from the Lord,		
τοῦτο οὗτος	this ***tou**·to*	ACC SG NEUT	demonstr pron
κομίσεται κομίζω	he will receive back *ko·**mi**·se·tai*	FUT MID IND 3RD SG	verb
παρὰ παρά	from *pa·**ra***	---	prep
κυρίου κύριος	Lord *ky·**ri**·ou*	GEN SG MASC	noun

8d	**εἴτε δοῦλος εἴτε ἐλεύθερος.**		
	whether slave or free.		
εἴτε εἴτε	whether ***ei**·tē*	---	conj
δοῦλος δοῦλος	slave ***dou**·los*	NOM SG MASC	noun
εἴτε εἴτε	whether ***ei**·tē*	---	conj
ἐλεύθερος ἐλεύθερος	free *e·**leu**·the·ros*	NOM SG MASC	adj

6:9

9a Καὶ οἱ κύριοι,

Kai hoi kyrioi,

And masters,

9b τὰ αὐτὰ ποιεῖτε πρὸς αὐτούς,

ta auta poieite pros autous,

do the same to them,

9c ἀνιέντες τὴν ἀπειλήν,

anientes tēn apeilēn,

ceasing to threaten [them],

9d εἰδότες ὅτι καὶ αὐτῶν καὶ ὑμῶν ὁ κύριός
ἐστιν ἐν οὐρανοῖς,

eidotes hoti kai autōn kai hymōn ho kyrios
estin en ouranois,

knowing that the Master over both them and you is in heaven,

9e καὶ προσωποληµψία οὐκ ἔστιν παρ᾽ αὐτῷ.

kai prosōpolēmpsia ouk estin par' autō.

and there is no partiality with him.

9a	**Καὶ οἱ κύριοι,**		
	And masters,		
Καὶ καί	and *Kai*	---	conj
οἱ ὁ	the *hoi*	NOM PL MASC	article

κύριοι κύριος	masters *ky·ri·oi*	NOM PL MASC	noun

9b **τὰ αὐτὰ ποιεῖτε πρὸς αὐτούς,**

do the same to them,

τὰ ὁ	the ***ta***	ACC PL NEUT	article
αὐτὰ αὐτός	the same *au·**ta***	3RD ACC PL	personal pron
ποιεῖτε ποιέω	(you all) do *poi·**ei**·te*	PRES ACT IMPV 2ND PL	verb
πρὸς πρός	to ***pros***	---	prep
αὐτούς αὐτός	them *au·**tous***	3RD ACC PL	personal pron

9c **ἀνιέντες τὴν ἀπειλήν,**

ceasing to threaten [them],

ἀνιέντες ἀνίημι	(you all) ceasing *a·ni·**en**·tes*	PRES ACT PTCP NOM PL MASC	verb
τὴν ὁ	the ***tēn***	ACC SG FEM	article
ἀπειλήν ἀπειλή	threat *a·pei·**lēn***	ACC SG FEM	noun

9d **εἰδότες ὅτι καὶ αὐτῶν καὶ ὑμῶν ὁ κύριός ἐστιν ἐν οὐρανοῖς,**

knowing that the Master over both them and you is in heaven,

εἰδότες εἰδώ	knowing *ei·**do**·tes*	PERF ACT PTCP NOM PL MASC	verb
ὅτι ὅτι	that ***ho**·ti*	---	conj
καὶ καί	both ***kai***	---	conj

αὐτῶν αὐτός	over them *au·**tōn***	3RD GEN PL	personal pron
καὶ καί	and ***kai***	---	conj
ὑμῶν σύ	over you (all) *hy·**mōn***	2ND GEN PL	pron
ὁ ὁ	the *ho*	NOM SG MASC	article
κύριός κύριος	Master ***ky**·ri·os*	NOM SG MASC	noun
ἐστιν εἰμί	(he) is *e·stin*	PRES ACT IND 3RD SG	verb
ἐν ἐν	in *en*	---	prep
οὐρανοῖς οὐρανός	heaven *ou·ra·**nois***	DAT PL MASC	noun

The term **κύριος** is mostly used in Ephesians to refer to Christ as "Lord," and that would be the first association one would make after reading the entire letter. However, by using the term to refer to Christ in his admonition to masters (**κύριοι**), Paul reminds them, through this play on words, what it means to call Jesus "Lord" when it comes to their relationship with their slaves. If Christ is their Master, they are ultimately fellow slaves of Christ along with their slaves since Christ does not allow partiality. This would represent a radical statement in a society that sees slaves as mere property.

9e **καὶ προσωπολημψία οὐκ ἔστιν παρ᾽ αὐτῷ.**

and there is no partiality with him.

καὶ καί	and ***kai***	---	conj
προσωπολημψία προσωπολημψία	partiality *pro·sō·po·lēm·**psi**·a*	NOM SG FEM	noun
οὐκ οὐ	not *ouk*	---	particle
ἔστιν εἰμί	(it) is ***e**·stin*	PRES ACT IND 3RD SG	verb
παρ᾽ παρά	with *par᾽*	---	prep
αὐτῷ αὐτός	him *au·**tō***	3RD DAT SG	personal pron

From Text to Sermon

Main Exegetical Ideas. Believers should relate to one another in their family relations according to their identity as members of the household of God.

Bridge to Theology. This passage is the focus of much theological debate, mostly related to relationships between husband and wife. Some argue that the passage establishes a relevant complementarian relationship between men and women, with men taking the position of authority in the household. Others argue that the text should be read against the historical context of the passage that assumed certain social dynamics that are no longer sustained in the modern world, a view sometimes referred to as egalitarian. These are the two main camps in the debate, but many interpreters fall somewhere in the middle. A thorough treatment of the passage falls beyond the scope of this preaching guide, and the preacher should be diligent in reading the many good technical and pastoral commentaries available (see Hoehner 2002:716–816; Cohick 2020:348–72; and Thielman 2010:365–94) in order to have a more comprehensive understanding of the many issues involved.

What is most important, however, is to focus on the main idea of the passage: household relations, whether ancient or modern, are fundamentally shaped by believers' ultimate identity as those who belong to the household of God. In that framework, our identity as members of God's household means that we are to live with the understanding that God, through Christ, stands above the household as its ultimate *paterfamilias*—the head of the household. Paul is following the logic that he has established in other parts of the letter: God's purpose is to sum up all things in Christ (1:9–10); he gave Christ as head over all things to the church (1:22–23); and Jews and gentiles live as fellow citizens and members of the household of God, with Christ as the cornerstone (2:18–22). Therefore, both the supremacy of Christ over all things and the harmonious living of different people under God's household are the undergirding theological principles of the whole argument. Now, looking more intently at the family unit, Paul applies the same principles. Even within the social hierarchical distinctions assumed in these relationships, believers are to understand that their ultimate identity is that of fellow members of the household of God. They are to submit to one another and have their allegiance to God as the fundamental principle for their relationships.

This reality has two aspects to it. The first is the reality of submission. Where hierarchical submission is assumed—such as in the relationship of wives, children, and slaves to their counterparts—such submission is to be understood in relation to their ultimate submission to Christ. Thus, wives must submit to their husbands "as to the Lord," children must obey their parents "in the Lord," and slaves must obey their masters "as they obey Christ." There is a fundamental understanding of people's direct submission to God informing their social hierarchical relations. Conversely, there is the reality of love. The paradigm for what one may call "hierarchical leadership" in this context is not that of power but that of love. In other words, submission is not submission to hierarchical power but to self-giving love. And the paradigm for such love is nothing less than Christ's own sacrifice for the church. Thus, the relationships are all framed in relation to Christ: husbands should love as Christ, fathers should nurture (see commentary) their children in the teachings of the Lord, and masters should understand that ultimately they are, along with their bondservants, fellow slaves to the supreme Lord. However one sees the hierarchical relationships in the household, it is critical to recognize that the dynamics of the relationships Paul establishes are not patterned on the standard notions of power and hierarchy but on the new reality of the household of God inaugurated by Christ's death and resurrection—a reality in which God's supremacy over all and Christ's self-giving love for the church are the overarching principles for relationships.

Furthermore, tucked in this wider argument is Paul's theological view of marriage. In framing marriage in relation to Christ's mystical union with the church, Paul makes marriage a prefiguration of that greater reality. The union between man and woman into one flesh that happens in the covenant of marriage uniquely expresses, even if mysteriously, the nature of the church's union with Christ. Marriage is, therefore, the closest paradigm available to understand the intricate notion of being in Christ or being united with Christ. That speaks to the important and sacred nature of both marriage and the physical union within it.

It is also interesting that Paul's language of becoming "one" recalls the union between Jews and gentiles in Christ, expressed in 2:15, whereby both become one. These dynamics of mysterious unity should therefore also characterize the unity of the church, not only with Christ but with one another, in his body.

Possible Sermon Structure. ***The social pairings constitute the obvious structure of the passage:***

1 Wives and husbands (5:22–33)
2 Children and parents (6:1–4)
3 Slaves and masters (6:5–9)

Another way to structure the passage is according to Paul's two main emphases in his instructions:

1 Submit to one another as those who belong to the household of God
2 Love and nurture as Christ loves and nurtures his church

In both arrangements, the overriding idea is that our relationships, even those that are characterized by some hierarchical difference, should be informed by the ultimate reality of our belonging to the household of God. The fact that we belong to God in Christ shapes the way we relate to one another within the context of both the family and society.

Points of Application. Although theologically dense, the passage has very clear and practical applications: submission and love. The difficult part is to deconstruct the notions of hierarchical power that inform so deeply people's understanding of these values. The preacher should make sure the congregation reflects on how their understanding of husband-wife relationships are sometimes heavily influenced by cultural assumptions. The task, therefore, is to show how Paul's admonitions assume a theological understanding that is fundamentally countercultural. To that end, it is good to highlight that Paul's admonitions would have been met with surprise in his own context. Affirming men's love obligations toward their wives in such a way would be perceived as subversive. Similarly, but from a different angle, Paul's admonitions clash with modern cultural notions of socially acceptable norms. And just like ancient readers had their hierarchical assumptions confronted, modern readers need to have their hierarchical or anti-hierarchical notions challenged in order to see these relationships through the new paradigm of the household of God.

More practically, marriage relationships and the relationships of parents and children are easy to address in terms of application. The relationship between slaves and their masters, however, is a bit more distant from us and requires caution. Make sure you explore the differences between the slave systems in the ancient and modern eras. Be careful not to minimize ancient slavery but also not to read modern assumptions into the text. Actual slavery still exists in the world but has been eradicated in most contexts. It is still legitimate, however, to reflect on how Paul's instructions may inform work ethics.

Illustration Opportunities. Marriage and family are full of illustration opportunities, and the preacher should avail himself/herself of family stories he or she knows. The familiarity of the topic, however, can be a minefield, so the preacher should be sensitive to how these stories might affect people with different backgrounds and upbringings.

Personal stories of sacrificial love in the context of marriage are profoundly impactful. And so are those stories that illustrate the mystical union that happens between husband and wife. In marriage, two individuals with different life stories, upbringings, and sometimes different cultures, converge in a union that reshapes them as individuals. In marriage, a new identity takes form to such an extent that one cannot define oneself without accounting for their relationship with the other. Having been married to my wife, Renata, for twenty-five years, I can honestly say I am a different person than I was before marrying her. This "new identity" is undoubtedly influenced by the experiences we have shared over the years. However, more than that, in a genuine sense, our individual identities are informed and transformed by our marriage. In a mysterious way, together, we become someone different from who we were when alone.

Within this mysterious union, mutual submission is the prevailing norm. A marriage in which individuals strive solely for their own happiness is destined for failure. Instead, in this mystical union, the key to a blessed marriage lies in focusing on the well-being of the other. More importantly, this passage shows that, in Christian marriage, the paradigm is not simply a romantic notion of love but the self-giving love exemplified in Christ's sacrifice for the church.

EPHESIANS 6:10–24

STANDING STRONG WITH THE ARMOR OF GOD

Closing his admonition and the letter, Paul calls the believers' attention back to the spiritual reality in which they participate (cf. 1:3, 21–23; 2:2, 6; 3:10). The apostle reminds the audience that even though their lives happen in the very earthly context of social, community, and household relations, they are participants in a larger cosmic drama, battling principalities and powers in the heavenly places. However, this is not a battle the church fights on her own strength. Believers are to put on the full armor provided by God in order to withstand the attacks of the devil and stand victorious in the power of the Lord.

6:10–22

10 Τοῦ λοιποῦ ἐνδυναμοῦσθε ἐν κυρίῳ

Tou loipou endynamousthe en kyriō

καὶ ἐν τῷ κράτει τῆς ἰσχύος αὐτοῦ.

kai en tō kratei tēs ischyos autou.

Finally, be strong in the Lord
and in the strength of his might.

11a ἐνδύσασθε τὴν πανοπλίαν τοῦ θεοῦ

endysasthe tēn panoplian tou theou

Put on the full armor of God

11b πρὸς τὸ δύνασθαι ὑμᾶς στῆναι

pros to dynasthai hymas stēnai

so that you may be able to stand

11c πρὸς τὰς μεθοδίας τοῦ διαβόλου·

pros tas methodias tou diabolou;

against the schemes of the devil.

12a ὅτι οὐκ ἔστιν ἡμῖν ἡ πάλη πρὸς αἷμα καὶ σάρκα,

hoti ouk estin hēmin hē palē pros haima kai sarka,

For we do not wrestle against blood and flesh,

12b ἀλλὰ πρὸς τὰς ἀρχάς,

alla pros tas archas,

but against the rulers,

12c πρὸς τὰς ἐξουσίας,

pros tas exousias,

against the authorities,

12d πρὸς τοὺς κοσμοκράτορας τοῦ σκότους τούτου,

pros tous kosmokratoras tou skotous toutou,

against the cosmic powers of this darkness,

12e πρὸς τὰ πνευματικὰ τῆς πονηρίας ἐν τοῖς ἐπουρανίοις.

pros ta pneumatika tēs ponērias en tois epouraniois.

**against the spiritual [forces] of evil
in the heavenly places.**

13a διὰ τοῦτο ἀναλάβετε τὴν πανοπλίαν τοῦ θεοῦ,

dia touto analabete tēn panoplian tou theou,

For this reason, take up the full armor of God,

13b ἵνα δυνηθῆτε ἀντιστῆναι ἐν τῇ ἡμέρᾳ τῇ πονηρᾷ

hina dynēthēte antistēnai en tē hēmera tē ponēra

so that you may be able to resist in the evil day

13c καὶ ἅπαντα κατεργασάμενοι

kai hapanta katergasamenoi

and, having conquered all things,

13d στῆναι.

stēnai.

to stand.

14a στῆτε οὖν

stēte oun

Therefore, stand,

14b περιζωσάμενοι τὴν ὀσφὺν ὑμῶν ἐν ἀληθείᾳ,

perizōsamenoi tēn osphyn hymōn en alētheia,

having girded your waist with truth,

14c καὶ ἐνδυσάμενοι τὸν θώρακα τῆς δικαιοσύνης,

kai endysamenoi ton thōraka tēs dikaiosynēs,

and having put on the breastplate of righteousness,

15 καὶ ὑποδησάμενοι τοὺς πόδας ἐν ἑτοιμασίᾳ

kai hypodēsamenoi tous podas en hetoimasia

τοῦ εὐαγγελίου τῆς εἰρήνης,

tou euangeliou tēs eirēnēs,

And having shod your feet with the preparation [provided] by the gospel of peace

16a ἐν πᾶσιν ἀναλαβόντες τὸν θυρεὸν τῆς πίστεως,

en pasin analabontes ton thyreon tēs pisteōs,

Taking up, with all these, the shield of faith,

16b ἐν ᾧ δυνήσεσθε πάντα τὰ βέλη

en hō dynēsesthe panta ta belē

τοῦ πονηροῦ [τὰ] πεπυρωμένα σβέσαι·

tou ponērou ta pepyrōmena sbesai.

with which you will be able to quench all flaming arrows of the evil one,

17a καὶ τὴν περικεφαλαίαν τοῦ σωτηρίου δέξασθε,

kai tēn perikephalaian tou sōtēriou dexasthe,

And take the helmet of salvation,

17b καὶ τὴν μάχαιραν τοῦ πνεύματος,

kai tēn machairan tou pneumatos,

and the sword of the Spirit,

17c ὅ ἐστιν ῥῆμα θεοῦ,

ho estin rhēma theou,

which is the word of God,

18a διὰ πάσης προσευχῆς καὶ δεήσεως,

dia pasēs proseuchēs kai deēseōs,

with all prayer and supplication,

18b προσευχόμενοι ἐν παντὶ καιρῷ ἐν πνεύματι,

*prose**ucho**menoi en pan**ti** kairō en **pneu**mati,*

praying in the Spirit at all times,

18c καὶ εἰς αὐτὸ

kai** eis au**to

and for this purpose,

18d ἀγρυπνοῦντες ἐν πάσῃ προσκαρτερήσει καὶ δεήσει

*agry**pnoun**tes en **pa**sē proskarte**rē**sei **kai** de**ē**sei*

being alert with all perseverance and supplication

18e περὶ πάντων τῶν ἁγίων,

*pe**ri pan**tōn **tōn** ha**gi**ōn,*

for all the saints,

19a καὶ ὑπὲρ ἐμοῦ,

***kai** hy**per** e**mou**,*

[Pray] also for me,

19b ἵνα μοι δοθῇ λόγος ἐν ἀνοίξει τοῦ στόματός μου,

***hi**na moi do**thē lo**gos en a**noi**xei **tou sto**ma**tos** mou,*

so that a word might be given to me when I open my mouth,

19c ἐν παρρησίᾳ γνωρίσαι τὸ μυστήριον τοῦ εὐαγγελίου

*en parrhē**si**a gnō**ri**sai **to** mys**tē**rion **tou** euange**li**ou*

to make known with boldness the mystery of the gospel,

20a ὑπὲρ οὗ πρεσβεύω ἐν ἁλύσει,

*hy**per hou** pres**beu**ō en ha**ly**sei,*

for which I serve as an ambassador in chains,

20b ἵνα ἐν αὐτῷ παρρησιάσωμαι

***hi**na en au**tō** parrhēsi**a**sōmai*

so that I might speak about it with boldness,

20c ὡς δεῖ με λαλῆσαι.

*hōs **dei** me lalēsai.*

as I must speak.

21a Ἵνα δὲ εἰδῆτε καὶ ὑμεῖς τὰ κατ᾽ ἐμέ,

*Hina **de** eidēte **kai** hymeis **ta** kat' eme,*

And so that you also may know about my circumstances—

21b τί πράσσω,

***ti pras**sō,*

what I am doing—

21c πάντα γνωρίσει ὑμῖν Τύχικος

***pan**ta gnō**ri**sei hy**min** **Ty**chikos*

ὁ ἀγαπητὸς ἀδελφὸς καὶ πιστὸς διάκονος ἐν κυρίῳ,

*ho agapē**tos** adel**phos** **kai** pis**tos** dia**konos en kyri**ō,*

Tychicus, the beloved brother and faithful servant in the Lord, will tell you everything.

22a ὃν ἔπεμψα πρὸς ὑμᾶς εἰς αὐτὸ τοῦτο

***hon e**pempsa **pros** hy**mas** eis au**to** **tou**to*

I sent him to you for this very reason,

22b ἵνα γνῶτε τὰ περὶ ἡμῶν

hi**na **gnō**te **ta** pe**ri** hē**mōn

that you may know our circumstances

22c καὶ παρακαλέσῃ τὰς καρδίας ὑμῶν.

***kai** parakalesē **tas** kar**di**as hy**mōn**.*

and that he should comfort your hearts.

10 **Τοῦ λοιποῦ ἐνδυναμοῦσθε ἐν κυρίῳ
καὶ ἐν τῷ κράτει τῆς ἰσχύος αὐτοῦ.**

Finally, be strong in the Lord
and in the strength of his might.

Τοῦ ὁ	the ***Tou***	GEN SG NEUT	article
λοιποῦ λοιποῦ	remaining *loi·**pou***	GEN SG NEUT	adj
ἐνδυναμοῦσθε ἐνδυναμόω	(you all) be strong *en·dy·na·**mous**·the*	PRES PASS IMPV 2ND PL	verb
ἐν ἐν	in *en*	---	prep
κυρίῳ κύριος	Lord *ky·**ri**·ō*	DAT SG MASC	noun
καὶ καί	and ***kai***	---	conj
ἐν ἐν	in *en*	---	prep
τῷ ὁ	the ***tō***	DAT SG NEUT	article
κράτει κράτος	strength ***kra**·tei*	DAT SG NEUT	noun
τῆς ὁ	of the ***tēs***	GEN SG FEM	article
ἰσχύος ἰσχύς	(of) might *i·**schy**·os*	GEN SG FEM	noun
αὐτοῦ αὐτός	of him/his *au·**tou***	3RD GEN SG	personal pron

Paul uses redundant language here—**ἐνδυναμοῦσθε** ("be strong"), **κράτει** ("strength"), and **ἰσχύος** ("might")—to emphasize God's power as the source of the believer's strength. This fits with the theme of power found throughout the letter (1:19, 21; 3:7, 16, 20). Surveying all these instances along with the present passage can be exegetically informative.

11a **ἐνδύσασθε τὴν πανοπλίαν τοῦ θεοῦ**

Put on the full armor of God

ἐνδύσασθε ἐνδύω	(you all) put on *en·**dy**·sas·the*	AOR MID IMPV 2ND PL	verb
τὴν ὁ	the ***tēn***	ACC SG FEM	article

πανοπλίαν πανοπλία	full armor *pan·o·**pli**·an*	ACC SG FEM	noun
τοῦ ὁ	of the ***tou***	GEN SG MASC	article
θεοῦ θεός	(of) God *the·**ou***	GEN SG MASC	noun

The verb **ἐνδύσασθε** has a connotation of "clothing" and is first used in 4:24, where it refers to the new self—created according to God's design in righteousness and holiness of truth—with which believers are urged to clothe themselves. This "new self" is now to be clothed with the full armor of God.

The word **πανοπλίαν** describes the full armor of a foot soldier. Paul may have drawn the metaphor from observing the armor of soldiers guarding him in prison (cf. 6:20).

The genitive **τοῦ θεοῦ** can indicate possession—the armor that belongs to God—or origin—the armor that comes from or is provided by God. Two pieces of armor that Paul will describe—the breastplate of righteousness (v. 14c) and the helmet of salvation (v. 17a)—are mentioned in Isa 59:15–18, which describes YHWH's displeasure at the injustice he was seeing, the failure of any human to stand up against it, and finally his decision to put on armor and join the battle himself. Although Paul does not fashion his description of the armor exclusively based on Isaiah, it is likely that the image has informed him. If so, the implications are significant. God, who in Isaiah takes on his armor to fight the battle no one is qualified to fight, now equips his church with his own armor for the battle.

11b **πρὸς τὸ δύνασθαι ὑμᾶς στῆναι**

so that you may be able to stand

πρὸς πρός	that ***pros***	---	prep
τὸ ὁ	*(sign of articular infinitive)* ***to***	ACC SG NEUT	article
δύνασθαι δύναμαι	(you all) may be able ***dy**·nas·thai*	PRES MID/PASS INF	verb
ὑμᾶς σύ	you (all) *hy·**mas***	2ND ACC PL	pron
στῆναι ἵστημι	to stand ***stē**·nai*	AOR ACT INF	verb

The entire admonition is conveyed using plural pronouns and verbs. While this relates more directly to the fact that Paul is addressing an entire congregation rather than an individual, it is likely that Paul has a corporate idea running alongside the individual emphasis. The individual armor pieces are to be taken up by individual believers, but given Paul's emphasis on unity throughout the letter, and that this passage comes right after admonitions concerning corporate worship and household relationships, there may be a sense of corporate battling, especially with the reference to praying for "all the saints" that closes this section (6:18–20).

11c	**πρὸς τὰς μεθοδίας τοῦ διαβόλου·**

against the schemes of the devil.

πρὸς πρός	against ***pros***	---	prep
τὰς ὁ	the ***tas***	ACC PL FEM	article
μεθοδίας μεθοδεία	schemes *me·tho·**di**·as*	ACC PL FEM	noun
τοῦ ὁ	of the ***tou***	GEN SG MASC	article
διαβόλου διάβολος	(of) devil *di·a·**bo**·lou*	GEN SG MASC	adj

To "stand" (**στῆναι**) implies a defensive posture. Later Paul will describe flaming arrows of the evil one being thrown at believers. While a defensive posture is indeed primarily in view, armies would often advance while in defensive formation. So a conquering movement might also be in view (see 6:13 below).

12a	**ὅτι οὐκ ἔστιν ἡμῖν ἡ πάλη πρὸς αἷμα καὶ σάρκα,**

For we do not wrestle against blood and flesh,

ὅτι ὅτι	for ***ho**·ti*	---	conj
οὐκ οὐ	not *ouk*	---	particle
ἔστιν εἰμί	(it) is ***e**·stin*	PRES ACT IND 3RD SG	verb
ἡμῖν ἐγώ	to us ***hē**·min*	1ST DAT PL	pron

ἡ ὁ	the *hē*	NOM SG FEM	article
πάλη πάλη	struggle ***pa***·*lē*	NOM SG FEM	noun
πρὸς πρός	against ***pros***	---	prep
αἷμα αἷμα	blood ***hai***·*ma*	ACC SG NEUT	noun
καὶ καί	and ***kai***	---	conj
σάρκα σάρξ	flesh ***sar***·*ka*	ACC SG FEM	noun

Οὐκ ἔστιν ἡμῖν ἡ πάλη πρὸς αἷμα καὶ σάρκα can be literally rendered "our struggle is not against flesh and blood." The word **πάλη** ("struggle") denotes a wrestling match, so Paul mixes his metaphors to include a more physical struggle in his image of a military battle. Ancient soldiers would often be trained as wrestlers (Thielman 2010:420).

12b **ἀλλὰ πρὸς τὰς ἀρχάς,**

but against the rulers,

ἀλλὰ ἀλλά	but *al*·***la***	---	conj
πρὸς πρός	against ***pros***	---	prep
τὰς ὁ	the ***tas***	ACC PL FEM	article
ἀρχάς ἀρχή	rulers *ar*·***chas***	ACC PL FEM	noun

12c **πρὸς τὰς ἐξουσίας,**

against the authorities,

πρὸς πρός	against ***pros***	---	prep
τὰς ὁ	the ***tas***	ACC PL FEM	article
ἐξουσίας ἐξουσία	authorities *e*·*xou*·***si***·*as*	ACC PL FEM	noun

12d	**πρὸς τοὺς κοσμοκράτορας τοῦ σκότους τούτου,**		
	against the cosmic powers of this darkness,		

Greek	English	Parsing	Part of speech
πρὸς πρός	against ***pros***	---	prep
τοὺς ὁ	the ***tous***	ACC PL MASC	article
κοσμοκράτορας κοσμοκράτωρ	cosmic powers *kos·mo·**kra**·to·ras*	ACC PL MASC	noun
τοῦ ὁ	of the ***tou***	GEN SG NEUT	article
σκότους σκότος	(of) darkness ***sko**·tous*	GEN SG NEUT	noun
τούτου οὗτος	(of) this ***tou**·tou*	GEN SG MASC	demonstr pron

12e	**πρὸς τὰ πνευματικὰ τῆς πονηρίας ἐν τοῖς ἐπουρανίοις.**		
	against the spiritual [forces] of evil in the heavenly places.		

Greek	English	Parsing	Part of speech
πρὸς πρός	against ***pros***	---	prep
τὰ ὁ	the ***ta***	ACC PL NEUT	article
πνευματικὰ πνευματικός	spiritual (forces) *pneu·ma·ti·**ka***	ACC PL NEUT	adj
τῆς ὁ	of the ***tēs***	GEN SG FEM	article
πονηρίας πονηρία	(of) evil *po·nē·**ri**·as*	GEN SG FEM	noun
ἐν ἐν	in *en*	---	prep
τοῖς ὁ	the ***tois***	DAT PL NEUT	article
ἐπουρανίοις ἐπουράνιος	heavenly (places) *e·pou·ra·**ni**·ois*	DAT PL NEUT	adj

Ἀρχάς ("rulers") . . . **ἐξουσίας** ("authorities") . . . **κοσμοκράτορας** ("cosmic powers") . . . **πνευματικὰ τῆς πονηρίας** ("spiritual forces of evil"): similar lists appear in 1:21; 2:2; and 3:10. Here, the term **κοσμοκράτορας** is introduced, a term formed from the words **κόσμος** (world) and **κράτος** (power). The term is used in pagan texts to refer to deities and supernatural beings. Paul may be referring specifically to the prominent Ephesian cult of Artemis—a deity referred to as "queen of the cosmos" in ancient writings. Paul has clearly stated that Christ is seated "far above all rule and authority and power and dominion, and above every name that is named, not only in this age but also in the one to come" (1:21), and that the church is seated with Christ in the heavenly places (2:7). It is against this background that the present admonition should be understood. Following an "already/not yet" understanding of reality, Paul can urge the church to engage in the ongoing battle against these powers while holding strong the certainty that in Christ they are already victorious over them.

Similarly, **ἐν τοῖς ἐπουρανίοις** ("in the heavenly places")—where these entities dwell—is also the place where the church is first said to have been blessed with every spiritual blessing in Christ (1:3), where they are seated together with Christ (2:6), and where the manifold wisdom of God is made known to the rulers and authorities through the church (3:10).

13a **διὰ τοῦτο ἀναλάβετε τὴν πανοπλίαν τοῦ θεοῦ,**

For this reason, take up the full armor of God,

διὰ διά	for *di·**a***	---	prep
τοῦτο οὗτος	this (reason) ***tou**·to*	ACC SG NEUT	demonstr pron
ἀναλάβετε ἀναλαμβάνω	(you all) take up *a·na·**la**·be·te*	AOR ACT IMPV 2ND PL	verb
τὴν ὁ	the ***tēn***	ACC SG FEM	article
πανοπλίαν πανοπλία	full armor *pan·o·**pli**·an*	ACC SG FEM	noun
τοῦ ὁ	of the ***tou***	GEN SG MASC	article
θεοῦ θεός	(of) God *the·**ou***	GEN SG MASC	noun

13b **ἵνα δυνηθῆτε ἀντιστῆναι ἐν τῇ ἡμέρᾳ τῇ πονηρᾷ**

so that you may be able to resist in the evil day

ἵνα ἵνα	so that ***hi**·na*	---	conj

δυνηθῆτε δύναμαι	you (all) may be able *dy·nē·**thē**·te*	AOR PASS SUBJ 2ND PL	verb
ἀντιστῆναι ἀνθίστημι	to resist *an·ti·**stē**·nai*	AOR ACT INF	verb
ἐν ἐν	in *en*	---	prep
τῇ ὁ	the ***tē***	DAT SG FEM	article
ἡμέρᾳ ἡμέρα	day *hē·**me**·ra*	DAT SG FEM	noun
τῇ ὁ	the ***tē***	DAT SG FEM	article
πονηρᾷ πονηρός	evil *po·nē·**ra***	DAT SG FEM	adj

The verb **ἀνθίστημι** literally means "to stand against," again denoting a defensive posture.

Paul spoke of evil days (plural) in 5:16. Here he refers to a specific "evil day" (**τῇ ἡμέρᾳ τῇ πονηρᾷ**), which might be either a critical day of distress or a reference to a final eschatological battle. In any case, Paul wants the church to be prepared for confrontation with evil.

13c **καὶ ἅπαντα κατεργασάμενοι**

and, having conquered all things,

καὶ καί	and ***kai***	---	conj
ἅπαντα ἅπας	all (things) ***ha**·pan·ta*	ACC PL NEUT	adj
κατεργασάμενοι κατεργάζομαι	(you all) having conquered *kat·er·ga·**sa**·me·noi*	AOR MID PTCP NOM PL MASC	verb

The verb **κατεργάζομαι** can mean "to accomplish" or "to conquer." Both ideas fit the context. If the first, the meaning would be "having accomplished the preparation by putting on the full armor of God, the church will be able to stand (defensively)." If the latter, the idea would be "having conquered all things, the church will stand (victorious)." I have opted for the second meaning since it makes more sense of the battle context Paul is describing. Paul wants the believers to hold their ground during the battle so they will stand victorious in the end.

13d	**στῆναι.**		
	to stand.		
στῆναι ἵστημι	to stand ***stē***·*nai*	AOR ACT INF	verb

14a	**στῆτε οὖν**		
	Therefore, stand,		
στῆτε ἵστημι	(you all) stand ***stē***·*te*	AOR ACT IMPV 2ND PL	verb
οὖν οὖν	therefore ***oun***	---	conj

14b	**περιζωσάμενοι τὴν ὀσφὺν ὑμῶν ἐν ἀληθείᾳ,**		
	having girded your waist with truth,		
περιζωσάμενοι περιζώννυμι	(you all) having girded *pe*·*ri*·*zō*·***sa***·*me*·*noi*	AOR MID PTCP NOM PL MASC	verb
τὴν ὁ	the ***tēn***	ACC SG FEM	article
ὀσφὺν ὀσφῦς	waist *os*·***phyn***	ACC SG FEM	noun
ὑμῶν σύ	of you (all)/your *hy*·***mōn***	2ND GEN PL	pron
ἐν ἐν	with *en*	---	prep
ἀληθείᾳ ἀλήθεια	truth *a*·*lē*·***thei***·*a*	DAT SG FEM	noun

Paul does not mention a belt, although the armor metaphor would evoke such an image. Instead, he focuses on the act of girding the waist with truth (**περιζωσάμενοι τὴν ὀσφὺν ὑμῶν ἐν ἀληθείᾳ**), i.e., the readying of the soldier's body for battle. Elsewhere in Ephesians, Paul speaks of truth in reference to the gospel as "the word of truth" (1:13) and in reference to the relationship between believers, who are to speak truth to one another (4:25). The two are related since it is the truth of the gospel that informs the truthful conduct of believers.

14c **καὶ ἐνδυσάμενοι τὸν θώρακα τῆς δικαιοσύνης,**

and having put on the breastplate of righteousness,

καὶ καί	and ***kai***	---	conj
ἐνδυσάμενοι ἐνδύω	(you all) having put on *en·dy·**sa**·me·noi*	AOR MID PTCP NOM PL MASC	verb
τὸν ὁ	the ***ton***	ACC SG MASC	article
θώρακα θώραξ	breastplate *__thō__·ra·ka*	ACC SG MASC	noun
τῆς ὁ	of the ***tēs***	GEN SG FEM	article
δικαιοσύνης δικαιοσύνη	(of) righteousness *di·kai·o·**sy**·nēs*	GEN SG FEM	noun

The breastplate is a protective piece covering the soldier's torso and back. Righteousness comes from God (cf. Rom 3:21–22) and is characteristic of the new self created in the likeness of God (Eph 4:24).

15 **καὶ ὑποδησάμενοι τοὺς πόδας ἐν ἑτοιμασίᾳ τοῦ εὐαγγελίου τῆς εἰρήνης,**

And having shod your feet with the preparation [provided] by the gospel of peace

καὶ καί	and ***kai***	---	conj
ὑποδησάμενοι ὑποδέω	(you all) having shod *hy·po·dē·**sa**·me·noi*	AOR MID PTCP NOM PL MASC	verb
τοὺς ὁ	the ***tous***	ACC PL MASC	article
πόδας πούς	feet *__po__·das*	ACC PL MASC	noun
ἐν ἐν	with *en*	---	prep
ἑτοιμασίᾳ ἑτοιμασία	preparation *he·toi·ma·**si**·a*	DAT SG FEM	noun
τοῦ ὁ	by the ***tou***	GEN SG NEUT	article
εὐαγγελίου εὐαγγέλιον	(by) gospel *eu·an·ge·**li**·ou*	GEN SG NEUT	noun
τῆς ὁ	of the ***tēs***	GEN SG FEM	article

εἰρήνης εἰρήνη	(of) peace *ei·**rē**·nēs*	GEN SG FEM	noun

As in the case of the belt, Paul does not refer specifically to shoes or sandals, even though such objects are implied. The emphasis falls on the act of shoeing the feet, with the subjective genitive (τοῦ εὐαγγελίου) establishing the gospel as that which prepares the believer. The image is of a soldier getting ready. Thus, the gospel prepares the believer for battle.

16a **ἐν πᾶσιν ἀναλαβόντες τὸν θυρεὸν τῆς πίστεως,**

Taking up, with all these, the shield of faith,

ἐν ἐν	with *en*	---	prep
πᾶσιν πᾶς	all (these) ***pa**·sin*	DAT PL NEUT	adj
ἀναλαβόντες ἀναλαμβάνω	(you all) taking up *a·na·la·**bon**·tes*	AOR ACT PTCP NOM PL MASC	verb
τὸν ὁ	the ***ton***	ACC SG MASC	article
θυρεὸν θυρεός	shield *thy·re·**on***	ACC SG MASC	noun
τῆς ὁ	of the ***tēs***	GEN SG FEM	article
πίστεως πίστις	(of) faith ***pi**·ste·ōs*	GEN SG FEM	noun

In a defensive formation, the shield (**θυρεὸν**), covering most of the body, is the most consequential piece of equipment. Paul's colorful depiction of its purpose in protecting the believer from the flaming arrows of the evil one only underscores its importance. This key protection is provided by faith (**πίστις**), described previously as the gift of God that constitutes the means of salvation (2:8), the means by which Christ dwells in the heart of the believer (3:17), and the means by which the unity of the church is maintained (4:13).

16b	ἐν ᾧ δυνήσεσθε πάντα τὰ βέλη τοῦ πονηροῦ [τὰ] πεπυρωμένα σβέσαι·

with which you will be able to quench
all flaming arrows of the evil one,

ἐν ἐν	with *en*	---	prep
ᾧ ὅς	which ***hō***	DAT SG MASC	relative pron
δυνήσεσθε δύναμαι	you (all) will be able *dy·**nē**·ses·the*	FUT MID IND 2ND PL	verb
πάντα πᾶς	all ***pan**·ta*	ACC PL NEUT	adj
τὰ ὁ	the ***ta***	ACC PL NEUT	article
βέλη βέλος	arrows ***be**·lē*	ACC PL NEUT	noun
τοῦ ὁ	of the ***tou***	GEN SG MASC	article
πονηροῦ πονηρός	(of) evil *po·nē·**rou***	GEN SG MASC	adj
τὰ ὁ	the ***ta***	ACC PL NEUT	article
πεπυρωμένα πυρόω	flaming *pe·py·rō·**me**·na*	PERF PASS PTCP ACC PL NEUT	verb
σβέσαι σβέννυμι	to quench ***sbe**·sai*	AOR ACT INF	verb

17a	καὶ τὴν περικεφαλαίαν τοῦ σωτηρίου δέξασθε,

And take the helmet of salvation,

καὶ καί	and ***kai***	---	conj
τὴν ὁ	the ***tēn***	ACC SG FEM	article
περικεφαλαίαν περικεφαλαία	helmet *pe·ri·ke·pha·**lai**·an*	ACC SG FEM	noun
τοῦ ὁ	of the ***tou***	GEN SG NEUT	article
σωτηρίου σωτήριον	(of) salvation *sō·tē·**ri**·ou*	GEN SG NEUT	adj
δέξασθε δέχομαι	(you all) take ***de**·xas·the*	AOR MID IMPV 2ND PL	verb

The helmet of salvation (**περικεφαλαίαν τοῦ σωτηρίου**) is the last protective equipment of the armor, mentioned also in Isa 59:17. Paul associates salvation with the proclamation of the gospel in 1:13.

17b	**καὶ τὴν μάχαιραν τοῦ πνεύματος,**		
	and the sword of the Spirit,		
καὶ καί	and ***kai***	---	conj
τὴν ὁ	the ***tēn***	ACC SG FEM	article
μάχαιραν μάχαιρα	sword ***ma***·*chai*·*ran*	ACC SG FEM	noun
τοῦ ὁ	of the ***tou***	GEN SG NEUT	article
πνεύματος πνεῦμα	(of) Spirit ***pneu***·*ma*·*tos*	GEN SG NEUT	noun

17c	**ὅ ἐστιν ῥῆμα θεοῦ,**		
	which is the word of God.		
ὅ ὅς	which ***ho***	NOM SG NEUT	relative pron
ἐστιν εἰμί	is *e*·*stin*	PRES ACT IND 3RD SG	verb
ῥῆμα ῥῆμα	word ***rhē***·*ma*	NOM SG NEUT	noun
θεοῦ θεός	of God *the*·***ou***	GEN SG MASC	noun

The **μάχαιρα**—a short-blade sword used by foot soldiers—is the only offensive equipment in the armor. The sword is "of the Spirit" in the same way that the armor is "of God"; namely, it is provided by the Spirit. More specifically, the sword is identified with the word (**ῥῆμα**) of God, another likely reference to the gospel (cf. 5:26). Of the six pieces of equipment, four—the belt of truth, the sandals of the preparation of the gospel, the helmet of salvation, and the sword of the Spirit—have a direct or indirect relationship with the gospel in Ephesians. The good news of God's salvation, which Paul so wonderfully describes in 2:1–10, is the fundamental element upon which the whole armor is dependent.

18a	**διὰ πάσης προσευχῆς καὶ δεήσεως,**		
	with all prayer and supplication,		
διὰ διά	with *di·**a***	---	prep
πάσης πᾶς	all ***pa**·sēs*	GEN SG FEM	adj
προσευχῆς προσευχή	prayer *pros·eu·**chēs***	GEN SG FEM	noun
καὶ καί	and ***kai***	---	conj
δεήσεως δέησις	supplication *de·**ē**·se·ōs*	GEN SG FEM	noun

18b	**προσευχόμενοι ἐν παντὶ καιρῷ ἐν πνεύματι,**		
	praying in the Spirit at all times,		
προσευχόμενοι προσεύχομαι	(you all) praying *pros·eu·**cho**·me·noi*	PRES MID/PASS PTCP NOM PL MASC	verb
ἐν ἐν	at *en*	---	prep
παντὶ πᾶς	all *pan·**ti***	DAT SG MASC	adj
καιρῷ καιρός	times *kai·**rō***	DAT SG MASC	noun
ἐν ἐν	in *en*	---	prep
πνεύματι πνεῦμα	(the) Spirit ***pneu**·ma·ti*	DAT SG NEUT	noun

18c	**καὶ εἰς αὐτὸ**		
	and for this purpose,		
καὶ καί	and ***kai***	---	conj

εἰς εἰς	for *eis*	---	prep
αὐτὸ αὐτός	this (purpose) *au·**to***	3RD ACC SG	personal pron

18d	ἀγρυπνοῦντες ἐν πάσῃ προσκαρτερήσει καὶ δεήσει
	being alert with all perseverance and supplication

ἀγρυπνοῦντες ἀγρυπνέω	(you all) being alert *a·gry·**pnoun**·tes*	PRES ACT PTCP NOM PL MASC	verb
ἐν ἐν	with *en*	---	prep
πάσῃ πᾶς	all ***pa**·sē*	DAT SG FEM	adj
προσκαρτερήσει προσκαρτέρησις	perseverance *pros·kar·te·**rē**·sei*	DAT SG FEM	noun
καὶ καί	and ***kai***	---	conj
δεήσει δέησις	supplication *de·**ē**·sei*	DAT SG FEM	noun

18e	περὶ πάντων τῶν ἁγίων,
	for all the saints,

περὶ περί	for *pe·**ri***	---	prep
πάντων πᾶς	all ***pan**·tōn*	GEN PL MASC	adj
τῶν ὁ	the ***tōn***	GEN PL MASC	article
ἁγίων ἅγιος	saints *ha·**gi**·ōn*	GEN PL MASC	adj

Paul reminds the believers that this is a battle fought as an army and not individually.

19a	**καὶ ὑπὲρ ἐμοῦ,**		
	[Pray] also for me,		
καὶ καί	also *kai*	---	conj
ὑπὲρ ὑπέρ	for *hy·per*	---	prep
ἐμοῦ ἐγώ	me *e·mou*	1ST GEN SG	pron

19b	**ἵνα μοι δοθῇ λόγος ἐν ἀνοίξει τοῦ στόματός μου,**		
	so that a word might be given to me when I open my mouth,		
ἵνα ἵνα	so that *hi·na*	---	conj
μοι ἐγώ	to me *moi*	1ST DAT SG	pron
δοθῇ δίδωμι	(it) might be given *do·thē*	AOR PASS SUBJ 3RD SG	verb
λόγος λόγος	word *lo·gos*	NOM SG MASC	noun
ἐν ἐν	in *en*	---	prep
ἀνοίξει ἄνοιξις	to an opening *a·noi·xei*	DAT SG FEM	noun
τοῦ ὁ	of the *tou*	GEN SG NEUT	article
στόματός στόμα	(of) mouth *sto·ma·tos*	GEN SG NEUT	noun
μου ἐγώ	of me/my *mou*	1ST GEN SG	pron

19c	**ἐν παρρησίᾳ γνωρίσαι τὸ μυστήριον τοῦ εὐαγγελίου**		
	to make known with boldness the mystery of the gospel,		
ἐν ἐν	with *en*	---	prep
παρρησίᾳ παρρησία	boldness *par·rhē·si·a*	DAT SG FEM	noun
γνωρίσαι γνωρίζω	to make known *gnō·ri·sai*	AOR ACT INF	verb

τὸ ὁ	the ***to***	ACC SG NEUT	article
μυστήριον μυστήριον	mystery *my·**stē**·ri·on*	ACC SG NEUT	noun
τοῦ ὁ	of the ***tou***	GEN SG NEUT	article
εὐαγγελίου εὐαγγέλιον	(of) gospel *eu·an·ge·**li**·ou*	GEN SG NEUT	noun

20a **ὑπὲρ οὗ πρεσβεύω ἐν ἁλύσει,**

for which I serve as an ambassador in chains,

ὑπὲρ ὑπέρ	for *hy·**per***	---	prep
οὗ ὅς	which ***hou***	GEN SG NEUT	relative pron
πρεσβεύω πρεσβεύω	I serve as an ambassador *pres·**beu**·ō*	PRES ACT IND 1ST SG	verb
ἐν ἐν	in *en*	---	prep
ἁλύσει ἅλυσις	chains *ha·**ly**·sei*	DAT SG FEM	noun

20b **ἵνα ἐν αὐτῷ παρρησιάσωμαι**

so that I might speak about it with boldness,

ἵνα ἵνα	so that ***hi**·na*	---	conj
ἐν ἐν	in *en*	---	prep
αὐτῷ αὐτός	it *au·**tō***	3RD DAT SG	personal pron
παρρησιάσωμαι παρρησιάζομαι	I might speak with boldness *par·rhē·si·**a**·sō·mai*	AOR MID SUBJ 1ST SG	verb

20c	ὡς δεῖ με λαλῆσαι.		
	as I must speak.		

ὡς ὡς	as *hōs*	---	adv
δεῖ δεῖ	it is necessary ***dei***	PRES ACT IND 3RD SG	verb
με ἐγώ	me *me*	1ST ACC SG	pron
λαλῆσαι λαλέω	to speak *la·**lē**·sai*	AOR ACT INF	verb

This is the final instance of the theme of mystery and revelation developed throughout the letter (Eph 1:9; 3:3–4, 9; 5:32). More directly, the passage evokes 3:1–10, where Paul, who identifies himself as a prisoner of Christ (**ὁ δέσμιος τοῦ Χριστοῦ**), discusses his role in the stewardship of God's grace. Even though he is constrained, his ministry is one of revelation; namely, to make known the mystery of the gospel. Here, Paul again alludes to his role in the revelation of the mystery, this time using the language of "ambassador" or "envoy"—a representative sent on behalf of someone. The qualifier **ἐν ἁλύσει** ("in chains") is ironic since the role of an ambassador requires freedom to proclaim and is expected to be a position of respect on the part of those who receive them. To imprison an ambassador would be highly inappropriate and an act of rejection of the one who sent him. Nevertheless, Paul sees in his circumstances an opportunity to preach with even more boldness—notice the repetition of the term in v. 19 (**παρρησίᾳ**, "boldness") and v. 20 (**παρρησιάσωμαι**, "I might speak with boldness"). For that, Paul asks the Ephesians to support him in prayer.

21a	Ἵνα δὲ εἰδῆτε καὶ ὑμεῖς τὰ κατ᾽ ἐμέ,		
	And so that you also may know about my circumstances—		

Ἵνα ἵνα	so that ***Hi**·na*	---	conj
δὲ δέ	and ***de***	---	conj
εἰδῆτε εἰδῶ	you (all) may know *ei·**dē**·te*	PERF ACT SUBJ 2ND PL	verb
καὶ καί	also ***kai***	---	conj
ὑμεῖς σύ	you (all) *hy·**meis***	2ND NOM PL	pron

τὰ ὁ	the (things) ***ta***	ACC PL NEUT	article
κατ᾽ κατά	according to *kat᾽*	---	prep
ἐμέ ἐγώ	me *e*·***me***	1ST ACC SG	pron

21b **τί πράσσω,**

what I am doing—

τί τίς~2	what ***ti***	ACC SG NEUT	interr pron
πράσσω πράσσω	I am doing ***pras***·*sō*	PRES ACT IND 1ST SG	verb

21c **πάντα γνωρίσει ὑμῖν Τύχικος ὁ ἀγαπητὸς ἀδελφὸς καὶ πιστὸς διάκονος ἐν κυρίῳ,**

Tychicus, the beloved brother and faithful servant in the Lord, will tell you everything.

πάντα πᾶς	all ***pan***·*ta*	ACC PL NEUT	adj
γνωρίσει γνωρίζω	(he) will tell *gnō*·***ri***·*sei*	FUT ACT IND 3RD SG	verb
ὑμῖν σύ	to you (all) *hy*·***min***	2ND DAT PL	pron
Τύχικος Τυχικός	Tychicus ***Ty***·*chi*·*kos*	NOM SG MASC	noun
ὁ ὁ	the *ho*	NOM SG MASC	article
ἀγαπητὸς ἀγαπητός	beloved *a*·*ga*·*pē*·***tos***	NOM SG MASC	adj
ἀδελφὸς ἀδελφός	brother *a*·*del*·***phos***	NOM SG MASC	noun
καὶ καί	and ***kai***	---	conj
πιστὸς πιστός	faithful *pi*·***stos***	NOM SG MASC	adj
διάκονος διάκονος	servant *di*·***a***·*ko*·*nos*	NOM SG MASC	noun

ἐν ἐν	in *en*	---	prep
κυρίῳ κύριος	Lord *ky·**ri**·ō*	DAT SG MASC	noun

Like Paul (cf. 3:7), Tychicus is identified as a **διάκονος**, a servant or minister. The use of the prepositional phrase **ἐν κυρίῳ** is consistent with Paul's use of the language in other instances in the letter to indicate one's participation in Christ as a primary identity definition (Eph 4:1; 5:8). Tychicus was a Christian from Asia, a companion of Paul (Acts 20:4), and the letter carrier for Paul's correspondence to the churches at Ephesus and Colossae (Col 4:7)—a position of high trust. Beyond simply delivering the letter, letter carriers were also entrusted with the important responsibility of supplementing the correspondence with oral instructions and information. In this case, Paul's circumstances and activities are supposed to be communicated to the audience for their comfort and edification. It is important for Paul that the Ephesians know that although in prison he is still preaching the gospel.

22a **ὃν ἔπεμψα πρὸς ὑμᾶς εἰς αὐτὸ τοῦτο**

I sent him to you for this very reason,

ὃν ὅς	whom ***hon***	ACC SG MASC	relative pron
ἔπεμψα πέμπω	I sent ***e**·pem·psa*	AOR ACT IND 1ST SG	verb
πρὸς πρός	to ***pros***	---	prep
ὑμᾶς σύ	you (all) *hy·**mas***	2ND ACC PL	pron
εἰς εἰς	for *eis*	---	prep
αὐτὸ αὐτός	very (*used as intensifying marker*) *au·**to***	3RD ACC SG	personal pron
τοῦτο οὗτος	this (reason) ***tou**·to*	ACC SG NEUT	demonstr pron

22b	**ἵνα γνῶτε τὰ περὶ ἡμῶν**		
	that you may know our circumstances		
ἵνα ἵνα	so that ***hi***·*na*	---	conj
γνῶτε γινώσκω	you (all) may know ***gnō***·*te*	AOR ACT SUBJ 2ND PL	verb
τὰ ὁ	the (circumstances) ***ta***	ACC PL NEUT	article
περὶ περί	concerning *pe*·***ri***	---	prep
ἡμῶν ἐγώ	us *hē*·***mōn***	1ST GEN PL	pron

22c	**καὶ παρακαλέσῃ τὰς καρδίας ὑμῶν.**		
	and that he should comfort your hearts.		
καὶ καί	and ***kai***	---	conj
παρακαλέσῃ παρακαλέω	he should comfort *pa*·*ra*·*ka*·***le***·*sē*	AOR ACT SUBJ 3RD SG	verb
τὰς ὁ	the ***tas***	ACC PL FEM	article
καρδίας καρδία	hearts *kar*·***di***·*as*	ACC PL FEM	noun
ὑμῶν σύ	of you (all)/your *hy*·***mōn***	2ND GEN PL	pron

6:23–24

23a Εἰρήνη τοῖς ἀδελφοῖς καὶ ἀγάπη

*Eirēnē **tois** adel**phois kai** agapē*

Peace to the brothers [and sisters] and love

23b μετὰ πίστεως

*me**ta** **pis**teōs*

with faith

23c ἀπὸ θεοῦ πατρὸς καὶ κυρίου Ἰησοῦ Χριστοῦ.

***apo** the**ou** pa**tros kai** kyri**ou** Iē**sou** Chri**stou**.*

from God the Father and the Lord Jesus Christ.

24a Ἡ χάρις μετὰ πάντων τῶν ἀγαπώντων

*Hē **cha**ris me**ta pan**tōn **tōn** aga**pōn**tōn*

τὸν κύριον ἡμῶν Ἰησοῦν Χριστὸν

ton** **ky**rion hē**mōn** Iē**soun** Chri**ston

May grace be with all those who love our Lord Jesus Christ

24b ἐν ἀφθαρσίᾳ.

*en aphthar**si**a.*

with incorruptible [love].

23a **Εἰρήνη τοῖς ἀδελφοῖς καὶ ἀγάπη**

Peace to the brothers [and sisters] and love

Εἰρήνη εἰρήνη	peace *Ei·**rē**·nē*	NOM SG FEM	noun
τοῖς ὁ	to the ***tois***	DAT PL MASC	article

ἀδελφοῖς ἀδελφός	(to) brothers *a·del·**phois***	DAT PL MASC	noun
καὶ καί	and ***kai***	---	conj
ἀγάπη ἀγάπη	love *a·**ga**·pē*	NOM SG FEM	noun

23b **μετὰ πίστεως**

with faith

μετὰ μετά	with *me·**ta***	---	prep
πίστεως πίστις	faith ***pi**·ste·ōs*	GEN SG FEM	noun

23c **ἀπὸ θεοῦ πατρὸς καὶ κυρίου Ἰησοῦ Χριστοῦ.**

from God the Father and the Lord Jesus Christ.

ἀπὸ ἀπό	from *a·**po***	---	prep
θεοῦ θεός	God *the·**ou***	GEN SG MASC	noun
πατρὸς πατήρ	father *pa·**tros***	GEN SG MASC	noun
καὶ καί	and ***kai***	---	conj
κυρίου κύριος	Lord *ky·**ri**·ou*	GEN SG MASC	noun
Ἰησοῦ Ἰησοῦς	Jesus *I·ē·**sou***	GEN SG MASC	noun
Χριστοῦ Χριστός	Christ *Chri·**stou***	GEN SG MASC	noun

24a **Ἡ χάρις μετὰ πάντων τῶν ἀγαπώντων τὸν κύριον ἡμῶν Ἰησοῦν Χριστὸν**

May grace be with all those who love our Lord Jesus Christ

Ἡ ὁ	the *Hē*	NOM SG FEM	article

χάρις χάρις	grace ***cha**·ris*	NOM SG FEM	noun
μετὰ μετά	with *me·**ta***	---	prep
πάντων πᾶς	all ***pan**·tōn*	GEN PL MASC	adj
τῶν ὁ	those ***tōn***	GEN PL MASC	article
ἀγαπώντων ἀγαπάω	loving *a·ga·**pōn**·tōn*	PRES ACT PTCP GEN PL MASC	verb
τὸν ὁ	the ***ton***	ACC SG MASC	article
κύριον κύριος	Lord ***ky**·ri·on*	ACC SG MASC	noun
ἡμῶν ἐγώ	of us/our *hē·**mōn***	1ST GEN PL	pron
Ἰησοῦν Ἰησοῦς	Jesus *I·ē·**soun***	ACC SG MASC	noun
Χριστὸν Χριστός	Christ *Chri·**ston***	ACC SG MASC	noun

24b **ἐν ἀφθαρσίᾳ.**

with incorruptible [love].

ἐν ἐν	with *en*	---	prep
ἀφθαρσίᾳ ἀφθαρσία	incorruptible (love) *aph·thar·**si**·a*	DAT SG FEM	noun

Paul closes his letter with a reference to peace, love, and grace coming from God the Father and the Lord Jesus Christ (cf. 1:2). The three nouns—grace (cf. 1:2, 6–7; 2:5, 7–8; 3:2, 7–8; 4:7, 29; 6:24), peace (cf. 1:2; 2:14–15, 17; 4:3; 6:15, 23), and love (cf. 1:4, 15; 2:4; 3:17, 19; 4:2, 15–16; 5:2; 6:23)—are prominent terms in the theology of the letter. In particular, these three terms are woven together in 2:1–22, where Paul describes God's work of salvation and reconciliation through the work of Christ. The concluding greeting is, therefore, fitting. The grace, peace, and love of God and Christ, which effect the salvation of believers and the formation of the body of Christ, are now proclaimed as a blessing over the church.

From Text to Sermon

Main Exegetical Idea. Believers should strengthen themselves in the Lord for their battle against principalities and powers by taking up the whole armor of God.

Bridge to Theology. Paul began his discourse to the Ephesians with a heavenly perspective, describing a reality in which Christ reigns supreme in the heavenly places, far above every principality and power (1:3, 20–21), and in which the church is seated together with Christ in the heavenly places (2:6). In his ethical section (4:1–6:20), Paul brings his focus back to earthly realities, admonishing the believers on how to live and conduct themselves both in relation to outsiders and in relation to one another in the community. To close his admonition, Paul again calls attention to the cosmic and spiritual realm, in which the church battles the principalities and powers at work in the world.

Following Paul's move between these realities is important to understand the full picture he is painting. Paul begins with the statement that God has blessed the church with every spiritual blessing in the heavenly places and enjoys a place of victory against principalities and powers. With that reality in mind, he can now affirm that the church still has a battle to fight. But the latter context can only be properly appreciated in light of the former: that battle has already been won! The church sits with Christ in the heavenly places far above all principalities and powers. In the already/not yet continuum, the church lives into the victory that Christ has already accomplished for her. Therefore, we do not fight on our own strength. We fight in the strength of Christ's might, taking up the armor of God and standing against the forces of darkness.

Although the armor has many elements, a core element connects them: the gospel, which Paul has explored in the first three chapters of his letter. As the church proclaims and embodies the truth of the gospel, she stands firm against the schemes of evil.

Finally, although this armor is to be taken up by each believer, Paul likely has the corporate church in mind as well. The body of Christ—those Jews and gentiles, men and women, children and parents, and slaves and masters who have been made into one new person in Christ through his work on the cross—is now equipped to stand and fight against the spiritual powers.

Possible Sermon Structure. A sermon on this passage may be structured as follows:

Be strong in the Lord and prepare for battle:

1 The nature of the battle and the enemies against which we fight
  1.1 The battle requires a defensive posture
  1.2 The battle is against spiritual forces
2 The armor and weapons at our disposal

Points of Application. Two common mistakes in the Christian life are either to ignore the spiritual battles or to misunderstand them: either to live as if there is no battle or to live as if the outcome of the battle is uncertain. One may wrongly rationalize all things in life, ignoring or not believing that there are spiritual forces at work in the world against which the church needs to battle. Conversely, one may believe in the existence of these forces but react in panic. Paul's letter to the Ephesians gives a much-needed, balanced perspective. Anyone paying attention to Paul will recognize the reality of principalities and powers. They are present throughout the discourse. As God's people, we participate in this dramatic unfolding of God's plan, whereby, through the church, God displays his multiform wisdom to principalities and powers (3:10). But Paul leaves no room for panic. Christ reigns supreme over all things, including the powers. This balanced perception is, perhaps, the most important point of application in this passage.

The means by which we fight this battle is also an important emphasis. It is God's armor, not ours. It is his truth, his righteousness, his gospel, his salvation, his word, and our faith in him (which is itself a gift from God [2:8]) that prepare us for battle. Our task is to clothe ourselves with the armor he has provided us with and stand firm.

Illustration Opportunities. The armor of a soldier and battle scenes are great illustrations for this passage. Stories like the ones in *The Lord of the Rings* are great ways of stirring the imagination of the audience. One of the greatest moments in Tolkien's epic is the battle for Helm's Deep. Men from Rohan are surrounded by the Uruk-hai and the armies of Isengard—the evil army—and despite the bravery of the king's soldiers, the battle reaches a point of hopelessness. The story reaches its climax when, at the darkest point in the battle when all seems lost, the White Rider appears:

> There suddenly upon a ridge appeared a rider, clad in white, shining in the rising sun. Over the low hills the horns were sounding.

> Behind him, hastening down the long slopes, were a thousand men on foot; their swords were in their hands. Amid them strode a man tall and strong. His shield was red. As he came to the valley's brink, he set to his lips a great black horn and blew a ringing blast. [. . .] "Behold the White Rider!" cried Aragorn. "Gandalf is come again!" [. . .] The hosts of Isengard roared, swaying this way and that, turning from fear to fear. (Tolkien 2021:541)

Tolkien's story is, of course, patterned on the biblical hope of the return of Christ. It illustrates well the reality of the ongoing battle against forces of darkness, which at times seems lost, but also the hope to which Christians are supposed to cling: the battle is already won, and we will stand victorious with Christ.

WORKS CITED

Barclay, John M. G. 2015. *Paul and the Gift*. Grand Rapids: Eerdmans.

Cohick, Lynn H. 2020. *The Letter to the Ephesians*. New International Commentary on the New Testament. Grand Rapids: Eerdmans.

Davies, G. I. 2020. *A Critical and Exegetical Commentary on Exodus 1–18*. Vol. 1, *Commentary on Exodus 1–10*. London: Bloomsbury.

Haiken, Melanie. 2021. "These Birds Flock in Mesmerizing Swarms of Thousands—but Why Is Still a Mystery." *National Geographic*, 25 March 2021. https://www.nationalgeographic.com/animals/article/these-birds-flock-in-mesmerizing-swarms-why-is-still-a-mystery.

Hoehner, Harold W. 2002. *Ephesians: An Exegetical Commentary*. Grand Rapids: Baker Academic.

Thielman, Frank. 2010. *Ephesians*. Baker Exegetical Commentary on the New Testament. Grand Rapids: Baker Academic.

Tolkien, J. R. R. 2021. *The Lord of the Rings*. New York: Houghton Mifflin Harcourt.

TEXT-CRITICAL NOTES

For those who wish to incorporate textual criticism into their preparation of the Greek text of the passages discussed in this volume, the following apparatus lists exegetically significant text-critical variations that exist among the Westcott-Hort text ("WH"), which is the basis for the Greek text of Colossians found in this book, and the 27th edition of the Nestle-Aland text ("NA") and the Robinson-Pierpont Byzantine text ("RP"). These data are reproduced, with permission, from the comparative apparatus of an edition of the Westcott-Hort text published by Hendrickson under the title *The Greek New Testament*.[1]

Any readings listed below that the author has chosen to incorporate into the Greek text found in the present volume are set in **bold** type.

Chapter 1

1	WH: Χριστοῦ Ἰησοῦ RP: Ἰησοῦ χριστοῦ
	WH: [ἐν Ἐφέσῳ] **RP: ἐν Ἐφέσῳ**
6	WH: ἧς RP: ἐν
7	WH: τὸ πλοῦτος RP: τὸν πλοῦτον
14	WH: ὅ
	{WH}/RP: ὅς
15	**NA/RP: *add* ἀγάπην τὴν *after* καὶ τὴν**

1. B. F. Westcott and F. J. A. Hort, *The Greek New Testament, with Expanded Dictionary* (Peabody, MA: Hendrickson Publishers, 2008), which is based on the 1885 edition of the Westcott-Hort text. "WH" represents the text printed in the aforecited volume; "NA" represents the text printed in Barbara Aland, Kurt Aland, Johannes Karavidopoulos, Carlo M. Martini, and Bruce M. Metzger, eds., *Novum Testamentum Graece*, 27th ed. (Stuttgart: Deutsche Bibelgesellschaft, 1993); and "RP" represents the text printed in Maurice Robinson and William G. Pierpont, eds., *The New Testament in the Original Greek: Byzantine Textform* (Southborough, MA: Chilton Book Publishing, 2005). The abbreviation "{WH}" denotes marginal readings in the Westcott-Hort text, and the use of brackets around an edition abbreviation (e.g., "[NA]") indicates that the reading listed is found in brackets in the text in question. For more details, see pp. xxi–xxvii of the 2008 Hendrickson version of *The Greek New Testament* cited at the beginning of this note, esp. p. xxvi, which further explains which kinds of (exegetically significant) variations are included here and which kinds of (exegetically insignificant) variations are omitted.

16	RP: *add* ὑμῶν *after* μνείαν
17	WH: δῴη **{WH}: δώῃ** *or* δῷ
	NA/RP: δώῃ
18	WH: [ὑμῶν] **RP: ὑμῶν**
	RP: *add* καί *after* αὐτοῦ
20	WH: ἐνήργηκεν
	{WH}/NA/RP: ἐνήργησεν
	RP: *add* τῶν *after* αὐτὸν ἐκ
	WH: καθίσας RP: ἐκάθισεν

Chapter 2

3	WH: ἤμεθα RP: ἦμεν
5	{WH}: *add* ἐν *after* συνεζωοποίησεν
7	WH: ὑπερβάλλον πλοῦτος RP: ὑπερβάλλοντα πλοῦτον
8	RP: *add* τῆς *before* πίστεως
11	WH: ποτὲ ὑμεῖς RP: ὑμεῖς ποτὲ
12	RP: *add* ἐν *after* ἦτε
13	WH: ἐγενήθητε ἐγγὺς RP: ἐγγὺς ἐγενήθητε
14–15	WH: λύσας, 15 τὴν ἔχθραν ἐν τῇ σαρκὶ αὐτοῦ, τὸν νόμον **NA: λύσας, τὴν ἔχθραν ἐν τῇ σαρκὶ αὐτοῦ, 15 τὸν νόμον**
15	WH: αὑτῷ
	NA: αὐτῷ RP: ἑαυτῷ
19	RP: *omit* ἐστὲ *after* ἀλλὰ
20	WH: Χριστοῦ Ἰησοῦ RP: Ἰησοῦ χριστοῦ

Chapter 3

1	WH: Ἰησοῦ
	NA: [Ἰησοῦ]
3	WH: [ὅτι] **RP: ὅτι**
	WH: ἐγνωρίσθη RP: ἐγνώρισέν
6	RP: *add* αὐτοῦ *after* ἐπαγγελίας
	WH: Χριστῷ Ἰησοῦ RP: τῷ χριστῷ
7	WH: ἐγενήθην RP: ἐγενόμην
	WH: τῆς δοθείσης RP: τὴν δοθεῖσάν

8	RP: *add* ἐν *after* αὕτη
	WH: τὸ RP: τὸν
	WH: πλοῦτος RP: πλοῦτον
9	{WH}/[NA]/RP: *add* πάντας *after* φωτίσαι
	RP: *add* διὰ Ἰησοῦ χριστοῦ *after* κτίσαντι
11	RP: *omit* τῷ *after* ἐποίησεν ἐν
12	RP: *add* τὴν *after* παρρησίαν καὶ
13	WH: ἐνκακεῖν RP: ἐκκακεῖν
14	RP: *add* τοῦ κυρίου ἡμῶν Ἰησοῦ χριστοῦ *after* πατέρα
16	WH: δῷ RP: δοεη
	WH: τὸ πλοῦτος RP: τὸν πλοῦτον
17–18	RP: *end* v. 17 *after* ὑμῶν·
	WH: ὑμῶν ἐν ἀγάπῃ·
	NA: ὑμῶν, ἐν ἀγάπῃ RP: ὑμῶν· ἐν ἀγάπῃ
18	WH: ὕψος καὶ βάθος
	{WH}/RP: βάθος καὶ ὕψος
19	WH: πληρωθῆτε εἰς {WH}: πληρωθῇ
20	WH: ὑπερεκπερισσοῦ RP: ὑπὲρ ἐκπερισσοῦ
21	RP: *omit* καὶ *after* ἐκκλησίᾳ

Chapter 4

2	WH: πραΰτητος, RP: πρᾳότητος
4	WH: [καὶ]
	NA/RP: καὶ
6	RP: *add* ἡμῖν *after* πᾶσιν
7	WH: [ἡ]
	NA/RP: ἡ
8	WH: [καὶ]
	NA: *omit* [καὶ] RP: καὶ
9	{WH}/RP: *add* πρῶτον *after* κατέβη
	WH: μέρη
	NA: [μέρη]
15	WH: Χριστός RP: ὁ χριστός

16 WH: μέρους {WH}: μέλους
17 RP: *add* λοιπὰ *after* καὶ τὰ
18 WH: ἐσκοτωμένοι RP: ἐσκοτισμένοι
21 WH: καθὼς ἔστιν ἀλήθεια ἐν {WH}: καθώς ἐστιν ἀληθείᾳ, ἐν
26 [NA]/RP: *add* τῷ *after* ἐπὶ
28 WH: ταῖς χερσὶν τὸ ἀγαθόν
{WH}: ταῖς ἰδίαις χερσὶν τὸ ἀγαθόν
NA: ταῖς [ἰδίαις] χερσὶν τὸ ἀγαθόν RP: τὸ ἀγαθόν ταῖς χερσίν
32 WH: [δὲ] **RP: δὲ**
WH: ὑμῖν
{WH}/RP: ἡμῖν

Chapter 5

2 WH: ὑμᾶς
NA/RP: ἡμᾶς
WH: ὑμῶν
{WH}/NA/RP: ἡμῶν
3 WH: ἀκαθαρσία πᾶσα RP: πᾶσα ἀκαθαρσία
4 WH: ἃ οὐκ ἀνῆκεν RP: τὰ οὐκ ἀνήκοντα
5 WH: ἴστε RP: ἔστε
WH: ὅ ἐστιν RP: ὅς ἐστιν
9 WH: φωτὸς RP: πνεύματος
12 WH: κρυφῇ RP: κρυφῆ
15 WH: ἀκριβῶς πῶς RP: πῶς ἀκριβῶς
17 WH: συνίετε RP: συνιέντες
19 {WH}/[NA]: *add* ἐν *before* ψαλμοῖς
RP: *add* ἐν *after* ψάλλοντες
22 WH: ἀνδράσιν {WH}: ἀνδράσιν ὑποτασσέσθωσαν
RP: ἀνδράσιν ὑποτάσσεσθε
23 WH: ἀνήρ ἐστιν κεφαλὴ {WH}: ἀνὴρ κεφαλή ἐστιν
WH: αὐτὸς RP: καὶ αὐτὸς ἐστιν
24 WH: ἀλλὰ ὡς RP: Ἀλλ᾽ ὥσπερ
RP: *add* ἰδίοις *after* τοῖς
25 RP: *add* ἑαυτῶν *after* γυναῖκας

27 WH: αὐτὸς RP: αὐτὴν

28 RP: *omit* [καὶ] *after* ὀφείλουσιν

29 WH: χριστὸς RP: κύριος

30 RP: *add* ἐκ τῆς σαρκός αὐτοῦ καί ἐκ τῶν ὀστέων αὐτοῦ *after* σώματος αὐτοῦ

31 WH: [τὸν] **RP: τὸν**

RP: *add* αὐτοῦ *after* πατέρα

WH: [τὴν] **RP: τὴν**

WH: πρὸς τὴν γυναῖκα {WH}: τῇ γυναικὶ

32 WH: [εἰς]

NA/RP: εἰς

Chapter 6

1 WH: [ἐν κυρίῳ] **RP: ἐν κυρίῳ**

2–3 WH: πρώτη ἐν ἐπαγγελίᾳ, ἵνα {WH}: πρώτη, ἐν ἐπαγγελίᾳ ἵνα

5 WH: κατὰ σάρκα κυρίοις RP: κυρίοις κατὰ σάρκα

6 WH: Χριστοῦ RP: τοῦ χριστοῦ

8 WH: ἕκαστος, ἐάν τι RP: ὅ ἐάν τι ἕκαστος

WH: κομίσεται RP: κομιεῖται

RP: *add* τοῦ *after* παρὰ

9 WH: αὐτῶν καὶ ὑμῶν RP: ὑμῶν αὐτῶν

10 WH: Τοῦ λοιποῦ, RP: Τὸ λοιπόν, ἀδελφοί μου,

WH: ἐνδυναμοῦσθε {WH}: δυναμοῦσθε

12 WH: ἡμῖν {WH}: ὑμῖν

RP: *add* τοῦ αἰῶνος *after* σκότους

16 WH: ἐν RP: ἐπὶ

WH: [τὰ] RP: τὰ

17 WH: δέξασθε RP: δέξασθαι

18 RP: *add* τοῦτο *after* εἰς αὐτὸ

19 WH: [τοῦ εὐαγγελίου]

NA/RP: τοῦ εὐαγγελίου

21 WH: εἰδῆτε καὶ ὑμεῖς {WH}: καὶ ὑμεῖς εἰδῆτε

WH: γνωρίσει ὑμῖν Τύχικος RP: ὑμῖν γνωρίσει Τυχικὸς

24 RP: *add* Ἀμήν *after* ἀφθαρσίᾳ.

INDEX OF BIBLICAL REFERENCES

NOTE: The primary purpose of a Scripture index in a book like this, where biblical passages are being treated directly, is not to present the reader with every biblical reference found in the book, but to offer ones that lie outside the range of each of the passages treated. Hence, this index presents references to such outside passages, plus verses from the passages treated in this book *but only when these are cross-referenced in a discussion of another verse found in these passages.*

Philippians

Colossians

1 Thessalonians

2 Thessalonians

1 Timothy

2 Timothy

ABOUT THE AUTHOR

Mateus F. de Campos (PhD, University of Cambridge) is the George F. Bennett Associate Professor of New Testament at Gordon-Conwell Theological Seminary. His writings include *Resisting Jesus: A Narrative and Intertextual Analysis of Mark's Portrayal of the Disciples of Jesus* (Brill, 2021) and commentaries on 2 Peter and Jude in *The New Testament in Color: A Multiethnic Bible Commentary* (IVP, 2024). He served for nearly a decade as a pastor in the Church of the Nazarene in Brazil and regularly preaches in churches of various denominations in the United States and abroad. Mateus and his wife, Renata, live in Middleton, Massachusetts, with their two teenage children, Matt and Zoe.